HUDDERSFIELD
AT WAR

HUDDERSFIELD AT WAR

HAZEL WHEELER

ISIS
LARGE PRINT
Oxford

First published in Great Britain 1992
by
Alan Sutton Publishing Ltd.

Published in Large Print 2007 by ISIS Publishing Ltd.,
7 Centremead, Osney Mead, Oxford OX2 0ES
by arrangement with
the Author

British Library Cataloguing in Publication Data
Wheeler, Hazel
    Huddersfield at war. – Large print ed.
    (Isis reminiscence series)
    1. World War, 1939–1945 – England – Huddersfield
    2. Large type books
    3. Huddersfield (England) – History – 20th century
    I. Title
    942.8'13084'092

ISBN 978–0–7531–9416–4 (hb)
ISBN 978–0–7531–9417–1 (pb)

Printed and bound in Great Britain by
T. J. International Ltd., Padstow, Cornwall

For Abigail, who used to say
"Tell me about the War."

Contents

Acknowledgements

Thanks to all who assisted towards the compilation of this book, including Mrs Annie Myers, Barbara Wilkinson, Lesley Parkinson, Mr P. Broadbent, Miss Dorothy Atha, Mr Brian Halstead, Mrs W. Halstead, Mr G. Hearne, Mrs J. Woodhouse, Mrs D. Suthers, Mrs M. Napier, Mrs A. Marston, Mrs Dorothy Biësche, Mrs D. Cockburn, Mrs M. Longstaff, Mrs J. Secker, Mrs Edith Walker, Ms H. McLoughlin, Mrs E. Dyson, Mrs L. McManus, Mr and Mrs D. Whitwam, Mrs Una Pearce, Mr and Mrs R. Large, Mr and Mrs F. Lindley, Mr H. Dyson, Mrs N. Swales, Mr C. Flaherty, Mrs M. Oxley, Mr and Mrs B. Darlington, Mrs A. Tracey, Mrs M. Horne, Mrs I. Broadbent, Mr and Mrs J. Firth, Mrs M. Stanley, Mrs M. Jessop, Mrs D. Martin, Mr Bill Dignam, Mr E. Buckley, Mr J. Oldroyd, Mr R. Saxon, Mrs M. Connolly, Mr Harry Hirst.

I would also like to thank staff at Huddersfield Reference Library, and the *Huddersfield Examiner*. If anyone has inadvertently been omitted, please put it down to "mental fatigue after battle".

My thanks, certainly not least, to Granville, who chauffeured me about to talk to people, learnt to cook, and applied himself to numerous other tasks while writing was in progress.

Very many thanks to everyone.

CHAPTER
ONE

1939

Annie Myers, aged twenty-two, dashed across to Mrs Martin's shop at Upper Brow, Paddock. It was Sunday morning, 3 September 1939, and Annie hadn't any cigarettes.

"Five Woodbines please . . ."

"Sshh." The usually communicative shopkeeper turned up the wireless set.

"What's up?" asked Annie, suddenly aware that this Sunday morning, already aromatic with the usual roast beef and cabbage smells, was going to be different.

"They've just announced that we're at war with Germany. You'd better get your gun found out, Annie."

Twopence changed hands and Annie lit up a Woodbine. For once, both were at a loss for words. Annie would have been even more astounded had she been able to look into a crystal ball and see the future; how this bloke Hitler would be the cause of both her sisters marrying Canadian air force men, and living the rest of their lives far away from Castlegate, Huddersfield, where their childhood had been spent.

Next day the population was bombarded, not with bombs, but advice about what to do in the new war situation. All sections of the Civil Defence needed volunteers, and were expected to work eight-hour shifts. Urgently required were canteen workers, ambulance drivers and attendants, first aid workers and wardens. Those willing to enrol had to go to the offices of the Women's Voluntary Services, at No. 12 Byrom Buildings, Station Street. The Huddersfield Town Council held a special meeting, and a Food Committee was appointed. The Mayor, Fred Lawson, spoke with great emotion, saying he thought we were in the right and he believed that right would triumph.

Trade representatives on the Food Committee were appointed: Herbert Biltcliffe (Butchers' Association); Mr H. Swallow (Co-operative Society); Mr F. Bannister (Dairymen's Association); Mr J. Heap (Retail Grocers); and Mr R. Whittaker (Bakers and Confectioners).

If at a church service when air raid sirens sounded, the congregation was to stand against the walls. And, it went without saying, pray. Many families, tempted by the fine weather, had spent the Sunday afternoon as though times were normal. All secondary, central, and elementary schools were to remain closed until further notice, while arrangements were being made for air raid shelters. Brick ones were built on the hockey fields at Greenhead High School.

The Control Centre at Longroyd Bridge was staffed throughout the night, and ARP Controller Mr Samuel Proctor, Town Clerk, and Councillor Sydney Kaye, member of the Emergency Committee, were in attendance.

Citizens were astounded to hear the banshee wailing of the first air raid siren during the early hours of Monday morning, when it was given at 3.20a.m. Large numbers of people gathered in groups in the streets, scanning the skies for they knew not what, somehow feeling that if "Jerry" peered down and saw the infuriated faces of Huddersfield people he would turn tail and vanish. For those who preferred to be out in the open, it had been announced that parks were to be kept open day and night, instead of the iron railings and gates being locked. Claustrophobia was probably worse to contend with than the remote chance of injury. That first early morning alarm caused some to rush into cellars clad only in their night attire, while the more fastidious took their time and dressed before turning out. A few ladies even powdered their noses and applied lipstick before facing the outside world. After all there were, no doubt, some handsome young Germans as well as Yorkshiremen.

When the "All Clear" sounded without mishap, relieved people emerged, all triumphant smiles, to "talk it over" with their neighbours, then returned to their own homes for an unusually early morning cup of tea. The general feeling seemed to be that it was all a bit of a lark, which would all be over in no time. Many were so nonchalant about the whole affair that they slept soundly through it all, probably dreaming that the sirens were nothing more than a particularly shrill voiced local tom cat.

Not all were so blasé. When the sirens were heard in Jackson Bridge some thirty residents, dressed only in night clothes, took refuge in a shaft at the Wood Top Pit.

Sandbagging of public and important buildings went on throughout the weekend, and progress continued on public shelters. That week demonstrations in fitting gas helmets on babies were held twice daily at ARP Headquarters in South Parade.

Chief Constable H. C. Allen said that motorists and householders were not complying with lighting regulations, but with it being "early days" police had dealt leniently with blackout offenders. When the town had been surveyed from a certain vantage point, the blackout was proving more effective than initially, but there was still room for improvement. People still forgot and switched lights on before making sure blinds had been drawn. Worst offenders were licensees, who failed to prevent shafts of light peeping from doorways as drinkers entered and left.

All manner of odd situations could arise if sirens shrilled at an inconvenient moment. Those who happened to be in court were to take refuge in an underground shelter which could be entered through the dock. Stipendiary magistrate Waldo R. Briggs advised those with business in court not to attend if an alert went as they were about to leave home. Every cloud having, so it's said, a silver lining, some criminals must have prayed for such a diversion to enable a getaway.

Some young men of call-up age looked forward to leaving humdrum jobs and joining the forces. Not so their mothers. Mrs Mallinson of Scar Lane, Golcar, had seven sons, all eligible for service. When it was confirmed that it really was to be war, on that Sunday morning in September, she left the table and began to cry. One of the sons, a farmer, was exempt. Another, Leslie, had "bad ears" and worked in a mill. Mrs Mallinson, fearful of what might happen, gathered her brood together and set off to Greaves Photographers in Huddersfield to ensure she would have a photographic keepsake of them all.

Much heartache would have been saved had she been able to foresee the future. All returned safely, and a thanksgiving photograph was taken of the family together again in 1945. Fate plays unpredictable tricks that seem so unfair at the time. While those seven sons emerged from the war unscathed, their mother Ida's sister Clarissa, who had only one son, was bereaved when he was killed on active service.

Joe Mallinson, uncle to the seven, was equally anxious about his own family. He drew out money to send his little daughter to grandparents in Canada some days after war broke out. Then came news of the sinking of the *Athenia*. A Golcar lady, Miss Ethel Booth, a well-known soprano singer, was on her way to Canada on the ship. Joe decided his daughter Annie would have far more chance of being safe if she stayed at home after that, so he bought new clothes with the money instead. Even so, Joe must have pondered the sagacity of such a decision when, later on, an explosion at Clough Head blew a hen hut across a field, blowing all the feathers off the hens!

The RAF Recruiting Office was at the Temperance Hall. There were vacancies for men willing to serve in aircraft crews as pilots, air observers, aerial gunners and wireless operators: men of sound physique between the ages of eighteen and thirty-two. Flying Officer B. Edwards was in charge of recruiting in Huddersfield.

When it was realized that petrol would be rationed, the licensing department at the Borough Police Office reported that 1,400 ration books had been applied for.

The whole population gradually started changing its way of life. Girls began training as conductresses on a number of Corporation petrol buses. School teachers, unable to teach until shelters were completed, were utilized by the Food Control Department in the preparation of ration cards. Recruits were wanted for Police War Reserve, £3 a week full time for the duration of the war.

Betty McIlveen, maid at the White Horse, joined the ATS, thinking it would be more interesting than "pulling pints" and walking the dog on Leeds Road.

An early fatality of the strange new blackout that people had to contend with was John Mannion, a well-known swimmer in his youth. He was knocked down at Aspley. Seventy-three-year-old Arthur Barrett, of Chapel Hill, accidentally stumbled and rolled into the very steep Varley's Yard. He only suffered shock.

Already Huddersfield people were reading less than before the war. Listening to the wireless, working for the ARP, and other new duties had taken its toll on free time. Dancing had, however, more enthusiasts than before, as all the new faces that were coming into town made going dancing more interesting than before. Glover's Dancing Academy at Fartown Conservative Club had non-stop dancing from 2.30p.m. until 10p.m. for 1s. 3d. Dancers could have "passouts", little rubber stamp marks on the back of the hand, to prove they had paid, should they feel the need to go out for a breath of fresh air or a drink, or to see what "talent" there was in other dance halls! Tuesday and Friday classes at Glovers cost 1s. for dancing from 7p.m. till 10p.m.

Some picture house managers were refusing admission to clients not carrying gas masks. At first, people felt a bit daft always having the soon to be familiar brown cardboard box slung by string over their shoulders. Some ladies carried them in their hands as though they were a box of cakes from Sylvio's or Whiteley's.

Stage hands at the Theatre Royal were kept busy filling sandbags. Mr J. Carson, the manager, let it be known that if the sirens went, patrons could descend to the pit bar, which accommodated a hundred people and was well protected on all sides by concrete. Should the audience prefer to remain, the Brookfield Players would carry on.

Already there were enough tales about what had been happening during the blackout to be made into a play or comedy. One warden even knocked at the door of his own house to enquire if there were any children under four. Another zealous patriot yelled "put that light out" at the moon. The police were receiving complaints about the conduct of youths who appeared to have nothing more to do but go about creating disturbances, and alarming people by their silly behaviour.

The increasingly sandbagged aspect of the town brought forth many derisory comments. Two headscarfed shoppers in Ramsden Street paused to regard the abomination.

"Sithee lass," remarked one, "they're covering t' windows o' t' rate office." Her friend sniffed in contempt.

"Ne'er heed t' winders; it's t'door they oughter block up."

The public was asked not to use umbrellas at night unless they were made of a light material that would show up in the dark. In the blackout an umbrella became a very dangerous weapon. And shopkeepers were requested to make sure outside blinds were pulled up at night. Some were rather low, and tall people might strike their heads upon them, causing much profane language.

Lodge's, the grocers, of Top Market Hall and Shambles Lane had been accused by some customers of profiteering because they had advanced the price of sugar to 11½d., salmon to 10d. and 1s. 4d., and corned beef to 8d., but they themselves had had to buy all those goods at an increased price. Corned beef in particular was becoming almost unobtainable, and such items became termed "under the counter" goods. Although rationing had not come into force on 15 September, should any commodities Lodge's sold become rationed, they would make sure that customers would have supplies if they rationed with them.

For those who could afford to, it made sense to buy clothes before they too became rationed. Suits made to measure, no extras, cost 30s. at Weaver to Wearer, Cross Church Street and New Street. Officers' outfits for all branches of HM Forces were obtainable from M. D. Forsyth, Civil and Military Tailor, Queen Street.

Economizing on everything was creeping in. One firm suggested a wartime economy — "Re-wire your mattress, only 18s. 4d." With fewer people at home to sleep on beds, and less time to lie on them, that idea probably never caught on.

The blackout was the main topic of conversation. A cartoon appeared of a little fellow looking utterly perplexed.

"Have we reached Almondbury yet?"

"Sorry, Sir," replied the buxom pinafored woman with a sweeping brush, "the bus is back in the depot and I'm the cleaner, not the conductor."

Entrepreneurs, out to turn wartime conditions to their advantage, soon stepped in with their slogans and cajoling ways. "Send for Panda Rug Wool Catalogue and Wool Fringe, You must do something to keep your mind occupied in the Blackout," suggested Aspinall Bros, Colne Road Mills. A householder advertised "Furnished rooms, Safe Area, near David Brown's, Lockwood." A firm selling sand in the normal way of life now advertised it as "suitable for ARP purposes, may be bought very cheap. Telephone Kirkburton 141."

Ordinary work had to go on. Albert Beaumont, of Deighton, advertised for a smart lad or man, exempt from military service, for a milk round and to assist on his farm. Another advertiser wanted a "Capable Help, to live in, 22s. 6d. weekly, or, living out, £1". Almost overnight, though, different attributes were hoped for in employees. Day and night weavers and winders were still wanted, but preferably with ARP training, for Garside and Sons, Dogley Mills, Fenay Bridge.

Wars of words went on in the Borough Police Court about two women, employed by the Arctic Milk Bar, New Street, who had come to blows over wiping pots. One hit the other over the head with a saucer, necessitating six stitches. She was bound over for a year, and ordered to pay 22s. 6d. costs. The famous wartime spirit had clearly not caught on in all areas of the town.

Everybody was buying blackout material or blinds. Greenwood's Wool and Handicrafts, Queen Street and Victoria Street, had some real proofed cloth for sale. Fred Booth, Engraver, Battye's Yard, Market Place, next to Blackburn's, Florist, warned the public: "Be Prepared. Get Your Identity Disc Complete with Name and Address."

The West Riding Court air raid arrangements for the public in the courtroom or nearby was to resort to the nearest shelter, in Roebuck's furniture shop in Buxton Road, and four shops at the bottom of High Street. Air raid precautions provided a novel way for people to make social contact with one another — it didn't take long for the youth of Huddersfield to use public air raid shelters as a quiet hideaway for a goodnight kiss.

Public service vehicles had to stop earlier, the last trolley buses leaving town at 10.15p.m.

It wasn't only the peril of explosions by enemy action, but those of negligence in a state of panic that one had to be aware of. An urgent warning that gas should be turned off at the meter in the event of an air raid was made. Appliances were to be turned off, including every gas burner in use, not forgetting those on gas refrigerators. Otherwise there was serious risk of explosion and poisoning when the gas was turned on again at the meter.

Racing pigeons, dead or injured, carrying any message or identification mark had to be handed over to the police or nearest Naval, Army or Air Force authorities. Blackout times were published nightly. On 7 September, for example, all lights had to be obscured by 7.45p.m.

Imminent risk of separation prompted an increase in young men "popping the question". Just before the announcement of war Huddersfield Registry Office had forty-five notices of marriage, and an increase in applications for birth and marriage certificates.

Dr J. M. Gibson, Medical Officer of Health, hoped for more first aid posts. The usual, personal problems of life still continued despite the larger issues. Somebody had lost her bottom set of teeth near the Scotch Wool shop, and a notice requested the finder to return them to the police station.

Certain establishments felt safer to be in than others. The Princess Café, Northumberland Street, situated underground, was ideal as there were no windows to splinter. Waitresses in black silk dresses, starched white aprons with frills round the edges, head-dresses and spanking white cuffs provided a welcome air of security and normality. The Princess was "Open as Usual" that first week of war, "for Luncheons, Teas, etc.". But Lockwood Picture Palace, Cosy Nook cinema, Fox's Academy of Dancing and a few other popular venues were closed until further notice. Andrew Stewart, General Manager of Huddersfield Building Society, gave notice that, because of lighting restrictions, Head Office, Britannia Buildings, would be open from 5–7p.m. instead of 6–8p.m. on Saturday evening.

That well-known figure Mr Ben Pearson, of Standard House, apologized that as ARP restrictions forbade the gathering of crowds, "I am unable to hold my usual Autumn Parades. But there is nothing to prevent you coming to see my collection either individually or in small groups. Telephone for appointment and I will arrange Private Parades for small parties."

Mr Pearson's advice to Huddersfield's fashion conscious was "look your best in wartime — it will keep you cheerful and raise other people's spirits to see you looking smart." A somewhat forlorn hope, when austerity, slacks for women munition workers and make-do-and-mend were about to become the order of the day.

12

At Wil-Be-Fort, ladies' coats and swaggers with the new flared back, at 42s. to 84s. seemed to give a final flourish to the pre-war elegance with its ample material.

Instead of playing outside, with gas lamps outside shops to provide lighting that autumn, children had to stay indoors, playing indoor games, jigsaw puzzles, and reading. As a concession to the dark evenings, Coates and Bairstow, Station Street, sold playing cards and auto bridge boards at half price.

Still the ever present sense of the absurd, even in the direst situations, was coming to the fore — especially what families had done that first night when the sirens went. One family — and probably not the only one — found themselves, after the first shock of being awakened from sleep, in a state of déshabillé and staring at each other from behind gas masks. "An improvement", one husband had quipped. One lady admitted to wearing three pairs of a "particular piece of clothing" in her panic to get dressed before blundering out to the air raid shelter.

Not many owned cars, but those who did were advised by Newton's of Viaduct Street to have regulation cowls and reflectors fitted to their headlights, from 10s. 6d. a pair.

At Birkby Council School, pupils missed lessons one morning a couple of days after school reopened, when all the children had to walk down Tanfield Road to St John's church. There, they had a service and prayers for victory over the Germans. Kenneth Halstead, who worked at Hopkinson's, was exempt from military service due to an unusual complaint — an allergy to tinned food. No tinned spam for him: the family contrived, when meat rationing came in, to ensure dad received the major portion. Kenneth joined Hopkinson's Home Guard. The men, without rifles at first, practised drill with broom handles. Already a proficient member of Huddersfield Rifle Club, Kenneth was the first to be sent to Deer Hill, to ensure when the rifles arrived that they were firing accurately. He ended up with a stiff, sore shoulder as a result of the continuing recoil from firing all those guns. Lessons were given in unarmed combat by Douglas ("Duggie") Clark, Huddersfield and British Rugby League Forward. Clark had his own coal business.

Kenneth, living at the flats on St John's Road, was called out one night when a lady at Fixby had seen, from her bedroom window, a load of parachutists in a field. It was with foreboding that Kenneth's family saw him set off, rifle over his shoulder, to join the other Home Guards at Hopkinson's. On his return, beaming with amusement, he recounted the terrifying tale of the parachutists. What the observant Fixby civilian had observed from her window was a flock of sheep, ambling slowly around in the blackout.

The reactions in odd situations were often unusual. One night the Halsteads heard the drone of an aeroplane. Idris Towill, friend, neighbour, and Fartown footballer, was visiting. They cautiously went to the door, so as to hear better. Idris, looking up, whispered, "I think it's one of theirs . . ." Despite the tension of the moment, Mrs Halstead couldn't help laughing. As though everything would be alright, as long as they whispered and weren't heard!

Later in the war a couple of soldiers were billeted with them. "Smithy", formerly a teacher, turned out to be an asset — reading bedtime stories to Brian and his sister Carol.

Geoff Hearn, at fourteen, was the youngest to join Huddersfield's ARP, and wore a silver badge. His dad was an air raid warden, and a bronze plate was fixed to their door to let people know that an air raid warden lived there. Geoff recalls the time:

Just before the war, the Air Raid Precautions service was started, and about the same time as recruitment began a depot was established to receive all the component parts of the civilian respirators and the simple jigs required to assemble them. Space was also needed to set up a crude assembly line. This was at Albany Mills on Firth Street, near the Wharf public house. Volunteers were called for to go down in the evenings and perform the simple assembly and packaging of the masks. They were available in three sizes, small, medium, and large. There was also a special one for very small babies who perhaps had not the lung power to draw air through the filter. The infant was placed inside the respirator and it had an air pump built into it for the mother to operate. There was also a special one for horses, very much like a nosebag. There was a good response for volunteers, and after about two weeks sufficient for the population of Huddersfield had been assembled and stored.

Next step was for each sector air raid warden to go to every house and measure up the occupant, noting the size of mask required. When the sector was covered, deliveries were made by the air raid wardens, fitted and made gas tight for each individual.

Air Raid Precautions Headquarters was situated in South Parade, just above the junction with Albion Street, in what is now Castlegate, where all the training courses for Anti Gas Training were carried out. There was also a gas chamber where at the end of the training course all the trainees went with their own CD type Heavy Duty Respirator on, to show how effective they were. At the end of the short period in the gas chamber we were invited to take off the gas mask for a few seconds to experience the tear gas, quite an experience for trainees.

As the war got under way the organization got a bit more sophisticated. In each area a permanent air raid post was established, with a paid full-time warden during the day, with a telephone link to HQ. After daytime hours the duty air raid warden had an apparatus that he plugged into his household electric power supply, called the Ripley Alarm. It was activated by the Huddersfield Corporation electric generation station in St Andrew's Road who, by varying the cycles per second of the power, caused a bell to ring in the set. When this happened it indicated that the air raid state of alert was at Red-Stand to — Raid Possible.

So the duty warden went and roused his colleagues and then manned the post. The permanent post for Milnsbridge was in the cellar of the Four Horseshoes pub. The next one was at Paddock in the cellars of the infants' school on Heaton Road. The full-time warden at Milnsbridge was Mr Robinson, one of the proprietors of the County Oyster Bar which was next to the entrance of Brooks Yard on Market Street. Full-time warden at Paddock was Mr Ernest Ditchfield, who lived up Larch Road.

In the spring and summer of 1940 a call was put out on radio for people at home to help farmers with the haymaking, as the call up had depleted the labour force. I went to a local farmer and asked if I could help — and was welcomed with open arms. (A big strong teenager!) I helped that farmer for eighteen months, and in those days there was little mechanization. When I was called up and said I would not come again, the farmer said: "Thanks for your help. Come and help when you are on leave." He gave me a drink of milk, but offered no recompense for the hours I had helped him. Life in the forces was easy after having been an unpaid farmer's boy!

An appeal went out at the time of the Battle of Britain in 1940 for aluminium. Housewives were asked to donate their aluminium pots and pans for

the war effort. The effect was tremendous —
mountains of them were collected. I remember
they were all piled up in a corrugated shed on St
Thomas's Road in what is now Brook Motors,
before being melted down. Similarly iron garden
railings were requisitioned. Very soon the "wide
boys" went round with their carts and took the
railings from the householder, without recompense
— and got away with it.

Mr D. S. Cooper had a horse flesh shop on
Buxton Road, opposite the Co-op, almost next to
McKittrick, Ironmongers, whose Georgian windows
are now preserved in Ravensknowle Museum.
Many were the poor farm horses who made their
last journey to the horse slaughterer down
Emerald Street, Hillhouse, the site of the waste
incinerator. Many the unsuspecting diner who
thought he or she was eating roast beef, when in
reality it was poor old Dobbin!

After the bomb at Pat Martin's Mill dam,
Christmas, 1940, the parachute canopy was hung
from the ceiling at ARP headquarters, South
Parade. It was green, and had an open net-like
weave.

I was walking home one evening in 1941 or '42
when I heard an aircraft flying very low over
Huddersfield. Straining my ears I followed its
course by sound, and was looking towards Castle
Hill when I heard a loud explosion. Castle Hill
was silhouetted by the light from the bang:
unfortunately it was a Wellington from a New

Zealand Squadron, lost when returning from a raid over Germany. It was low on petrol and trying to land on a road illuminated by the moon on Stirley Hill, Farnley Tyas. All five crew were killed. I believe this was to have been their last trip before going on leave.

Bacon, I recall, was in a very short supply at one time. Some bright spark suggested, "why not dry-salt cure mutton instead of pork?" It had a very short life, and was called Macon. I tasted it, and it was awful: food shortage or not, people would not eat it. I had a few gifts from time to time of a small piece of home fed and cured bacon. It was about 90 per cent fat. I doubt if anyone now would even bother with it, but in war torn Britain it was very welcome, with wartime bread fried in its dip. Many recipes circulated, including baking cakes using liquid paraffin instead of normal baking fats. It didn't taste too bad though, as there was little to compare it with.

On the night and early morning of 14 and 15 March 1941, a shower of incendiary bombs fell on the town, two of them on Royds Hall School. One fell into the school dining hall, burning a hole through a table, while the other failed to ignite and stayed in an underdrawing, unknown to anyone. After the war workmen found it, after it had been there, unsuspected, for fifteen years. A small HE bomb dropped at the same time demolished one of the houses at the Carr Street end of Smiths Avenue, Marsh.

For wartime purposes, Huddersfield was divided into sectors, by the method of drawing a grid over the map of the town. Each square of the grid took its reference number in the same way as the eastings and northings method of using Ordnance Survey maps.

In 1938 formation of No. 59 Squadron of the Air Defence Cadet Corps took place, with a limited membership number. It was oversubscribed on the first night of enrolment. It continued training boys, and in 1940 the name was changed to 59 Squadron Air Training Corps.

Due to popular demand an additional squadron was formed in 1941, No. 1033, both with the same HQ, on Upperhead Row. Besides the youth of the town, they also trained lots of the young men who had volunteered for air crew duties in the RAF. I well remember nearly all the young policemen of the Borough Force coming for morse code and aircraft recognition training, besides the cream of our youth who volunteered for this hazardous job. Sadly, many of them never returned.

The wedding of local veterinary surgeon Mr J. B. M. McKinna to Miss Muriel Rushworth took place in those first days of war, with the reception at Out of Bounds, residence of Mr and Mrs D. H. Rushworth. The bride wore a two piece dress and coat of blue angora, trimmed with grey fur and hat to tone. A case of fish knives and servers, from the staff of Rushworth's Ltd, Westgate, was among the presents.

Neighbouring establishment George Field and Sons Ltd already had stocks of "Extra heavy black Italian, 40 (in) wide, and 1s. 6d. Gas Mask Covers in guaranteed waterproof material with leather strap." Fashionable persons began competing among themselves as to who sported the smartest gas mask cover. George Vyner, Brook's Yard, Market Street, boasted that their waterproof gas mask carriers were "Made to last till Hitler Capitulates". Asthmatics were provided with special masks.

Possibly there were more injuries and fatalities due to the blackout than from any direct enemy action. Christopher Brook, retired worsted weaver of Taylor Hill, was knocked down on the first Monday evening after going to his allotments in Taylor Hill Road. The Coroner thought it risky that "an old man of seventy-seven be out after dark in these conditions" and asked if he was an obstinate man.

"It was no use me talking to him," replied a member of his family. "He was very obstinate." Maybe patriotic would have been a better description.

By October 1939 more restrictions were becoming apparent. The ARP warned J. B. Brooke & Sons, Manchester Road, "if you do not black out your works within four weeks you will have to stop work before 5p.m." Under the fuel rationing scheme, Mr J. W. Lomas reminded Colne Valley housewives that in future they must order supplies of coal in writing, and give quarterly orders in advance.

Mrs Tunnacliffe, Kilner Bank, must have wished she hadn't had any coal. She had placed a sheet of newspaper in front of the fire to "draw it" one chilly morning, and while outside the flames spread to clothing on the line near the mantelpiece. Clothing was damaged to the extent of about 30s.

Consolation could still be found in a bar of chocolate in those early months, though. "The Perfect Emergency Ration — Fry's Sandwich Chocolate: 2d. oz, 4 oz. 4d." ran an advert.

And there was entertainment in the many cinemas, and the Palace Theatre and Theatre Royal. Albert Modley, "The Great Little Yorkshire Comedian", was making 'em laugh at the Palace, while George Formby was at Lockwood Picture Palace in *Keep Fit*.

Fire-watching in works, factories, schools and other establishments was getting under way. Up at Greenhead High School, headmistress Miss Annie Hill and her staff formed a fire-watching rota, and slept in the school, "so eerie at night" being their verdict. Perhaps they felt like Will Hay in *Old Bones of the River* (Premier, Paddock Head cinema) after a few nights roughing it like that.

"Bright Hours" kept up the spirits and morale of many church and chapel goers. Minister's wife Mrs Smith presided at one in Aldmondbury St John's church, speaking about the early days of Methodism in Aldmondbury. Madame O. Law sang solos, with Mrs Crook as accompanist, and Mrs H. Lockwood at the piano for the remainder of the evening.

Fox's Academy of Dancing in Trinity Street reopened. Classes were 1s. 6d., and there was a Ladies' Wednesday afternoon class for the same price.

Children's class on Saturday mornings cost 1s. Brown's School of Dancing, near the Empire cinema, also had classes at 1s. A favourite and appropriate song was "Dancing in the Dark". There was also dancing at Hope Bank Pleasure Ground, admission 6d. from 7p.m. to 10p.m. Those looking for something different to wear at reasonable cost may have gone to Hall Bower Sunday School Rummage Sale on Saturday 7 October 1939. It cost 2d. to go in.

There were still houses to rent: No. 4 George Avenue, Birkby cost 15s., though a Longwood ex-serviceman complained that his wife went to ask for a Corporation house at Bracken Hall, to be told they were not letting any more. The enquirer was furious. He was a Corporation workman, gone all through the last war, and now had a son in the Army. "What does justice think of *that*?" he wanted to know.

Those who could afford it bought up as much tinned food as they could get. In early October, Wallace's, Grocers, asked customers to help the situation by not purchasing more than normal weekly requirements. By over purchasing, others would go short.

Huddersfield's first gas driven motor car of the war arrived, having been adapted for the Corporation Gas Department. A gas balloon was strapped to the roof, and a tube ran from the balloon to the induction pipe. It was estimated that the car would run fourteen miles on each bag of gas.

In the West Riding Hotel, a meeting of Huddersfield and District Allotment Holders Federation reported 119 acres of Corporation allotments in existence. The appropriately named Alderman W. A. Meadows told members that new ground was to be opened at Dawson Road and Cross Lane, Newsome; Heatherfield Crescent and Fir Road, Paddock; Dryclough Road, Crosland Moor; Broomfield Road, Fixby; and Hangingstone Road, Berry Brow. At a lecture in the Town Hall the previous evening Mr W. J. Cummins, chief ARP Instructor, told a large audience of farmers what they should do to protect themselves and their animals against gas.

By 6 October 1939 everybody in Huddersfield should have had an identity card — not much use in the blackout, one would imagine. The hit song of the summer was "Boomps-A-Daisy", which was significant of the dark days to follow, when citizens were, in slow motion, doing their utmost to *avoid* bumping into each other. At the Borough Police Court, the first three persons were summoned for blackout offences before the stipendiary magistrate Waldo R. Briggs.

Quite apart from how to feed dogs and other pets as food became scarcer, what to do with them when the sirens went was another problem. It was forbidden to take them into public shelters, so dog lovers were asked to offer refuge to dogs and their owners in their own shelters to any who may be caught out in the street — a sad outlook for stray dogs and cats, and sheep and cattle out in the fields.

When that first air raid alert was sounded, a tiny ginger kitten was wandering on Bradford Road. Young Betty Key, whose parents had a shop and lived at No. 10, emerged to go into a cellar which was reached by going outside first. She had grabbed the bird cage and Bob, her wire-haired fox terrier, and was making her way to the refuge when she spied the kitten, mewing piteously. Betty adamantly refused to take shelter herself unless the kitten was allowed inside too, so there they all congregated: a dog who hated cats, a kitten who hated dogs, and a bird twittering in agitation at being so rudely awakened from its slumbers. And Lance, Betty's dad, no doubt playing hell with them all, in what was supposed to be a haven of refuge.

Tuberculosis was still a problem, and the reason why some young men were not called up. Patients at Bradley Wood Sanatorium, as other hospitals, were given numbers and these were published (rather than their names) in the local newspaper, giving news of their progress and whether relatives could visit.

Childhood delights came under threat when there was a ban on the importation of toys and games, and timber was controlled. Dads began making toys for Christmas themselves, and mothers made dolls out of whatever they could find. Wooden pegs made attractive little Japanese dolls, with a bit of black wool stuck to the top for hair. Ingenuity came to the fore. But none could prevent the abolition of bonfires and fireworks on 5 November: only indoor fireworks, like sparklers, were allowed. There were novelties available for those dark evenings, though. Barkers, Market Place, suggested, "You can't do it outside, so make Whoopee indoors this year. Joy Bombs, Sparklers and all manner of harmless indoor fireworks." Fascinating were those weird, squelchy green "snakes" that coiled out of a little green box when a match was put to them.

Huddersfield Boy Scouts went round houses collecting waste paper to help with salvage and the war effort. Every scrap of food was saved for pigs. And staff at the Food Control Office in the Technical College extension was increased.

Mid-October saw a blackout fine of 40s. imposed on dance instructor James Vivian Rawlins of No. 57 Gramfield Road, Crosland Moor, for permitting a light to be seen from a grating in Northgate on 19 September. Cyril Firth of New North Road was fined £5 for lights from Priestroyd Mills, Queen Street South on 20 September, issuing from twenty-eight windows. Sergeant Braithwaite had to burst open a door to put them out. The defendant said the premises weren't used after 5p.m. and arranged to have blinds fitted to all windows.

Some firms had painted windows black to make sure they weren't fined, but in so doing obscured valuable working daylight. J. B. Brooke & Sons Ltd, No. 264 Manchester Road, offered free estimates for their "Pull a Cord" blackout, saying that all up-to-date mills were having them.

Stress of lighting restrictions, and bumping into lamp posts and other objects on dark evenings was alleviated by the type of films shown at local cinemas. Stan Laurel and Oliver Hardy were always good for a laugh in *Swiss Miss* at the Lounge, and Mickey Rooney in *Huckleberry Finn* at the Cosy Nook. Eleanor Powell, Robert Young, George Burns and

Gracie Allen were in *Honolulu* at the Rialto, Sheepridge.

On the Saturday of that week Huddersfield YMCA held a Rugby Union Football Club dance at Ye Olde Barn from 6.30 to 10p.m., with admission costing 1s. 6d.

Away from the frivolity of cinemas and dancing, the world of work needed constant replenishment as young men went into the forces. Fittons Fruit Stall in Westgate advertised for a smart boy, aged fourteen to sixteen. A "Daily General" was required by a New North Road family, as was a second operator at the Empire cinema. Fitters for Admiralty Work of "First National Importance" were wanted by J. Blakeborough, of Brighouse.

Every aspect of life was geared to wartime living. Evelyn Webster, hairdresser of No. 55 New Street, next to Woolworths, advertised: "let us have the privilege of your hairdressing appointment. A set that will photograph well for a miniature for a handsome Territorial to take abroad. Jamal permanent waving. Colouring and all beauty services."

How fortunate that most seemed to be on good terms with their neighbours. Good fellowship, comfort, fun and laughter as well as a bit of apprehension was to be enjoyed sheltering together in cellars or Anderson shelters. Many neighbours arranged to dash into each other's shelters on alternate alerts. It gave them a bit more chance to gossip.

Margaret Gould, her little dog Trixie, and parents Walt and Elsie shared a cellar with their neighbour, Mr Sykes, where Elsie sat trembling on a chair at first, clutching the insurance policies when the sirens went. Margaret, in a way, looked forward to getting up in the middle of the night: it gave her the opportunity of wearing her new blue siren suit, zipped up the front, with a cosy hood attached. There was an oil stove in the cellar, and a stock of candles. It was a big cellar, so Margaret's Auntie Alice went in as well. Alice's husband, Johnny, was in the ARP so she didn't want to face being bombed on her own. There they all sat during that first alert, expecting to be killed. Then they became used to it, so decided they may as well enjoy themselves and make alert times a bit of a party atmosphere. When the "sireens", as some called them, shrilled, Auntie Alice heated up pies and peas down there in the cellar, and sometimes they had ham sandwiches, all tasting even more delicious in the middle of the night. Trixie enjoyed an extra feed of biscuits and a ham shank bone.

Sometimes they played Monopoly. But it wasn't usually worth starting a long game like that before the "All Clear" rang out. When you had to get up for work the next morning it was a bit daft fiddling around with Leicester Square and the rest of it for hours on end in a cold cellar. Margaret's dad, Walt, was a postman and sometimes had to drive the van to take mail bags to Wakefield. Occasionally he clattered down into the cellar: "ah'm just passing through to see you're alright."

Mrs Gould kept an umbrella rolled up beneath her bed, and it sometimes accompanied her into the refuge. It could double as a bayonet if necessary, or maybe could keep them dry if rain came in following a direct hit — you never knew . . .

As days went by and nothing very terrible seemed to be happening, local ARP men drew up a "spoof" set of rules and emergency regulations:

The practice of lighting up cigarettes from incendiary bombs must cease forthwith as this is a grave insult to the enemy. Unexploded High Explosive Bombs are DEFINITELY not the property of the finder. It has been reported that wardens are taking them home for use on November 5th. These bombs are the property of the enemy, on finding same, the label should be reversed, the bomb taken to the nearest station, and duly returned to Adolf Hitler. Invading aircraft must always be attacked by anti-aircraft guns. The habit of using darts for the purpose must be discontinued as darts are a basic necessity to the well being of the country. Anyone not adhering to these rules will be instantly dismissed from the Unpaid Wardens List.

"Who are you registering with?" soon became the question on every housewife's lips as October wore on. Shops attempted to encourage business:

Register with Redmans, at the Good Bacon Shop, Market Avenue and Market Hall. Redmans Light as a Feather Suet Dumpling Mixture will help your meat supplies. A 2½d. packet makes 12, a

4½d. packet 24 dumplings. When Ration Cards are issued, we shall greatly appreciate your registration for all rationed articles (except butchers meat). Nobody can serve you better, and all our staff remain cheerful in spite of difficulties.

Some imagined shop keepers to be luckier than customers — they'd be able to "fiddle" the rations in favour of themselves. Maybe, to some extent, but coupons, points and permits made a lot of extra work. There were Food Office returns to fill, and counting the bits of paper all took time. Especially when some young men who had worked in shops had left to join up, and the proprietor was left with the lot to see to himself. When my parents' shop was closed, Dad spent many an hour sorting out the new extra regulations and coupons.

"We could do with a flipping secretary these days," he often said, there being less time for a game of billiards down at the club.

Dances were increasingly held in aid of war funds, such as the Red Cross. The local Farmers' Dance at Cambridge Road Baths on Wednesday, 25 October is one example. Phil Gordon's Band played, and tickets were 1s. 6d., with dancing from 6 to 10p.m. When feet were weary with dancing, there was always Townend, chiropodist, Temple Chambers, Westgate, open from 2p.m. to 7p.m. daily, except Wednesdays. It cost half a crown for both feet, and patients could be visited at home by appointment.

Aldmondbury Silver Prize Band gave a concert to the troops in Huddersfield on 20 October.

English halibut at the time cost 2s. 4d. per lb, and plaice was down to 1s. 4d. Chilled salmon cost 2s. per lb, wild duck 5s. 6d. a brace, rabbits from 1s. 2d. to 1s. 8d. each. Hares were 3s. to 4s., American apples 2d. per lb, Cox's 8d. per lb. Pickling onions, ready peeled, were 6d. per lb; onions and radishes 1d. a bunch. Mushrooms were 7d. per quarter, and cucumbers 9d. each.

A total of 3,000 gas helmets for babies were due to be delivered on Sunday 22 October, so parents were requested to stay at home that day. Richard Broadbent, of No. 90 Greenhead Lane, Dalton, didn't think much of being in one of these contraptions the first time the sirens went, especially being taken into the cellar as well. He cried and screamed all the time and Frank, his dad, declared the din was far worse than any bombs could be, so they'd simply take their chance in future. It was the first and last time baby Richard had experience of being in a Second World War gas helmet.

You never knew where you were — or would be — when wartime authorities decided on a move. S. Heaton, wholesale confectioners of Northumberland Street, had their chocolate and sweet warehouse commandeered for an ARP shelter, and there was a compulsory removal to No. 27 Lord Street.

Huddersfield Food Office had prepared a total of 113,000 ration cards in the Technical College extensions. Work was expected to be completed within days, apart from complications and changes arising from removals and deaths.

Despite an almost imperceptible move to casual wear, including slacks for women and siren suits, there was still a demand for smart fashions. Experienced sales ladies, also juniors, were required by H. & J. Wilson of No. 6 King Street, who sold mantles and gowns. And "not a hair out of place" was still the ideal for well-groomed ladies, who could have a 3s. 6d. permanent wave, guaranteed for eight months, or re-setting for 1s. at Koronet of Chapel Hill.

War was throwing up more and more its own peculiar brand of humour. A mother was heard admonishing her grubby young son: "you're lucky to have soap in your eyes. In Germany the poor little boys can't have any soap at all." A stout lady, chatting on a bus about the best thing to do in an air raid admitted: "well, ah allus run about meself. You see me husband says a moving target is more difficult to hit."

That lady would not have looked her best in a siren suit, not even from Rushworth's, who were selling them in both wool and waterproof material. Slacks were also on sale, warm and comfortable for shelter wear. ARP workers may have preferred a two piece slack suit of fine velour, in navy, light navy or nigger, for 63s. A model coat cost 6½ gns. Rushworth's closed at six, with half-day closing on Wednesdays at one.

Cartoonists were quick to latch on to current situations. A sketch of a house on fire showed two bewildered ARP men, discussing what to do first. Send for the Fire Brigade, or report him for showing a light?

Many used oilcloth in 1939 to cover kitchen tables. The Carpet Shop, Market Avenue, had forty rolls for sale at the old price — and who knew what would be rationed next?

Girls wore gabardines at Greenhead High School in the autumn term, as did pupils of Huddersfield Boys' College. Wil-Be-Fort, John William Street, was selling them at 15s. 6d., 21s. 6d., and 27s. 6d.

Public houses were awash with original humour, such as this, heard in one in October 1939: "fra what ah can mak aat, it ain't Hitler that's to blame for this 'ere carry on. It's that bloke they call t'Furer that's at t' bottom of it." One drinker referred to von Ribbentrop as "Yon Whip and Top".

Dancers who considered themselves rather posh patronized Greenhead Masonic Hall in preference to the Co-op Hall and some of the other places. Here they could show off their finery, and dance slow foxtrots and quicksteps. A Grand Charity Ball was held on Friday 3 November, when there were cigarettes for the troops, and Billy Hobson and his Orchestra. Evening Dress was required, with members of HM Forces to be in uniform. Tickets were 5s. each, including buffet, from either J. Marshall & Co., J. Wood and Sons, or Kenneth Levell Ltd.

The free list was entirely suspended at the Palace Theatre for the week when it featured *Clap Hands — Here Comes Charlie*, starring Charlie Kunz, "Radio's Wizard at the Piano". At our shop we showed theatre bills in a prominent position on top of the counter every week, and as a reward received two free tickets for each event, except when someone especially noteworthy was appearing. Yet we were still expected to show the bill. Huddersfield did well out of the war culturally, "stars" in the metropolis coming to the provinces to escape the London Blitz.

People started writing letters again, now that relatives were "Somewhere in England". Airgraphs sped to and fro, though some were "censored" if anything was remotely likely to give information to the enemy, should they fall into wrong hands. John Lewis, of the Lower Market Hall, cashed in on the new craze. "Platignum and Mentmore Pens, from 1s. 3d. to 7s. 6d." would encourage men in the forces to send more airgraphs and letters home.

To own a fur coat was the ultimate ambition of many ladies before the war. If the coat was slightly out of fashion, Alec Cole of Market Street, facing Heywoods, was just the place to have it remodelled and renovated by experts. And the first week in November was the time to attend to the matter.

A very different kind of protection was that authorized to air raid wardens: steel helmet, CD respirator, protective suit, gloves, boots, eyeshields, hand lamp, rattle, whistle, bell, and first aid box. Huddersfield boy scouts were disappointed when local ARP men passed over their offers of help.

Even wardens were liable to fail to be aroused from sleep, so one local man, not having a telephone in his own home to receive important ARP messages, decided to rig up a contrivance with a bell, and a means of sounding it at his neighbour's abode. An exercise for wardens had been arranged, and it was put to the test. A few days later, as Zero Hour approached, the neighbour sat expectantly in his sitting room, ears alert for the sound of the bell. It was fixed up in the bedroom, for night warnings, but no signal came to send him scurrying to his post. When he had almost given up hope of a call, an urgent rapping at the door nearly frightened him to death. He opened it, to find a mystified neighbour on his doorstep.

"Didn't you hear the bell?" he asked. The warden listened intently. Ah yes, there it was, ringing away in the bedroom. But he had closed the sitting room door to avoid being in a draught, and was too far away for the faint sound of the bell upstairs to reach him.

Farce and tragedy are seldom far apart. The blackout being imposed ostensibly to save lives, it was taking them. Forty-two-year-old Miss Julia Oddy, of Wiggan Lane, Sheepridge, died after being knocked down by a motor bus in the blackout, on Halifax Road. Hebble Motors owned the bus.

Ruses to obtain extra food were manifold, and often very inventive. One chap went so far as to get himself admitted to the Royal Infirmary in the early hours. He told the house surgeon, Dr Sebastian, that he had struck his head dodging a bus. No sign of injury could be found, but he was admitted for observation. Three days later, after being examined again, the opinion was formed that he was malingering. The patient was a Gentleman of the Road, who would not have been able to pay the costs.

That November, the cost of living was rising, and an increase of 5s. a week to pensioners of sixty-five and over was essential, said Mr W. Glenvil Hall (Labour, Colne Valley).

"Fiddling" money was a doddle for many, under cover of the blackout. Fake and foreign coins were frequently tendered to bus conductresses, while others handed over a farthing, pretending it to be a sixpence. Shillings were confused with half pennies, half-crowns and florins mistaken for pennies, and vice versa. Rushworth's came up with a novel idea — an all-in-one gas mask and handbag container, with room for lipstick, powder compact, torch, and other paraphernalia. It cost 21s.

Optimistic householders who had bought cheap, temporary paper blinds, expecting the war not to last long, were already finding cracks and chinks developing, and were having to try and fasten them to the sides of the window panes with drawing pins. Annie Myers, sprucing up her home in readiness for a visit from her sister, who was to stay overnight, had washed her "Pullons". They weren't dry enough to bring in from the clothes line, as it was a dank, misty November day, so she hung up a makeshift blanket at the window for a temporary blackout. But it didn't black out enough, despite "loads of nails and stuff in the walls". A policeman called, and Annie was fined 10s. when she appeared in court. However, the kindly policeman paid the fine for her. Aptly, George Formby was starring in *Trouble Brewing* at the Regal cinema on Wakefield Road.

Besides giving salvage and money for good causes, people were now being asked by Denton Guest, Pathologist, to give their blood. Donors were urgently needed. Messrs Joseph Hanson & Sons Ltd helped the war effort by presenting the Corporation with a bus which had been converted into a mobile first aid post. It could carry a staff of twenty first aid workers.

By November, total applications for Anderson shelters in Huddersfield were approximately 10,000. Among them was a first consignment of a large type to accommodate up to ten people.

Dancing continued unabated, despite the darker nights. A non-stop Carnival Dance at the Mechanics Hall, Longwood, to Norman Hancock and his band, with carnival novelties free, drew many. Then there was dancing every Monday at Paddock Institute, from 7 to 10p.m., to Eddie Riley's Band. This cost 6d. up to 7.45p.m., 9d. afterwards. Deighton Sunday School started to have Saturday night "hops". Local residents Harry and Nellie Gibson helped to run the dances. They were in aid of Comforts Funds for Local Lads in the forces. Harry Barraclough once had a bit of fun putting his gas mask on, then strolling across the floor to ask an astonished girl to dance. And he didn't take it off, not even in a "Paul Jones" dance.

Part of the supplies of children's respirators, for those between their second and third birthdays, were to be delivered on 5 November 1939. They could not be left without receipts from parents. Small civilian respirators, not small children's, would be at South Parade for any children they would fit.

Manchester Furnishing Company, Market Avenue, had 300 yds of ARP black curtain lining cloth for sale, 44 in wide at 11½d. per yd; also 1940 designs for fitted carpets at 1939 prices.

Special constables were constantly having skirmishes with blackout offenders. As one "Special" moaned, "if everybody in Huddersfield used torches, the whole town would be floodlit." One car had even approached a Special with a "lamp like a searchlight". Everybody now used the language of wartime as second nature.

"New girls" who had passed the eleven plus were to attend Greenhead High School for the first time that November. In normal times they would have been integrated into the grammar school in September. They were notified that if they forgot to take gas masks, with satchels as well, they would be sent home to fetch them. I had been at Greenhead since September 1938, and forgot my gas mask one morning when loaded up with satchel and hockey stick already. How frustrating, having got up on a dark morning in plenty of time, to retrace my steps, and pay another fare home and back again. It seemed a bit of a fiasco, especially as there was no gas alarm after all that palaver. I almost wished there had been, so my time wouldn't have been wasted.

There was always "the pictures" to look forward to, however, whatever annoyance occurred during the day. That week many chose to go to the Tudor. Lupino Lane was on in *The Lambeth Walk*. "You can Do as You Darn Well Pleasey — but you must see the Lambeth Walk," the billboard outside the cinema advertised. At the Palace were the Home Service Follies with *Gerroff Me Fooit*, staring Frank Randle, with his rather uncouth humour, and grand supporting cast of full pre-war standard. We gave our free pass for the Monday evening show to our shop assistant. Deanna Durbin was in *Three Smart Girls Grow Up* at the Princess, wearing those cute little bolero dresses so popular at the time. Those good at sewing bought brightly coloured pieces of felt, to make boleros for themselves. Film stars' hairstyles and mode of dress were slavishly copied in Huddersfield.

More ration books were available by 6 November, those with National Identity letters KFDA to KFDZ, and FEA to KFED in the allocation.

A national stand-by that never failed to raise morale was fish and chips, or fish and a penn'orth as they were known at one time. A "must" eaten from a newspaper, well seasoned with salt and vinegar, when walking home after "the pictures". In wartime even this harmless occupation had its hazards. A Holmfirth mill worker, nicknamed "Waggon Wheels" for some reason, got himself into a bit of a tangle. Trying to hold his torch and his portion of "land and sea", he conveyed his supper from paper to mouth with the hand holding his torch, intermittently lighting up the patch of darkness round him, however dimly. His action and subsequent fine of "ten bob" was even known about in Hamburg — in a broadcast it was, no doubt, quoted as another example of Yorkshire daftness.

"Lord Haw-Haw", the Englishman turned traitor, broadcast from Germany, and with his propaganda made out that the English were on the verge of starvation and about to surrender. This exasperated one local housewife so much that she shoved a "doorstep" ham sandwich in front of her wireless: "Sithee, yer daft bugger, have a sniff o' that!"

Huddersfield's tradition of performing *The Messiah* in chapels, churches and Town Hall during the run up to Christmas continued. The Choral Society were booked for the usual performance, albeit in the afternoon, for Saturday, 23 December, with the Christmas Hymn sung at 2.30 by the wonderful Janet Hamilton-Smith, Muriel Brunskill, Webster Booth and Norman Walker and conducted by Dr Malcolm Sargeant. Balcony seats not required by subscribers were available to the public at 7s. 6d.

During those early months, before the victorious outcome was at all certain, a few chose suicide because of their extreme worry about air raids, fear often being worse than the event itself. A Golcar burler, a widow with one child, chose to end it all in the canal, leaving a note indicating it was either that or Storthes Hall.

It was enough to drive the authorities mad when sandbags outside public buildings in town started to rot, and became loosened as a result of bad weather. A large section of sandbags on the Victoria Lane side of the public library gave way completely, falling down like an avalanche. They had been filled with earth instead of sand. Huddersfield Building Society had covered theirs with tarpaulin, securing them with stout ropes.

On the morning of 2 December in the market place, Mayor Norman Crossley opened a centre for the sale of

National Savings Certificates and Defence Bonds, in the "Save For Victory" War Savings Campaign. Nevertheless, many preferred to buy traditional Christmas gifts. Taylor & Hobson, New Street, had an attractive display of Smokers' Stands, Cake Stands, Standard Lamps, Down Quilts, Lloyd Loom Chairs, and many other items to brighten the home for the festive season. Thomas Kaye & Sons, King Street, tempted shoppers with imitation hogskin gloves at 5s. 11d., and pure silk hose, fully fashioned at 3s. 11d. to 7s. 11d. Rushworth's extended their shopping hours until 7p.m. that Saturday. In the food line, Wallaces had prunes at 8½d. lb, glace cherries 6d. a quarter, "Ely" Christmas puddings 9d., 1s., and 1s. 4d. without basins. Mincemeat cost 8½d. a jar, ground almonds 8d. a quarter.

As ever, the run-up to Christmas was probably more exciting than the event itself. Vera Brittain was in Northumberland Street School on 8 December, speaking "In Favour of an Armistice". On the 16th the mayor entertained wardens. An ARP Dance took place at the Town Hall on Friday the 22nd, when 500 people danced to the Westbourne Players.

In a letter to the *Examiner* newspaper an Austrian refugee sent Christmas greetings to the people of Huddersfield.

The blackout promoted more daylight Christmas shopping than in previous years, and, just in case, official instruction was given on "How to wear spectacles with gas masks on". The Arctic Café, New Street, put on a Christmas Lunch Special, for 2s.

including a variety of soups, stuffed turkey, chipolata sausages, rissoles or mashed potatoes, cauliflower or garden peas, followed by Christmas pudding and rum sauce or cream, or a mince pie, and finally coffee. Or one could have the usual 1s. 3d. lunch.

Kenneth Levell's, Market Street, "The Home of Light and Music", appointed itself "The Anti-Blackout Gift Headquarters", where elegant lighting, ornaments and other desirable items for the home attracted gift shoppers. On a more mundane level Heatons, Northumberland Street and John William Street, wholesale on Lord Street, suggested: "In Tommy's Parcel put some Heatons (Stop Coffin) Badcoff Pastilles. 2½d. ounce. Good stocking fillers!"

Brook Motors Social and Sports Club held a whist drive and dance, with bar and buffet, at Cambridge Road Baths on Friday 15 December 1939. Dancing was to H. Beevers and his band. Tickets 1s. 6d. Part of the proceeds were to go to the Mayoress's Comforts Fund for employees in HM Forces.

Robert Donat starred in *Goodbye Mr Chips* at the Tudor. Those who had seen it warned friends to take a few handkerchiefs: "it was ever so good, made us cry buckets."

The Mayor's Boots for Bairns Fund collected a total of £156 17s. 6d.

CHAPTER
TWO

1940

1940 opened after a quiet New Year's Eve in Huddersfield. Streets were practically deserted, and there was no Watchnight service at the parish church. Fireside parties were held in many homes, especially those of Scots people living in the town. 1940 calendars indicated "Safe nights for Social Life", when there was a "Moonlight Ration". Dates of the full moon were shown, and, given favourable skies, when movements to and from places of assembly in bright moonlight up to midnight, and sometimes even after, were possible. One benefit the war did give was the experience of walking by moonlight, when no artificial light spoiled the unearthly, magical scene, especially magical if walking home after a dance with a handsome escort who was new to the town and spoke with an irresistible foreign accent!

Old Mother Riley came dancing into the New Year at the Picture House, as daft as the cyclist in court later in January who said he'd been using his cigarette end as a rear light . . .

Alec Cole, Market Street, advised men to buy more suits and wear them alternately. Two suits costing 50s. were a wartime economy over one costing £5. Regular daily brushing with a stiff brush and pressing with a hot iron through a damp cloth would put the crease into trouser legs. Frank Fairburn's, 28 Victoria Lane, sold clogs, mill and munition workers being the main users. Nobody wearing clogs would patronize the select Fields Café, Westgate, where a smart girl aged fourteen or fifteen was wanted. A young girl was also offered employment at E. Coletta's ice-cream stall.

War or no war, it was always pantomime time in January. *Goody Two Shoes and the Yellow Dwarf* at the Theatre Royal made audiences temporarily forget the reality of shortages and the blackout. A seat cost from 6d. to 4s., including tax, with children half price.

According to Chief Constable Mr H. C. Allen, Huddersfield was now one of the most effectively blacked out towns in the country. He was speaking at the opening of the new headquarters of the Special Constabulary in the old Labour Exchange on John William Street. The premises had been adapted to provide a parade room, lecture rooms, social rooms, officers' rooms for senior officers and sergeants, and an orderly room and store room.

Some extremely hard cases were coming before the court, said the Chief Constable, for example, elderly people to whom a fine of 10s. meant real hardship. However, because of the team spirit prevailing in the Civil Defence, the town was getting on well.

Such a lot was still to be learned about the hazards of the relatively new situation. People were warned not to use green or red paper to dim a pocket torch. Inadvertent waving of a green light by a passenger had the effect of starting a train, as the driver mistook the torchlight for the official "Right Away" signal. It was safer to use either white or yellow paper, and to keep the torch always pointed downwards.

British Dyes gave 650 children of employees a treat by taking them to a special matinée performance of *Babes in the Wood* at the Palace Theatre. Tea was omitted so youngsters could get home before blackout, but the "panto" and box of sweets was ample compensation. The treat was organized by the Works Committee, the Hon. Secretary of which was Mr J. Milner. Those living near the British Dyes factory, incidentally were worried more than most at the onset of war, thinking the "Dyes" would be a number one target for the "Jerries".

On 3 January 1940, the Baths and Model Lodging House Committees decided that the charge for hire of the Assembly Hall at Cambridge Road Baths up to midnight on Fridays should be £11 11s., plus a guinea an hour after 1a.m. Police found no objection to an extension of the permitted hours for dancing to 1a.m.

Builder J. Wimpenny of Spurn Point, Milnsbridge, suggested that bricks were cheaper than sandbags, and did not rot. Replacing sandbags with brick walls would be a sound investment.

Early that month two evacuees from Bradford, aged eight and ten, were playing in a barn when they lost a cap. Looking for it with matches, they started a fire, burning 20 tons of hay belonging to farmers Dunning and Walker, of Saddleworth, Uppermill. In court the chairman, in mitigation, told the boys that the man they were billeted with gave them a "very good name", and hoped that they would not play around with matches again. It was hoped that this would be a lesson both to them and other boys in the district.

Problems cropped up daily. Feeding of pets was one of them. In Germany ration cards were issued for dogs over 16 in high, but those dogs could be requisitioned for military purposes. English dogs had to rely on butchers' offal, not rationed but rather expensive. Horse flesh and cow meat not considered fit for human consumption were available too, and to identify this, it was painted a harmless green colour. In some areas owners clubbed together and ordered it in large quantities, to make it less expensive. Dried liver was on offer for dogs as well, only requiring the addition of water. Local abbatoir officials were able to advise.

Pure silk stockings were still on sale at the Yorkshire Warehouse, Cross Church Street, at 2s. 11d. a pair. Artificial silk chiffon hose cost 1s. 3½d. per pair. Girls and ladies still twitched round to make sure stocking seams were straight, and soon they began painting their legs with suntan lotion, gravy browning or cold tea. A "seam" was drawn on up the back of the legs, with mascara or whatever seemed suitable.

Second World War songs were becoming as popular as "Tipperary" and "Pack up your Troubles" had been in the First. Topical words were put to some:

You are my Sunshine, My double Woodbine,
You make me happy, when skies are blue
You'll never know, dear, how much I love you,
Please don't take my Sunshine away.

Even cigarettes, including humble Woodbines, were
becoming hard to get. Famous people, on the other
hand, were becoming almost ten a penny in the town.
"Stars" usually stayed at the George Hotel if they were
playing at the local theatres. Audrey Cudworth, then at
Galloway's Commercial College, used to haunt the
George in her lunch hour, along with a friend who
collected autographs of the famous. Diana Churchill,
Barry K. Barnes and Will Fyffe featured in her
collection.

From 22 January all vehicles had to use the ARP
headlamp mask or equivalent. Car owners were asked
to try and park their vehicles off the roads at night time,
as the blackout enabled more thefts to take place.

Wartime or not, January sales always give a lift to the
spirits and bring a ray of hope of better times to come.
Especially so when Rushworth's reduced corset prices
— Gossard's front lacing to 13s. 6d., pure wool vests to
a mere 2s. 8d. Those seeking to set up home found
bargains in furniture at Oldfield and Studdard,
Kirkgate. Sale items included an oak bedroom suite for
£27 15s., complete with bed. A three piece, ten cushion
Chesterfield suite in uncut moquette was £27 10s.
Many newly weds, however, put off having a home of
their own, as young husbands were leaving to join up,
and even going abroad.

Dorothy and Charlie Suthers were among them. Charlie was posted to Iceland early in their married life, so she lived at home with her parents, Mr and Mrs Arthur Nunns Priestley. Dorothy was directed to work at the ICI, where she was a clerk. There was no "Music While You Work" relayed to the staff canteen. Mr Priestley, choirmaster at Deighton Chapel, had served in the First World War, and in this one he joined the Home Guard.

Everybody was working hard and for long hours, besides helping voluntary causes, and tiredness often overcame people. A foreman was annoyed when a worker shuffled in to work late again.

"You've decided to turn up at last then?" he skitted.

"Ah, well, you see, it's those blessed blackout curtains. I can never wake up at right time when they're up," was the excuse.

"But where were you on Tuesday, *and* Wednesday morning, lad, then eh?" sarcastically enquired the boss, who had his own blackout difficulties to put up with in an early morning as well.

Maybe grilled fox was on the menu somewhere that January. Five were destroyed on the moors near Meltham. George Taylor tracked the last vixen to her lair. Joseph Brook, the old Fartown footballer and his dog were sent for, and soon had the fox out. Mr. Taylor then shot it.

Whether that poor fox got to heaven or not, at the Ritz cinema Bing Crosby was crooning away in *East Side of Heaven*. Starring with him were Joan Blondell, Mischa Auer, and C. Aubrey Smith.

Lancelot Luxton Key, of No. 107 Bradford Road, President of Huddersfield Musicians' Union, was outraged after hearing the Chief Constable's report about not knowing a better blackout anywhere than Huddersfield, so much so that he penned another of his regular missives to the local paper.

Well, judging by the number of fatal and other road accidents I feel that he is "about" correct. 5p.m. Already I have witnessed more than one road bump. At 5.45 I am going out with regulation form of pocket torch, suitably disguised round the bulb with tissue paper, in order to guide my daughter back home. In the event of my not returning I should like it to be made perfectly clear at the inquest that I am taking every precaution to preserve my safety with the very limited means the authorities allow. With all good wishes for my safe return, L. L. Key. 6th January, 1940.

Sarcasm was a useful weapon at times. In court a defendant was asked if he would like to pay something off his arrears.

"I'd love to," was the reply. "But we can't all do everything we want. We must make *some* sacrifices in wartime."

Entertaining others wasn't confined to laughter in court. Huddersfield Thespians were casting for *Arms and The Man*. George Wheatley Dyson, and Dora Rushworth took leading parts, while Mrs Pamela Blakeborough was the producer. The production was given in the New Co-operative Hall for the Mayor's War Charities Fund.

An appeal for a piano for Huddersfield Entertainments Committee was met by Joseph Walker, Marsh House, Lindley, and a volunteer tuner was also found.

Miss Nora Bray and her Dance School were among a list of concert parties busy entertaining the troops. Miss Sadie C. Shaw, former member of Huddersfield Light Opera Society, had become a member of the Black-Out Blues. Bradley Concert Party also "did their bit". Another side of the artistic life of the town was at the Rotary Club's meeting in January, when Norman Culley discussed the subject of Art and War.

There were some protests about Sunday music hall programmes for the forces on the wireless. Gracie Fields, however, after rendering the sacred song "The Holy City" in a Sunday broadcast was deemed to have given a reverent, as well as a brilliant rendering.

By 11 January there were some sixty refugees in the district. One had been a High Court judge, another the editor of an Austrian newspaper, one an authority on banking. This was revealed by the Rev. T. A. Dangerfield, Vicar of Moldgreen, in a statement on the work of Huddersfield and District Refugee Relief Committee, which had been started two months before the war, a room at St Mark's school having been lent and equipped as an office.

Six refugees had been brought from Germany, hospitality found for seven, and domestic posts for four. When the premises at St Mark's were lost, the YMCA offered accommodation. Then the Refugee Relief

Committee found a home at The Friends' Meeting House, Paddock. Five more people were hoped to be brought out of Germany. One was brother of a Polish nurse in the district, the other four were related to a Huddersfield refugee.

More men between twenty-five and fifty were needed for full-time service in Huddersfield Auxiliary Fire Service. Payment was £3 a week, with £1 bonus on completion of the course. That January a cabaret by Nora Bray's pupils entertained dancers at Cambridge Road Baths Annual Pantomime Ball, with music provided by Vivian Rawlins's Pirates Dance Band, and admission was 2s. 6d.

January being the time for making marmalade, the Ministry of Food allowed 3 lb sugar for every pound of oranges purchased for marmalade making, provided an invoice was produced and presented to the local Food Office.

A Linthwaite fellow, alleged to have allowed light through a skylight of his cow shed was brought to court. He was fined 20s. At this indignity he retorted "Tha can cross me off air raid warden's list now then." His money could have been better spent on bargains in the shops — Millet's Stores on Cross Church Street could have set him up with a few items for that pound note. A man's shirt at half price was 2s. 9d., gauntlet gloves were 2s. 11d., all wool cardigans 3s. 11d. Army and Naval socks, Government rejects, were 1s. 10d., "just right to buy for the troops".

Juggling food rations was more difficult than selling clothing. Some traders found themselves with abnormal stocks of bacon, yet were only allowed to sell it for coupons.

Tempers were running short among some panel patients, desperately trying to find a chemist's shop in the blackout. The Home Office had refused to allow chemists to display a sign over the pavement as a guide. What patients ought to do was to try and remember the *exact* position of a shop . . .

Nevertheless good humour, on the whole, tended to prevail. Some local "wit" wondered if, instead of the harrowing and monotonous wail of the sirens, they might be adapted to play jolly, appropriate tunes. Say, for instance, "Run, Rabbit, Run" or "Hush, hush, hush, here comes the Bogey Man", to be followed happily with "Girls and Boys Come Out to Play" for the All Clear.

By the middle of the month news was filtering through about local men who had joined up, and their fate. Among them was Kenneth Doody of Leeds Road, who was in hospital after his ship, the tanker *El Oso* had been blown up by a Nazi mine.

Great Northern Street abattoir was taken over as a government slaughter house. As a result, ten privately owned abattoirs in the town and many in country districts, had to close. People were allowed to kill their own pig if they had owned it for at least two months, and if they had a licence on behalf of the Ministry of Food. The meat was to be consumed only in the house of the licence holder.

A gleam of hope shone through when it became known that ham shanks and cooked ham would not be rationed. The price of cooked ham was fixed at 3s. 3d. If there was any danger of bacon "going off", permission could be given for it to be sold coupon free with regard to surplus stocks in the area. At one shop customers were triumphantly getting double what their coupons entitled them to.

At a dinner of Huddersfield Deaf and Dumb Institute, the mayor challenged the Institute's billiard champion to a game, and promised that whether he won or lost, members would be provided with a tripe supper. Games followed, and with happy hearts members at last made their way home in the moonlight.

David Brown's, the well-known engineering firm, held a special dance on Friday, 26 January 1940, at Cambridge Road Baths. Music was provided by Ralph Hunt and his band, and the MC was Steve Cantwell. Tickets were obtainable from L. Chillingsworth, King's Head Arcade.

At the police station, a "Special" reported late. The Sergeant admonished him: he should have been on his beat for an hour. "Why, what happened?" panted the Special.

Towards the end of the month, farmers still were not "in their stride", and a few butchers' shops had to close early.

Huddersfield's newest cinema, The Majestic, Viaduct Street, rose from the ruins of the old Star Picture House, which had burnt down in August 1939. Its first film, starring Humphrey Bogart in January, was *You Can't Get Away With Murder*.

Snow fell relentlessly as the month reached its last days, and it cut off many districts, including Crosland Moor and Outlane. On the 31st many villages were still isolated, but services had resumed to Sheepridge and Woodhouse. Oh, the times a bus did its utmost to negotiate steep Woodhouse Hill in treacherous conditions, passengers willing it to pull up from Central Avenue so they wouldn't have to walk through thick snow uphill further than they ought to — especially as they had paid!

Farmers at Lindley Moor, unable to reach customers, poured 120 gallons of milk down the drains. One enterprising farmer took his milk to the top of a village, drawing it in a zinc bath. In Scapegoat Hill a milkman had a can of milk strapped to his back as he plunged his wellington-clad feet into the snowdrifts.

Those who could stay at home, yet still feel they were being of service, were lucky. Bad weather was ideal for staying in by a blazing fire and knitting: no fewer than 300 lbs of wool were knitted for service men by members of Golcar Ladies' Comforts Society, probably when they were marooned in their homes as snow occasionally drifted up to bedroom windowsills during that freezing cold January of 1940.

In the wartime jargon that was becoming commonplace, Manchester Furnishing Company announced their January sale: "We scuttle carpet and lino prices, and, like the Graf Spee, down they go."

Food rationing began, with 4 oz of butter per person, 12 oz of sugar, and 4 oz of bacon or ham (3½ oz cooked). Coupons were only to be detached by the shopkeeper. There were some long, miserable faces about that day. "What the hell can we do with that? Our cat would make short work of that in a second!" was the type of comment heard on the street and in the shops. But dentists welcomed rationing of sugar, believing that children's and adults' teeth would greatly improve. Many housewives arrived in town only to realize they had forgotten their ration books, so they couldn't get what they had come for. Rationing had still to bite, though. A swan on the River Colne by Somerset Bridge was thrown scraps of bread by Inspector Cyril Sanders, but it was obviously so well fed that it just swam majestically down the river in haughty disdain.

Even Phyllis Bentley, the author, was working as an ambulance driver in Halifax. Born in Huddersfield, Phyllis visited the Huddersfield Authors' Circle at their monthly meeting.

For those who had joined the forces, there was glamour to offset the danger: a smart uniform, new friends, new locations. There was a very different outlook for those who stayed at home, directed to work in munitions or working in mills. Mrs Annie Holmes was a weaver at John Crowther's, Milnsbridge, mainly turning out Royal Air Force cloth — that lovely blue. A workman's return ticket from her home in Marsden cost 4½d. It was an early start, the mill gates closing at 7.15a.m. Annie felt as though she was entering the black hole of Calcutta, as all the windows had been painted black. They worked in the sheds in artificial light all the time. Eventually she and other workers complained, so it was washed off and new blackout arrangements were made.

There was no break until midday dinner at 11.45a.m., for three-quarters of an hour. The workers didn't want any interruption in their work, as they were paid for what they produced. If in the canteen, workers queued behind barriers for each item, Yorkshire pudding at one, meat another. There was a system of metal "checks". A shilling was paid for one, and when it was handed in the shilling was paid back — when the cutlery was returned in an attempt to prevent theft. Meals were selected the previous day, to avoid wastage.

Occasionally Marsden Church Amateurs gave a concert in the canteen. When work was over, the workforce either ate sandwiches in the mill at teatime, or took a teacake from home and bought fish and chips. These were brought round by a man who carried them in separate baskets, with an aluminium hot water bottle beneath each to keep them warm and covered with a towel. He did a roaring trade.

Weavers were all married women, single ones having either joined the Land Army, ATS, or gone to be conductresses. The latter made their own fun, giving stopping places nicknames. "Slaithwaite", for example, became "City Centre". Passengers joined in the fun. When a young new conductress leaned out to see where they were, then realized they were at Greenhead Park, she bawled out "Park Gates!"

"Nay lass, it can't be," sniggered an elderly passenger. "They've taken all t' gates for scrap."

On Saturday mornings the weavers worked from 7.15a.m. to 11.45a.m. In the afternoon Annie washed her overalls ready for Monday. As they bent over the looms a great deal during the course of the work, overalls became very dirty, so they used to buy "patterns" from the mill office for 1s. 6d., out of which could be made a couple of cloth aprons, saving wear and tear on the overalls.

When Annie began working at Crowther's in 1939 it was only supposed to be for a fortnight, but when war broke out she and the others were kept on. Her husband Fred was in the ARP. He enjoyed it best when Thomas Lunn, the butcher, was on duty with him, for Thomas brought pork pies for them. Those who lived in outlying areas such as Marsden, where there were farms, fared rather better in some respects. A few weeks before Christmas they had an "arrangement" with one farmer for a chicken and a bit of pork. Portions had to be handed out straight-away, so the transaction would not be found out.

John Crowther's mill always had a Christmas party for the children of employees. Weavers themselves would have been only too glad to rest and put their feet up, never mind parties. It was tiring work, standing all day long, with only the occasional moment or two to rest on a piece of wood, which was hooked to the end of the loom and could be let down.

The Arctic Café, New Street, served poultry from its own farm. In 1940 they still had butchers' meat, ham or bacon, butter on bread, and sugar in tea, if wanted. But sugar couldn't be pinched, as it was loose in bowls.

Luncheons were served from 11.30a.m.–2.30p.m. at the reasonable price of 1s. 3d.

Snow was one thing not in short supply that winter. In the town a parcel delivery lorry drew up outside a shop. Men were engaged outside in clearing the snow and, on seeing the lorry loom up, they jumped to the conclusion it had been sent by the Corporation, and promptly filled it with snow. The parcels were, most effectively, snowed under.

Snow scene photographs didn't appear in the local paper until later, as indications of weather conditions were considered to be helpful to the enemy.

The general public seemed to have more stomach for actual warfare than irksome food restrictions. "As we have had no meat for a week, I should like to know where to apply for a portion of the hash they have made of our meat rationing," wrote "Old Bones". A butcher quipped to a photographer: "I want you to photograph this piece of beef and enlarge it. I don't know where to start cutting to suit my customers."

Victoria nurses were commended for their devotion to duty during the snow. There was an influenza wave in Huddersfield that February, resulting in 117 tramway staff being absent, and between 5 and 10 per cent of a textile factory's workforce ill.

Those still on their feet could find amusement by going to see Gracie Fields in *Shipyard Sally* at the Tudor Super Cinema. It was hoped that influenza, coupled with the bad weather, would not mean poor attendance at the Police Ball, with the Aldro Dance Band, in the Town Hall on the 7th. This cost 5s., and refreshments were included. Skating star Sonja Henie was gliding around on the silver screen, Charlie Chan starred in *Reno* at the Princess. Heart throb Tyrone Power was also in *Second Fiddle* with Miss Henie.

It was announced that paper was to be rationed, supplies cut by two-fifths. The silver lining was that streets were litter free, as most commodities went unwrapped. People used to take their own basins to carry eggs in, and any scrap of paper went for salvage. School magazines were printed in smaller type to reduce material and cost, but it couldn't reduce the brilliance of some of the contributions! Joyce Beaumont, Form VI Arts and Science, St Clare House, at Greenhead High School, wrote this "Epitaph on a Saucepan":

In the first life, before the war
A saucepan new was I
And now, with wings of silver gleam
Transformed, in planes I fly.

All schools played their part in the War Effort. Form gardens at Greenhead High School produced vegetables and sold them. A Bring and Buy sale by Form 111R raised £3 9s. 7d., which was sent to Huddersfield men training in the south, to be spent on dart boards and other luxuries. Other gifts to the forces included a crate of cigarettes, magazines and books for the RAF. Gifts were also sent to naval ratings under Lieutenant Commander Berry — £3 12s. to be spent on games. The Mayor's Spitfire Fund raised £2 5s. The Royal

Corps of Signals, training in Huddersfield, received 2,500 sheets of notepaper, 2,500 envelopes, a weekly paper supply of *The Times*, draughtsmen and boards.

Later, gifts were also sent to Channel Island refugees, including parcels of clothing, gifts to evacuees, and about two hundred garments for children. In addition, tinfoil and scrap wool continued to be collected. During the summer holidays and mid-term several night-dresses and pairs of pyjamas had been made by the girls for evacuee children.

During War Weapons Week, the canary and cage given by Greenhead School caretaker Mr Atkinson in the slogan competition was won by Molly Dyson, of Form IIIC. The competition was open to the whole school, but Molly's "Give with a Grin and Help Britain to Win" was judged the best. Form 1B raised 14s. with a sale of dishcloths, coal gloves and other items; 1C, with a sale of unrationed goods and old newspapers, raised £2 10s 0½d. 111A sold "Victoria Bun Pennies", while others sold flowers, identity card cases, and held a dance. They accumulated £2 5s. 6½d.

School secretary Miss Haigh collected £1 5s. with her sale of hors d'oeuvres. Greenhead, in connection with the Women's Wartime Bureau, knitted 254 articles throughout the year with wool supplied by the Bureau. Junior forms continued to knit "squares" for blankets.

Money was collected for the British Red Cross, and 240 eggs were given to Huddersfield Royal Infirmary. For emergency rest centres (through the WVS) 337 pairs of socks were darned. Huddersfield men taken prisoners of war were sent chocolate and chewing gum.

A guinea was sent to Huddersfield Memorial and Relief Fund, in addition to a wreath from the school. The Russian Red Cross Fund benefited from a White Elephant sale which raised £23 13s. 10d.

Salvage collecting went on continuously. Rubber bands, used toothpaste tubes, bones, newspapers — and in the summer holidays Joyce Beaumont and others helped to make camouflage nets. They also collected toys and books for the Cinderella Society, to ensure poor children of the town had as good a Christmas as possible.

Words and music can often be as powerful and effective as the sword. The verse printed in the front of one of Greenhead High School's wartime magazines certainly seemed to inspire all to work hard to assist all aspects of the war effort:

One who never turned his back, but marched
  breast forward
Never doubted clouds would break, Never
  dreamed, though right were worsted,
Wrong would triumph, Held we fall to rise, are
  baffled to fight better, Sleep to wake.

Housewives were getting into the habit of joining queues. If they saw one, they joined it, not bothering first to find out what the queue was for. As one lady said, outside a butcher's shop, "it's a beggar when they have to ration lights."

Early in February 1940 there was said to be only one 4 stone pig at the slaughterhouse for the whole of

Huddersfield, farmers having been unable to get pigs through to market because of the weather.

Speaking of heavyweights, Tommy Farr was discussing terms for a bout with Joe Louis. It made a change from war conversations, but injustices occasionally overshadowed events. People were outraged to read about a Northern textile factory that had deducted pay from employees who sheltered during an air raid warning. When they went on strike, they were given their pay.

"Make Do and Mend" was becoming the vogue. Greenwood's of No. 13 Victoria Street encouraged customers to begin making rugs, and knitting balaclavas, gloves and socks for the forces, in service colour wools. Their sales slogan was "A Greenwood Craft Will Conquer The Blackout."

New innovations were constantly introduced to lighten traumas of the blackout. Rushworth's began to sell pen torches for 3s. 6d., with an attachment for writing in the dark. There was also a bakelite case, lipstick size, an ideal emergency light for 1s. 9d. And many dainty torches for ladies' use, to easily slip into a handbag, were sold.

Rabbit clubs were formed for food production. Many households began to have a hutch or two in the back garden, where rabbits eagerly munched through dandelion leaves or whatever came their way. Young Sam Hawkins, about eight years old, began breeding rabbits. He looked upon himself as a future tycoon, and sold baby rabbits for 6d. a pair. My two were kept solely as pets, coming into the kitchen when mother and dad were at the Theatre or Palace with the free pass, and Philip was up at Warrenfield ARP Post, or fire-watching. Bunny and Beauty leapt and danced to strains of "The Blue Danube", and Heddle Nash singing "Come Into The Garden, Maud". They had their supper with me before being returned to the hutch around 10p.m.

Customers of the Direct Meat Company, Buxton Road, flocked there on opening day, 23 February. There was home killed meat in plenty, they boasted, with no ration cards needed. One chap suggested "no wonder there's been fewer rats down by t' cut."

Plenty of chilled mutton and lamb was also imported around that date.

On 24 February people were advised to "Put Your Clock Forward tonight. Summertime will come into force at two o'clock Sunday morning." It was thought common sense to take advantage of the lengthening days as early as possible under wartime conditions.

By the 26th there were seventy refugees in town — Austrians, Czechs, Germans and some Jews. At the Rotary Club meeting in Whiteley's Café, an appeal for £300 was made to defray office expenses, set up an emergency fund, and aid in providing a hostel. Doctors and dentists gave their services free to the refugees.

Churches and chapels welcomed the new "summer time" as it enabled them to return to normal Sunday evening services. In the Minutes Book of Deighton chapel, it was noted that minute books after 1935 were either mislaid or had been given to salvage. Town cafés rejoiced, as it meant more trade. People could first enjoy their tea, then go shopping and still be home before dark.

The air raid precautions committee decided to build basement shelters at Zion Methodist chapel, Lindley, for sixty-six persons, and at the Bridge Inn, Lockwood, for two hundred. It was confirmed that they were to purchase 500 steel helmets.

The good news was that Corporation dustmen were to collect waste paper. The bad news was that eggs were to go up, from 3s. 3d. to 3s. 6d. a dozen.

At the annual whist drive and dance in the New Co-operative Hall, Buxton Road, on 29 February, the Mayor presented "Lucky Horseshoes" to men in uniform. Proceeds were in aid of charities concerned with the Huddersfield Branch of the British Limbless Ex-Servicemen's Association.

In March the famous Florrie Ford headed the bill at the Palace Theatre, and those not in uniform were beginning to think about their Easter bonnets. Sailor hats for ladies were the most popular spring style in town shops, Guardsman Red the most popular colour. Bowler hats were popular again with men.

Spring-cleaning was under way. Hitler may or may not attack in spring, but Huddersfield housewives were already attacking — replacing shabby linoleum, rugs and quilts, throwing carpets over the clothes line and beating the dust out. Manchester Furnishing again came to their aid, offering to fit linos of value £2 upwards, free in local areas.

The Borough rate was expected to go up by an increase of 1s. 6d. in the pound, due to the cost of local air raid precautions. But never mind. Errol Flynn and Olivia De Havilland could be seen at the Empire in *The Adventures of Robin Hood*.

Three hundred children had been allocated to Kirkburton for evacuation from Bradford, and the Council was in a position to billet them.

Dorothy Carter's mother and her friend Mrs Richardson went to the Scout hut down Wiggan Lane, Sheepridge, to offer a home to some of the evacuees from London. Mrs Richardson had room for three, but Mrs Olive Carter only took one little boy as she already had her own sons — Ernest, Ralph, Alan and Ramon (so named after film star Ramon Navarro). The London evacuees looked a bit lost at first, armed only with their gas masks, labels with their names on, and a small case each. But it didn't take long before the children became part of "our Gang", as Dorothy called them.

Those who risked taking a break away from home at Easter were reminded to take ration books with them. By then meat as well as sugar, bacon and butter were rationed. There was, of course, always that good old standby "fish and a penn'orth", but even the Huddersfield Fish Fryers Federation had mooted a charge of 1½d. for chips in fish and chip shops, but not necessarily over the whole district. There had been increased costs of dripping, paper, and gas.

The Warrenfield ARP Post at Sheepridge had a happy band of volunteers. Philip, my brother, was one of them, and looked upon it more or less as having the air of a gentleman's club. Mr Anyon was one of the leading lights and became a familiar figure wandering up and down. They may not have seen much action, apart from at the table tennis and billiard tables, but locals felt safer knowing that they were there and ready.

In the summer holidays of 1940, evacuees arrived at Mount Pleasant school, Lockwood. Mrs Elizabeth Moorhouse had four children of her own, but decided to take one of them, a twelve-year-old boy. His mother visited occasionally, and the families wrote to each other between visits. Mollie Moorhouse responded to the school's request — "ask your mothers if they have any pans to spare for the war effort" — by almost clearing the lot from their kitchen, including the three tier steamer. And now there was an extra mouth to feed — but somehow they managed.

Mollie was sick to death of the increasing monotony of food, especially of the two "sweet" cakes that her mother baked each week. Wednesday, baking day, heralded the latest coconut cake and Robin cake, baked in loaf tins.

Nothing was wasted. A kind of metal stud was bought from a hardware shop and the green Fairy soap was attached to it, so that when hands had been washed the soap didn't dribble away. Bits of soap too small to use separately were put into a wire basket with a handle, then swished around in the washing up bowl with the crockery and cutlery.

Tripe being unrationed, it figured on the dinnertime table frequently, with onions. Mrs Moorhouse sometimes bought horsemeat from the shop in town, unrationed.

It was alright for a meat and potato pie, but needed to be cooked longer than ordinary meat.

Mr Moorhouse occasionally managed to get a couple of duck eggs, and he kept rabbits ostensibly to show. But if one, poor thing, was not deemed good enough to be admired alive, it was killed. And the family, and London evacuee, ate it.

Mrs Moorhouse, like many housewives, contrived to make most of the family clothes on her sewing machine. Parachute silk, when she could get some, was a boon as it made lovely blouses. Once she acquired some barrage balloon material, which was transformed into a tablecloth. Mollie had some transfers and embroidered it.

Another Huddersfield family added a twelve-year-old girl evacuee from London to their own son and two daughters. She was surprised that her new home had "all mod-cons" and "such a nice bathroom, so far North". Perhaps another surprise was that her new "family" were vegetarians. A vegetarian was allowed 12 oz of cheese instead of 2 oz, even young children.

Father of the household, like some others during the Second World War, was a conscientious objector. A gentleman of upright and unblemished character, he was sent to prison because of his beliefs, and because he stood by his principles. Being in prison was far from being a sinecure. He wore the same socks for five weeks, and then had only cold water to wash them in. Cold water was used for washing the floor, too, a job which had to be done every day. He also spent hours sewing mail bags. These were not pleasant occupations by any means, but at least something was being achieved — unlike wives who often queued for ages to buy a pound of apples or other commodity. Demoralizing in good weather, this was terrible if rain was lashing down, or in freezing temperatures on a winter day.

As February drew to a close, and there were fewer hours of blackout to contend with, people began to see and talk about the funny side of it, as opposed to the aggravating and often tragic ones. One fellow, for example, before Summer time came in, decided to risk taking the short cut home from work. Hands stretched out before him, blindly teetering along, a sixth sense suddenly caused him to halt abruptly.

"Where the dickens am I going?" To his amazement, out of the blackness came an answering voice.

"Thar't going into t'watter."

"Oh, an' ha does ta know?" the other seemingly disembodied voice wanted to know.

"Cos 'ahm just coming aht," was the alarming reply.

Longevity seems to be the reward of hard workers. Ninety-three-year-old Fanny Garside, of Birchencliffe, was still knitting socks for soldiers at the beginning of March 1940.

Gas masks were turning up among lost property. Trying to increase a sense of responsibility among owners, a charge of half a crown was to be incurred to replace them that April. Prematurely, a man forecast that the war would end in September. As though to dispute him, the Tudor cinema was showing the film *Old Mother Riley Joins Up*, emphasizing the conviction that there was still a long way to go Lister Street allotments, Moldgreen, took over the old football pitch adjoining Ravensknowle Park, to use it in the Dig For Victory Campaign. Indeed, hard work was the order of the day.

Mangles, with dual purpose folding table tops, came on sale at Jas Woodhouse, No. 36 New Street, at a cost of £4 19s. 6d. Some girls worked in laundries as their "war work". Mavis Smith, who lived at No. 5 Wiggan Lane, Sheepridge, first helped at Gregg's Laundry, sorting clothes, sewing, ironing, and occasionally in the office. It meant an early start at 7.30a.m. Her friend Dorothy Brunt, of Brackenhall Road, also worked in the laundry as a packer. Hard work though it was, the girls were never so tired that they didn't want to go dancing in the evenings. What girl could resist going out and about, with all the fascinating newcomers entering the town? Mavis's dad Jim worked at L. B. Holliday's, and spent his leisure time in the Home Guard.

Springtime was in the air, and Jimmy Hunter and his Brighton Follies came to the Theatre Royal. Nora Bray's "Follies On Parade" entertained for the Lord Mayor's War Charities Fund.

It became apparent that some people, on hearing an air raid warning, had been wearing their gas masks for up to three hours, not having heard the All Clear. Masks should not be put on until gas was discerned, or warning rattles were heard.

An almost inevitable result of strange young men arriving in the town was that young girls began to run after them. Some were evacuees, freed from the restraining influence of parents. Even Shirley Temple was growing up, though losing none of her childhood charm, in *Susannah of the Mounties* at the Tudor, in April 1940.

Marjorie Stanley and her husband had a butcher's shop, in Milnsbridge. To help pensioners, Marjorie chopped bones up for them to use in stews. It was a case of "give and take" between shopkeeper and customer many a time. Occasionally a customer asked Mrs Stanley if she wanted any clothing coupons, and was given a tin of corned beef in exchange. It always paid to tell the truth, Marjorie thought, because if you did, nobody believed you. Her husband was driving up Westgate once with black market eggs in his car. When police stopped him and asked "What have you got in there?", Jack cheekily replied.

"Oh, summat to do with Black Market."

"Gerrof with yer, yer silly devil," laughed the policeman, waving him on without investigating. You could get away with murder by joking, Marjorie thought.

When Jack was due to be called up, Marjorie was in a quandary, having no experience of butchering. James Hanson's father called in one day, and advised her she could get six month's deferment for Jack, so that she could learn the trade. Eventually he joined the RAF, and his wife was in charge of the shop. One day, a huge frozen buttock of beef from Argentina arrived. Mr Kerrod, a retired butcher, laid it on the wooden block with the new lady butcher's help. It was Marjorie's initiation when he admitted, "I can't chop that, Mrs Stanley."

"Alright then, I'll chop it myself," laughed the newly fledged butcher. Everyone had to learn new skills, and most, as she did, rose to the challenge with the same magnificence.

Marjorie had to fire-watch as well. She used to rush round like mad in order to be able to spend the weekend in Sheffield, where Jack had been posted. One weekend she set off, then hastily returned home when German planes were bombarding Bradford.

With the best will in the world, though, exhaustion can overtake one. After working all day in the shop and fire-watching on Friday nights at a dental surgeon's in Market Street, Milnsbridge, with receptionist Ann, Marjorie became worn out. They had only a camp bed each to sleep on; then the shop had to be opened on Saturday morning at 8a.m. Then off she used to dash to Sheffield after closing. She developed a bad attack of tonsillitis, and asked Mrs Middlebrook Haigh at the Citizens' Advice Bureau what to do. Mrs Middlebrook Haigh obtained compassionate leave for Jack, and he came home for a fortnight.

Another Huddersfield lady, Marjorie Thackray (what a popular name Marjorie was!) was a salesgirl at Leaders Gowns, New Street, until she had to do war work. From being inside all her working day, she had to become a gas meter reader — most of the male workers having gone to the war. She encountered something in her new job that she thought was potentially even more lethal than meeting Hitler himself in somebody's kitchen. Knocking at a door in Holmfirth, she had to step over a tiger to reach the cellar to read the meter. Fenella the Holmfirth tiger was quite famous and, fortunately, quite tame. She was taken for walks in wartime Holmfirth on a lead, like a huge dog. Even a humdrum task like reading gas meters had its unexpected moments.

Unlike Marjorie, Margaret Horne, who had a hairdressing business in King's Head Arcade, knew all her customers, one of whom kept her supplied with fillet steaks during times of shortage. She cosseted her clients as they looked after her. Margaret loved cooking, and if a lady had a lunchtime appointment, she was handed a tasty sizzling chop as she sat beneath the dryer. Margaret bought some hens for another of her customers who had some land, on the proviso that she let her have freshly laid eggs whenever possible.

A shampoo and set cost 4s. 6d., and the "loos" beneath the salon were among the best air-raid shelters in the town. In the early forties Margaret won the "Eugene" competition for the best dressed window. Her assistants earned in the region of £2 a week. With swagger coats at 45s. 11d. and 32s. 6d. at Joan's, No. 6 New Street, any working girl would have to save up for a while to buy one of those.

In April the Thespians produced a new J. B. Priestley comedy, *When We Are Married*. On the 19th of the month Florrie Forde died, but George Formby was still chasing away wartime blues at the Tudor, in *Come On George*.

Huddersfield had a cookery demonstration at the Corporation Electricity Showrooms, and a talk about how to avoid waste by the Healthy Life Society. Appropriately for the age of the gas mask, *The Man in the Iron Mask* was on at the Princess cinema, commencing 25 April, and starring Louis Hayward and Joan Bennett.

When mouths were free from encumbrances such as masks, and stomach empty, what better way of occupying both than a midday meal at the Arctic Café on New Street? Lancashire hot pot or grilled sausage, baked or mashed potatoes, braised onions or butter beans, followed by jam roll and custard, Queen's Pudding or ground rice, and coffee, cost only 1s. 3d.

The Corporation itself was fined £25 for a blackout offence at Lockwood Baths on 10 July. Town Clerk Mr S. Proctor ordered in August that those who did not have a sufficient covering of earth on top of their Anderson shelter, and who took no steps to provide one after being warned, were liable to have the shelter taken away. There must be about 15 in of earth on top. While some didn't care a jot about the shelter at the bottom of the garden, others made a feature of it, vying with neighbours over who could have the best looking shelter and the best flowers on top. The aim was to make it as comfortable and inviting inside almost as the George Hotel itself.

Theatre-goers were thrilled to be able to see in person "names" hitherto only heard on the wireless. That August Albert Whelan, Popular Broadcaster, and Vine, More and Nevard, Radio Entertainers from *Sing*

Song and *Monday Night at Eight* were in Huddersfield. Of course, one needn't necessarily go to a theatre to be amused. One had only to keep ears open in and around the town to hear snippets of entertainment. A lady in a queue was relating a recent experience: she had heard a whistling noise, then what sounded like an explosion. "I thought a bomb had dropped. How relieved I was to find it was only my husband who'd fallen off the ladder and hit his finger with a hammer."

The opening of a war efforts exhibition in Cloth Hall Street included first aid, air force cadets, YMCA, a wartime cookery stall, and an allotments stall with a show of vegetables from local allotments, and also from Beaumont Park gardens.

That year Huddersfield had 1,000 extra gardens and allotments. More were hoped for in 1941. Also exhibiting were rescue and demolition squads, the Citizens' Advice Bureau, "Keep Fit" movement, Salvage Authority, and the Mayoress's Comforts Fund.

The Food Control Committee now had power to authorize additional rations to invalids who suffered certain diseases.

News kept trickling in as the summer wore on of more and more missing Huddersfield servicemen. For those soldiers stationed in and around town, a tea van had been set up. More shortages cropped up — wood for packing cases was to be rationed.

Amidst the gloom came news to lighten the hearts of cricket lovers. West Indian cricketer Leary Constantine was to play in Huddersfield League at least one match before the end of the season, and Holmfirth had been selected as the club to have his services.

All manner of small ways to help others did a lot to ease the lot of soldiers away from home. Some stationed at Bradley had to bring buckets of water from the station, as they had none on the camp. Edith Dyson allowed the lads to have a bath in her home.

Edith and her neighbours with young children didn't go far, apart from shopping, especially in an evening, in case there was a raid. Even so, summer evenings were happily spent in their back gardens, or enjoying "collop parties" on Edith's lawn. She made the best tasting collops, so the others gave what fats they could spare or render down. Old kitchen chairs and stools were brought out, and they had sing-songs and gossiped till darkness fell. Those collop evenings were happy and memorable. On nights when the sirens did go, it made you feel a lot better knowing that your friends were in their shelters at the bottom of their gardens as well.

A total of 1,564 men engaged in certain engineering and other occupations covered by the Industrial Registration Order of 1940 registered at Huddersfield Employment Exchange that August.

Increased output was obtained by means of overtime and shift work. All Huddersfield industries began to have "staggered" holidays, so works had no need to close down.

Eric Buckley had joined the ATC when it was formed, hoping to join the RAF when old enough. With the ATC he had visited Finningley Aerodrome and seen bombers and fighters. He had even had the thrill of going up for a flight in one. Alas, when the time came for his medical, he failed it, passing Grade Four. What a blow! Instead he went to work at W. C. Holmes of Turnbridge. Over ninety new benzole plants were installed at the onset of war, together with equipment for production of pure toluol. A wide range of new manufactures and processes was introduced to meet the urgent demand for many details required in modern warfare. Exploder containers and detonators for bombs, the latter for use in 4,000 lb high explosive bombs, were machined from solid bar on lathes specially set up for female labour, each worker having a single operation to perform.

Harrison inert gas machines were of particular value during the war period for dealing with gas plant and mains suffering bomb damage. A further development of these machines was made for the Ministry of Petroleum Warfare. Adequate controls and instruments were fitted to all machines so that they could be used under widely varying conditions, and as many safeguards as possible had to be provided to prevent damage when used by operators who often had had only a short period of training.

Loch-class twin screw frigates were specially designed and built to counter the U-boat. Owing to the urgent need, qualified draughtsmen were loaned to the Admiralty to help in the design for rapid construction. The frigates were fabricated in engineering works in different parts of the country, and assembled at the shipyards. W. C. Holmes made the forecastle deck, supplying finished sections for forty-one frigates. The finished section, 40 ft by 30 ft had to be accurate to 1/8 in in each dimension. After complete assembly for Lloyd's inspection, the deck was dismantled into sections for dispatch by road transport.

W. C. Holmes also made bogie wheels and turret track rings for Churchill tanks, and electrical switchgear parts.

Eric found it laborious work, carrying bags of steel dust, and sandblasting rocket shells. He had to have a bath every night, and his stockings went rusty with the dust. "It was worse than being in any forces," he said. Starting work at 7a.m., he got up at 5.30a.m. each morning to catch the 6a.m. train from Clayton West to Huddersfield, then walked down to Holmes's. Sometimes, if he worked overtime, it was 10p.m. before he arrived home.

There was a ten minute break mid-morning, when drinks were brought round on a trolley, and three-quarters of an hour was allowed for the midday meal. "Music While You Work" was relayed — but often it was so noisy in the works that it could hardly be heard.

Precious leisure time was spent attending whist drives at Skelmanthorpe, or at the Oddfellows Hall. Scissett Baths dancing on Saturday nights. If the sirens went when Eric was in a cinema, he stayed where he was: "What was the point in going out, when I'd paid?"

Prizes at whist drives were "bits and bats", perhaps a hair brush or other trifling item. Round Clayton West they "didn't do bad" for food: a bit of black market meaning there was usually pork to be had from the farmers. And Eric's dad got soap from the pit where he worked, "right hard household soap, but soap nevertheless".

Sometimes Eric had to work on the night shift, from 9.00p.m. until 7.00a.m. If he finished a job in between train times he was allowed to carry on working, and clock out in time for the next train.

Doris Holliday taught swimming at Cambridge Road Baths. After Dunkirk both pools were opened for returning soldiers. Each tired, grimy soldier was given a bar of soap, then they plunged into the pools for a refreshing bath, the first after the battle. Then they were ushered into the café for refreshments. The water, filthy by then, was emptied, then refilled for normal swimming.

Doris's talents weren't confined to swimming: she was an entertainer as well. Nora Bray's "Follies On Parade" didn't want to lose a star turn, so Doris was persuaded not to join the forces but to go on munitions instead. She went to work at Seller's, Chapel Hill, initially going to Leeds for tuition for a month. She worked from 7a.m., until 5.30 or 6p.m. Night shifts gave her an upset tummy. Doris earned a bonus every month making "something for bomber wheels". On Saturday mornings the firm worked from 7a.m. until 12.30p.m.

All Doris's spare time was given to entertaining the troops. She did comedy sketches with Joan Morris, based on the war, and using their own scripts. Sometimes they went to St Patrick's Hall at the top of

Fitzwilliam Street with a show. If the girls couldn't get mascara, boot black was used, and so was Leichner theatrical make-up. Gwen Taylor was the pianist. Nora Bray's husband, Jack Stewart, a tailor, made all the costumes. For one military number he made a full officer's outfit for Nora, and taught the "Follies" army drill.

Bill Campbell was so impressed with Doris that he invited her to go on tour with him, and his Rocky Mountain Rhythm. But as she had begun courting Bert Martin at the time she refused. Anyhow, it was such fun for a girl in Huddersfield during the war! The "Follies" were the amateur side of ENSA, which Doris also had the opportunity to join.

Nora put her own words to "Oh Listen to the Band", and Joan was a wow as Carmen Miranda in one of the shows.

One night they had gone to Marsden to entertain. Fog came down thicker than any blackout. Doris's family wasn't on the telephone, so she couldn't let them know she was alright. After the show, the Follies set off to walk back home, as no buses were available. They managed to negotiate their way to Lockwood, with full make-up still on, hair stuck down with the damp fog. They only had one torch between them — and the battery failed in that by the time they reached Lockwood. There was nothing to fear from passers-by, though. They said a polite "Good night" as the theatrical troupe loomed up, arm in arm, from the pea souper fog, and went on their way. Eventually, the team had to separate, and they had to find their own way home at three in the morning. But it was fun — singing all the way: "Kiss me Goodnight Sergeant Major", "There'll be Blue Birds over the White Cliffs of Dover", "A Nightingale Sang in Berkeley Square", and the ever popular Vera Lynn hit, "Yours".

The Follies always ended shows with:

Goodnight to you all, Goodnight, Goodnight,
The Long Day is through, Sleep Tight, Sleep
   Tight.
The Shadows are falling, so turn down the lights,
Goodnight to you all, Goodnight, Goodnight.

Excitement there was in plenty in 1940. A runaway horse drawing a milk float down High Street in August, in the direction of New Street, could have caused havoc. But a young soldier, Lance-Corporal Mervyn Lloyd, Royal Corps of Signals, from down south, dashed into the road, caught the reins, and brought the tearaway milk float to a standstill.

Channel Island refugees' families in Huddersfield urgently required houses to rent in the late summer of 1940. People were requested to give all manner of household goods to help, such as babies' high chairs, furniture, crockery, pillows, sheets and blankets. Collection was by lorry.

The Refugees Committee was at Kayes College, New North Road. Collections were going on all over the place. Pig troughs or bins were being placed in streets for the collection of kitchen waste suitable for pig food, and were filled so rapidly they had to be emptied several times a day. One trough was outside the Town Hall. When housewives went into town to shop, their baskets were filled with kitchen waste.

At the Palace Theatre Donald Peers was warbling "In a Shady Nook, By A Babbling Brook" to entranced audiences of mainly female fans.

New suggestions to help the clothing situation were continually put forward. A novel one was that anyone owning a bob tailed sheepdog could soon get enough wool from combings to make a suit. A rush to buy a bob tailed sheepdog did not ensue, as there was first the problem of what to feed it on.

Some wardens, annoyed that they only had tin hats and armbands, were leaving to join the Home Guard, which had a uniform. Every other town's wardens had uniforms, so why not Huddersfield? Smokers had a grievance as well. They weren't allowed to pursue their habit in public shelters, as it was important that the air was kept fresh.

August 1940 was hot and dry, with the prohibition of hosepipes and swilling of flags being enforced.

"That was a very short air raid alert the other night, wasn't it?" a shopper was overheard conversing in a queue.

"Aye," replied her elderly friend, "hardly worth putting me teeth in for."

Never slow to cash in on current affairs, Manchester Furnishing Company advertised: "New Purchase Tax will make carpets, linoleums, rugs, very much dearer. But don't forget that this will be your contribution towards Government finances, and consequent shortening of the War."

Among those earlier reported as missing, news was heard of Bandsman Arthur Mitchell, of Lowerhouses, who had been taken a prisoner of war in Germany. He had joined the 27th Battalion Duke of Wellington's Regiment a week before the outbreak of war, and was a saxophonist in the battalion band. Formerly he had been a Corporation bus conductor and member of the tramways band. Also POWs in Germany were Private John Ronald Lindley and Private Bernard Caulfield.

Complaints increased about untidy air raid shelters, some people having taken to eating picnic meals in them. Fifty to sixty staff were employed to clean shelters out after each alarm. When the All Clear sounded it was anything but — with a trail of litter scattered around the shelters.

Towards the end of August, Charles Laughton, Sir Cedric Hardwick and Maureen O'Hara in *The Hunchback of Notre Dame* at the Picture House engendered imitations of the notorious hunchback by fervent cinema-goers, whose mimicry hitherto had usually been limited to pulling a scowling face, imitating the Nazi salute and shouting "Heil, Hitler."

Most wedding photographs now portrayed the groom in uniform. Corporal R. Robinson and his bride, aircraft woman W. H. Baines, showed the bride in uniform too. They married at the registry office, then had a reception at the bride's home. She gave her soldier husband a shaving set; he gave her a gold powder compact.

Sad news came through about a local preacher in the Holmfirth Methodist circuit. Sapper Albert Wood had died at a casualty clearing station in France on 29 May, from gunshot wounds.

A year into the war, Alderman N. Crossley, JP, appealed to raise £25,000 in the Mayor's Spitfire Appeal, to provide a squadron of five planes for the RAF.

Because air raid shelters were closed to dogs, cards could be sent, post free, from the National Canine Defence League, to be displayed in windows, and offering refuge to dogs and their owners.

Author Phyllis Bentley came to town again on 4 September, to give a lecture in the Technical College in aid of the Benevolent and Orphans Fund of Huddersfield and District Teachers' Association.

Proceeds of a comic cricket match on Slaithwaite cricket field, in aid of Slaithwaite Red Cross and Comforts Fund, raised £100.

Summer time was drawing to a close. The Home Secretary gave notice that it would end on the night of 16/17 November, as provided by the Defence Summer Time Regulations, 1939.

"Up Housewives and At 'em!" ran the slogan, filling Kirkburton householders with the inspiration to "do their bit". It was decided at a Council Meeting that if they were prepared to do the spadework they would be provided with material for air raid shelters. Material (concrete slabs) was provided by the Government, but labour had to be given free, to build shelters that would accommodate fifty people. Of course the ladies would not be expected to do the actual labouring work, that was their husbands' province, but they could do the "back up" jobs.

Mayor Norman Crossley was the first air raid "casualty". During a warning he visited a public shelter and cut his leg. He visited the Public Library first aid post, and had the wound dressed. The result was so satisfactory that His Worship showed his appreciation to the personnel of the post by treating them to a feast of fish and chips early that September.

A Lockwood woman was in court accused of attempting to obtain rationed food from Ireland. She had written to her mother-in-law asking her to send 1 lb of tea, 2 lb sugar, and 1 lb of butter, well parcelled up. She added, "this is only Tuesday and we are well into our rations." She promised to send 10s. in payment. The letter had come into the possession of the Ministry, and the prosecution resulted. The lady from Yews Hill Road was ordered to pay the costs of her case. If people attempted to obtain food like this, shipping space would be taken up, and ordinary rationed supplies would be affected.

Another man sent a postal order for 9s. to an address in Cork, asking for 4½ lb best butter, having seen an advert published at Christmas. He was fined £1 and granted 2 gns advocate's fee.

People were advised to wear gas masks for at least fifteen minutes every week, to acclimatize themselves to them. Masks would not deteriorate as no gas was being used.

Platoon Sergeant Major Douglas Arnold Harpin, of No. 124 Birkby Hall Road, sent a letter to his family. He was a prisoner of war in Germany, permitted to write two letters a month, and to receive as many as people cared to send. One parcel could be sent to him every three months. He mentioned articles he would like, and advised his parents to consult the Red Cross Society about sending them.

Advice about living with the blackout kept appearing in the papers. For instance, standing for a few minutes in a darkened hall rather than going straight from a lighted room into the blackout was recommended. Blind people came off best in the situation, frequently leading the sighted in the darkness.

A number of soldiers enrolled at the Technical College on 10 September for technical training. There was a great demand for foreign language classes, and there were special classes in wartime cookery.

The last of Huddersfield's trams was scrapped the next day, to help provide scrap metal for guns. Seats were retained for use in air raid shelters, and doors were used for greenhouses.

It wasn't only dire happenings that came up in court. In a domestic dispute the husband complained that his wife made the excuse that her feet were bad so that she didn't have to go out with him. Yet the siren had only to go off and she "ran like a hare".

Even getting young children to help "Dig For Victory" was helpful. The week beginning 12

September was Allotment Week in Huddersfield, a thousand more plots being the aim.

Borough member Mr W. Mabane starred in a Ministry of Information film entitled *Wear Your Gas Mask.*

Hearts sank when it became known that places of entertainment would have to close at 9.30p.m. Chief Constable John Wells thought it a necessary step in order to minimize loss of life or personal injury. An order was also made prohibiting public music and dancing after 11p.m.

Mr A. W. Toalster, Manager of Cambridge Road Baths, said bookings for dances were higher than ever before. "The later the dances are, the more popular with the public," he said. The most popular were those that continued after midnight. He appealed to all dance organizers to start their functions at 6p.m. instead of 7.30p.m.

Back gardens were sprouting talent as well as vegetables. Behind No. 37 Browning Road, Sheepridge, the garden was screened by sheets and quilts for a makeshift theatre, as children gave a concert and sang and danced for the Spitfire Fund.

Surplus items were still required for refugee work in the town. Owing to the blackout there was no evening distribution of clothing from the Depot at No. 36 Byrom Arcade, and opening was limited to Monday, Wednesday and Friday, from 2.30p.m. until 4.30p.m., and Saturday afternoons, only for the issue of men's clothing.

In court on 17 September, an ARP Section Leader was called to give evidence in a lighting order case. He read the oath incorrectly, and was asked to read it over again.

"You will excuse me, but it is the first time I have been in court," stammered the newly fledged official leader. Magistrate's Clerk Mr Thomas Smailes told him he would become used to the ritual if he came there often enough.

Those magistrates must have had plenty of laughs in wartime. One husband told them that "you can have too much of a good thing. I like my wife to keep the house clean, but if she was in the trenches she'd want to polish the barbed wire."

A vindictive wife told a magistrate that her husband was very lazy. "He only puts a clean shirt on so that he'll show up in the blackout." It must have made them wonder why some couples bothered to marry. How could a wife's face change so much from one her husband fell in love with to one that "drinks her tea with an expression on her face like a third and final notice . . ." And what did the couple talk about in courtship days if, as a wife complained, "My husband never tells me anything. He might be in the Ministry of Information for all I can get out of him."

With the influx of soldiers in the town it was thought prudent to talk to parents at Spring Grove School about sex instruction, and the problem of war for a girl of fifteen or thereabouts who pestered a soldier, "obeying an urge she did not understand". But no school instruction, they were told, could replace the homely kind of talk that only a parent could give.

What a husband's role in life was in war time, either when home on leave or when at home full time, was summed up by one wife: "It is a husband's duty to take his wife to the pictures at least once a week."

Women were becoming more emancipated as they took on outside jobs. They were smoking more as well, which shocked a gentleman who wrote to the local newspaper after seeing female smokers on buses: "How common and ugly they look — they will be the mothers of the next generation, which cannot turn out to be anything but C3 quality if these stupid habits are not completely stopped."

On 25 September children were learning useful habits, helping the nation's war effort by collecting acorns for pig food.

Last buses were to be at 10p.m., and continued to run if the sirens sounded unless there was imminent danger of attack. Tram lines were taken up at Honley, causing many objections.

Appealing to people's fears was one way of trying to sell a £1,850 free-hold property. It was advertised as a "safe retreat in the West Riding of Yorkshire — sheltered by the Pennines".

October came in, and so did Spencer Tracy and Hedy Lamarr at the Ritz in *I Take This Woman*. The Ritz was the most impressive cinema to go to, as during the interval the Wurlitzer organ emerged and played tunes of the moment. Saturday nights, though, were dancing time for the young ones. Aub Hirst and his

Westbourne Players (Swing Band of the North) drew the crowds to the Town Hall on 5 October, with Spot Waltz, valuable prizes, and MC Steve Cantwell. Admission was 1s. 6d., with HM Forces half price.

Vying with Aub Hirst was Roy Dickinson and his band at the Co-op Hall. "Do you come here often?" was still the opening gambit for many, after asking a young lady to dance, but so many things were happening in wartime that there was no shortage of conversation during the waltzes and quick-steps: "Did you hear about the London barber who had the upper part of his shop blown away? He put a notice on the door — I have had a close shave today. What about you?" If you could make a dancing partner laugh, you were likely to be accepted to walk them home after the dance.

Shops kept coming up with new ideas. Rushworth's had reliable anti-splinter nets and blackout curtains at 10½d., 1s., and 1s. 11d. a yard.

A Longwood conscientious objector argued: "My citizenship is not here — it is in Heaven." He was brought down to earth when conditionally registered for land work.

Babies were still being named after favourite film stars by many new parents, but one baby, born in an Anderson shelter, was given the Christian name of "Anderson".

The Colne Valley received its first batch of evacuees from Southern England. Some complained that they could scarcely sleep the first night as it was so quiet here. They didn't have to wait too long for things to alter.

War Weapons Week was from Saturday 23 November to 30 November, to raise money for three destroyers, each one costing about £450,000.

Huddersfield was to have a rude awakening just before Christmas. Here is the account of Barbara Wilkinson:

The bombs fell on Oakes village on the night of 22/23 December 1940, Wellington Mills taking the brunt of the explosions. One shell completely demolished the four storey building in Plover Road. Everyone was in bed as no alert had been sounded.

I lived at No. 20 Oakes Road. All the houses in the terrace, Nos 2–24 Wellington Street (between Oakes Road and Wellington Mills) suffered heavy damage, but windows over a much wider area, including those of Lindley parish church, were shattered.

By torchlight we were all escorted into an air raid shelter in Oakes Council School yard, and a little later we transferred to the cellars of Oakes Working Men's Club, as these were heated and had some form of lighting.

Early in the morning we were told we had to go to Zion Sunday School in Lindley for hot drinks and breakfast, before returning to see our homes in daylight. Before this happened an unexploded land mine was discovered in the Mill dam on New

Hey Road, so a large area was then evacuated. (I walked in pyjamas and dressing gown to Zion as when I'd tried to get my clothes in the dark before going to the shelter, I found them covered in broken glass.)

It was the afternoon of Boxing Day when we were finally allowed into the area again, after the land mine had been defused by bomb disposal experts. Not until the end of March could we live again at No. 20. The windows had been blown out, large chunks of plaster had come off the walls, and although the ceilings didn't collapse, they were so badly damaged they needed to be pulled down and replaced.

No mention of the unexploded land mine was made in the local paper, but this was the main reason for so many being evacuated. There were army sentries at all the road ends, stopping people going into the area. The local paper reported that "high explosive bombs dropped. Nobody killed, several received cuts and abrasions from splinters and flying glass. Two casualties being wardens. One thrown onto his face by the blast, suffering cuts. Another tripped over debris, breaking a bone in his arm. Control was informed within two minutes of the explosion. The fire brigade was on the scene a short time after, and the flames extinguished. Blast from an exploding bomb destroyed windows over a wide area, and structure of the houses near the scene so affected it was necessary to remove all people from their homes to the shelter of a chapel."

An octogenarian, taken from the cellar of his house by a warden humorously remarked, "Can't you find me my false teeth?" They were found by the warden, but the cup they were in was smashed to smithereens.

"Anyway, lad, I thought they were dropping bombs, not sandwiches," he consoled him. The cup containing the teeth had been left on a window sill in a room above the cellar. Miraculously the teeth themselves were undamaged.

The clock of the mill was completely shattered, and the mechanism dropped out. A warden who rushed into the yard of a neighbouring mill found a night worker sitting on the ground roaring with laughter. The blast had thrown him down, and as he sat on the ground he saw the glass roof of a shed lifted into the air. The sight of it going up struck him as very funny.

Many of the evacuated families were taken in by friends or relatives. As soon as the order to evacuate was given, one of the town's seventeen emergency feeding and shelter centres was thrown open, and about two hundred people were given breakfast. Ample sleeping accommodation was available at the centre, but thirty found accommodation elsewhere. Hot dinners were provided for those remaining.

Harry Hirst, occupier of a house where damage was done to the gable end, said that the bomb fell in a field nearby, leaving a huge crater. Four windows in his house were broken, and fall pipes were dislodged.

Neither he nor his wife were injured, but were severely shocked.

Having a "Quiet Christmas" in pre-war days used to seem all wrong. But in 1940 the peace of Christmas meant not having to strain ears for the drone of aircraft, banging of guns or bursting of bombs. Instead, the crackling of a log fire, and tiny snap of a cracker — if you could get them — were more to be desired.

The effects of the explosion at Lindley were felt as far away as Bradley and Deighton. Plaster was blown down in Edith Dyson's larder, covering all the food. Plumber Tom Jessop was due to work at Pat Martin's mill the morning after the attack. When he arrived, having his camera with him as usual, he "snapped" some of the damage.

The people of Huddersfield carolled "Silent Night" with less conviction than usual that festive season.

CHAPTER
THREE

1941

Sam Carter made his Anderson shelter at Belle Vue, Sheepridge, almost a pleasure to be in. His children loved to play inside it. Sam made a form to sit on, propped up on bricks, and two wooden armchairs were given over to the "little house at the bottom of the garden". A crippled lady living next door wasn't so lucky with her shelter: it was always full of water. So Sam carried "Auntie Lottie" into his own snug little palace whenever there was an alert. They took blankets in when the sirens went, and an old piece of carpet hung on a piece of wood at the entrance gave an extra sense of security and cosiness. The family lit a candle, talked, and played "I Spy", soon running out of things to spy in the gloom.

Mrs Carter registered at Sheepridge Co-op for the family's rations, occasionally getting a banana — a rare treat — for Ramon, who was under five years old. Olive had a treadle sewing machine, and made most of the clothes for her children, besides working in a fish and chip shop.

One day, after sweets were rationed, Mrs Carter took her daughter Dorothy to buy a quarter of sweets at our shop, Central Stores, Deighton. As they walked back up the hill, a real hullaballoo was going on outside the Woolpack public house. Jean Tiffany, one of the daughters at the pub, was crying bitterly. Her dog had been knocked down by a car. Impulsively, Olive pushed the sweets into Jean's hands. "Cheer up, love, he'll be all right." Whether the poor dog was or not, that gesture typified what became known as the "Wartime Spirit", considering others before yourself. Though little Dorothy, deprived of her sweet ration, didn't think much of it at the time.

Her brother Ralph went into the mines as a Bevin Boy. He didn't think much of that either, breaking his finger while labouring in the pit. He had worked at Hopkinson's, Birkby, after leaving school. His stint as a Bevin Boy finished, he joined the Army.

If you didn't volunteer for the Services, the Labour Exchange became almost like a "Little Hitler". Marjorie Wood dreaded having to work in munitions, maybe having to leave home. Fortunately, she knew someone who worked at Brook Motors who managed to get her fixed up there at the beginning of 1941. When Marjorie gleefully returned to the Labour Exchange the official dealing with her was blazing mad. "You should be going on munitions," she ranted, seeming to take sheer delight in disrupting people's lives as much as possible. What a relief for Marjorie, though, not to be leaving home.

Young as she was, Marjorie felt so tired after a day's work at Brook Motors that she simply stayed at home listening to the wireless most evenings. There were some good plays on, and dance bands — for example Joe Loss, Glenn Miller, Victor Sylvester and Henry Hall. Marjorie didn't go dancing, as her fiancé, Arthur Longstaff, was away working in Newcastle. Occasionally Marjorie went to the pictures with his sister, or to chapel for a rehearsal if a concert was proposed. It was a 7.30a.m. start to the working day. Marjorie caught a trolley bus from Ashbrow Road through to Folly Hall. After clocking in, they worked till nine, when there was a short break. She never liked the canteen, it was too big and overpowering for her taste.

If a Workers' Playtime concert was on, Marjorie and her pals went to it. "Music While You Work" was relayed throughout the day. It was a bit of a rush going into town for midday dinner, but made a change from work surroundings. The Elite fish shop, Upperhead Row, was a favourite haunt, as was Bannister's on Byrom Street, or sometimes a place on Wood Street — which was "a bit scruffy".

Marjorie earned around 35s. a week. Holidays were in July, traditional Engineers' Holiday Week. At the end of the year she married Arthur, who later joined the Royal Corps of Signals.

Audrey Cudworth of Bradley Bar was working at the Westgate Branch of National Provincial Bank at the time, earning £1 a week. She enjoyed the Kingsway Café, King Street, at dinnertime. Cafés were usually full, as workers could save their rations by not eating at home. If there were queues down the stairs at the Kingsway, and only limited time for a meal — or there was shopping to be done — it was quicker just to have a milk shake at the Arctic.

At the beginning of 1941 the Fire Brigade issued two stirrup pumps to each Fire Protection Party organized by neighbours. Those with no pump were issued with two sandbags per household, for incendiary bombs.

The Mayor's Annual Charity Ball in January was cancelled because few tickets were sold, due to the blackout, bad weather, and fewer young men being about.

West Riding Yorkshire County Committee of the Women's Land Army requested farmers to let them know their requirements, as it was unfair to keep them waiting. And on 15 January another 140 evacuees from London arrived to be accommodated in the Golcar district.

Holmfirth War Weapons Week began on 27 January. £282,000 was raised. In Huddersfield Court Waldo Briggs fined a man £10 with 10s. costs for being absent from fire-watching duty. The court was told that in future other absentees would be sent to prison.

The Mayor, Alderman A. E. Sellers, had been digging for victory, and had successfully grown brussels sprouts 3 ft 2 in high, cauliflowers 8½ in across, cabbages weighing 9 lb, and 68 stone of potatoes. His success was, he said, due to fertilizer from the sewage works, and the corporation decided to put the fertilizer on sale.

In 1941 Mr H. G. Barwood, Headmaster of Huddersfield College, sent letters out to parents regarding school uniform:

As a result of war and shortages, the only article of uniform which boys are obliged to wear is the school cap. Uniform is serviceable, and as almost all boys wear grey trousers and pullovers, involves the expenditure of very few coupons. It is hoped that as many as can will wear uniform.

Clothing for physical training, games and swimming, presents some difficulties from the point of view of hygiene, and I hope these suggestions will be found helpful. Obviously, no boy can take part in games or physical training without a complete change of clothing. It seems unavoidable therefore for a boy to have a pair of white trunks which can be used for both these compulsory activities. Instead of wearing the regulation House jersey for games, a *spare* shirt can be worn, but if it is, a sash in the House colours must be worn over the right shoulder down to the right hip, to distinguish opposing sides.

If a boy is excused (on a medical certificate) from games but not from physical training, he may wear a *spare* pair of flannel trousers or his bathing costume for physical training. As at present, trunks (which require a few coupons) should be worn instead of full costumes in the baths. Plimsolls for physical training are advised strongly because of the roughness of the floor of the gymnasium, but they will not be insisted upon. So that terminal reports may be as valuable as possible, examination scripts and also question papers when possible will be sent home by the pupils. For the present, question papers may not always be available since it has been found essential to economise in the use of paper by writing question papers on the blackboards whenever possible.

Parents should realise that the "Final Order" on the Report Form is determined *not* from the examination marks alone, but by combining with marks awarded during term.

One pupil of Huddersfield College, William (Bill) Dignam, whose father was a dentist in Marsh, couldn't join the ATC at first because of parental opposition. When eventually he did "sign on" it was with a different Squadron from the one that his friends at the College were already in. The initial enthusiasm soon evaporated and he quit. The headmaster could be quite scathing in his comments about boys: "Profundity was never in great evidence as far as Dignam was concerned . . ."

Maybe Mr Barwood was also annoyed because a prefect had reported young Dignam and a friend for speaking to girls, who were wearing the distinctive blue and navy striped blazers of Greenhead High School for Girls. The ones who received the attentions of the boys were Margaret Dugdale and Jean Yates. Bill joined the RAF, returning to Huddersfield in 1945.

Another circular was sent to parents later in July from H. Kay, Director of Education: "As a war measure, the requirements as regards compulsory school uniform will be restricted to the wearing of the school badge. It was to be hoped that as much of the regulation uniform as possible will continue to be worn."

Pupils at Greenhead were impressed when Robin Desirée Barwood joined us, daughter of the headmaster at Huddersfield College. Her name sounded so exotic — we'd never heard of a girl being called Robin before. And there was also the hope that she would know a lot of college boys, and perhaps introduce us to them.

At Greenhead there were frequent sales of second-hand uniform, set out on tables in the gym. The navy blue and sky blue stripes of blazers were somewhat faded after a few seasons of summer suns, as were the ties and hat bands that, when new, showed up strikingly against the cream straw panamas. But at least clothing coupons had not to be given for them.

I was alright, as mother had customers rationed at our shop who, having a few children, preferred money to clothing coupons — so furtive deals were done behind the shop counter. There was only Philip, a pupil at the Boys College, and me in our family. Sixty-six coupons were supposed to last for a year, and it was illegal to buy them for cash.

Eileen Robinson, who lived at Sheepridge, always hated being at Greenhead because she sometimes had to wear second-hand uniform.

Although Miss Dawn, our English mistress, wrote on one of my school reports "Hazel has ability in this subject", I never had the confidence to send a contribution to the school magazine. How fortunate that others had. Margaret Shaw, Form II Latin, compiled this contribution for her House, Montrose:

Then the well-known man Lord Woolton
Made a study of all foodstuffs,
Rationed fats and meat and bacon
Rationed cheese, and tea and sugar,
so that food was shared out fairly.
Gave to every man and woman
and to every child a booklet
Each with pages full of coupons,
for the butcher and the grocer.
Next he found that eggs were scarcer,
So this food he rationed also.
Pots of jam and sweet oranges,
oranges that were for children,
By whom these foods were mostly needed.
Next our clothing they considered,
Gave us each a set of coupons,
Sixty-six of these per annum.
Then our friends across the water,
sent us tins of meat and salmon.
So our friend Lord Woolton gave us
One more precious book of coupons
Now we have three books of coupons,
Which are white, and pink, and yellow.
Vitamins we get in plenty,

Which will keep us well and healthy
Through the long dark months of winter.

Sylvia Sissons, Form IV Arts and Science, St Clare House, made this contribution to the school magazine: "COUPONS. But now things are better, for I, being tall, And weighing a good bit too much, Get forty more coupons, to spend on new coats, and shoes, and school blazers and such."

A number of incendiaries and fire bombs rained down on Huddersfield one night in June — known as "Flaming June, 1941".

Though I quite fancied joining the WRENs or WAAFs if the war lasted long enough, I'd have hated working on a machine. Girls in industry wore "turbans" and "snoods" to keep their hair safe from becoming entangled in machinery. In summer at Greenhead we played tennis, and sometimes had lessons out on the lawns. Those on munitions had no such luck.

In 1941, as a result of the successful development of the Rocket Projectile, the Ministry of Supply was anxious to arrange for the production of large quantities of the weapon. W. C. Holmes and Co. Ltd was approached to become one of a small group of three firms being asked to provide a minimum of 20,000 2 in projectiles per week. Holmes's share of the total was to be 10,000 a week. This was an entirely new departure from normal works practice at Turnbridge, calling for up-to-date mass production. At that time no one among the firm's employees had experienced such methods, so a new and separate organization had to be created.

There was no space available in the Turnbridge Works, but an existing building within 300 yards of the main works was found to be suitable. Though in a state of very bad repair, a scheme was prepared and approved by the Ministry, and the firm was able to join the group. The building had to be almost rebuilt, while the usual wartime necessities of ARP shelters, blackout and firefighting arrangements, and also a canteen and ambulance room, had to be provided. Work on the building begun, machinery layout was then planned and approved by the Ministry, who provided the whole of the machinery for the processing of the various components.

Visits to other factories already making similar projectiles were made, which not only enabled small difficulties to be avoided, but helped to improve existing operations, and increase the output when the factory started up.

Machinery began arriving during the summer of 1941, and was installed under the direction of key personnel brought over from Turnbridge. New electricity, water and gas supplies had to be brought to the building, which, together with the building work and installation of machinery going on at the same time, created a sense of chaos not easy to be imagined. But the urgent demand for production at the earliest possible moment made it essential for everyone to put their backs into the task. So much so that by everybody's supreme efforts the factory was able to start operation by November of that year, first dispatches being made before Christmas Day. So there, Mr Hitler!!

The size of the 2 in tail made it particularly suitable for handling by female labour, and at peak production some 250 women, and only about thirty men were employed in the factory, the latter being chiefly auto-setters, setters-up, and general labourers.

Machining operations were carried out on a battery of fifteen lathes specially tooled for female labour. Due to the fine limits specified, inspection after each operation was necessary, requiring the services of some fifty employees. In addition, a resident naval ordnance inspection department, consisting of a leading examiner with a staff of thirty — mostly women — provided point to point and final inspection of all details and finished products leaving the factory.

Introduction of mass production into the organization called for costings to be calculated down to the fourth decimal place of 1d., a new experience for those engaged upon it.

Throughout these new departures from the firm's normal practice, various members of the Ministry of Supply were co-operative, giving willingly their knowledge and experience. Sub-contractors helped with the supply of raw materials and components. Last, but not least, members of staff and employees, with their wholehearted efforts, enabled the enormous wartime task to be carried out successfully.

Also working at full stretch was David Brown and Sons, which also rose to the occasion, and held important naval contracts. They produced turbine gears for "Man O'War" and similar vessels, gears for Paravanes and funnel operating, and other mechanisms for submarines.

Jack Oldroyd, who lived at Somerset Road, worked at Brown's, pitch testing gears for battleships. The first gearbox for a tank was designed by a Huddersfield man, Dr Merritt, and built in 1939. After the war the Government gave him £30,000 for the design, as it had been such a success.

Jack began work at 7.30a.m. on Monday, working through until Tuesday midday. He was taken home to rest; then he and others working on the job were up first thing Wednesday to begin again, working through the night until Thursday midday. Returning home to sleep, he was at Brown's on Friday morning, where he worked until Saturday dinnertime. This routine went on for three weeks, at the end of which Jack felt "absolutely beggared". Staff weren't paid overtime, but £4 a week at the beginning of the war was a very good wage.

It was a strict, disciplined regime, some would say harsh. There was no music at all, and no smoking in the Works. Even when a worker went to the toilet, he had to take his time card and hand it to the man inside the office. He was clocked on, then his card was put in a rack. The worker was handed "four by fours", as they called the pieces of torn newspaper which the dispenser of the "toilet paper" had wrenched into four identical pieces. Ten minutes a day was allowed for visiting the toilet. There were twenty back-to-back lavatories, with no doors on any of them. If eight minutes passed before a return to work, the attendant shouted out the worker's number, like calling in a boat that had been out at sea too long. On return from the main lavatories, the time card was given back, after the official had written on how much time had been spent. There were no facilities for washing hands. Essential war work didn't make allowances for such non-essentials as battling with germs! The only place to wash hands was in bowls at the side of the canteen, at dinnertime. If a man really couldn't hold on any longer to "pass water" there was an open urinal by the attendant, where he could relieve himself before returning immediately to his machine.

If workers weren't inside the gates at David Brown's before 7.30 precisely, the gates were closed. After five minutes they were reopened, and a quarter of an hour was knocked off the worker's pay. At 7.45a.m. the gates were closed again, then the late employee would be interrogated. "Who's your foreman?" When told, the man at the gate rang the foreman up, to say, "So and so's here. Do you want him?" It was known that occasionally the answer was "no", to show who was boss. So the poor chap would have to go home, losing a day's pay.

When Jack Oldroyd first worked at Brown's he lived at Lowerhouses. He used to get up at six, as there were no buses from there. He walked down Dog Kennel Bank, on King's Mill Lane, to Lockwood, then to Brown's, a walk which took about three-quarters of an hour. If it snowed, or rained, workers simply had to stay wet until they dried out as the day went on.

The hierarchy between those at the bottom of the scale and the "top notchers" was illustrated by the canteen system. When dinner time arrived, the labouring classes, those on machines, ate their own sandwiches in the first floor canteen, number one, where they could mash a mug of tea — if they had taken their own tea — or buy a mug of tea for 1d. On the next floor a lunch could be brought, and eaten at tables for four. They'd never heard of vegetarians. Potatoes, meat and peas cost 6d.; apple pie or rice pudding, 2d.; 8d. for the complete meal. There wasn't any water on the tables to drink, so if you wanted a drink, you had to buy a mug of tea. Most didn't bother, as they couldn't afford another 1d. Coffee wasn't available.

Facilities for the staff were next to the labourers', with the same menu, but larger helpings — and the refinement of tablecloths. Senior staff occupied the other half of the canteen, which was for foremen and supervisors. A separate area was set aside for managers and assistant managers. Finally, there was the Directors' Room. The progression was rather like the Seven Stages of Man, pictured on the Jacob's Ladder of the David Brown Canteens.

Jack joined the Local Defence Volunteers, which later became the Home Guard. He was in the 26th Battalion A Company. During the engineering holiday week in July, Home Guards had a camp at Farnley Tyas. Headquarters were behind the Wesleyan chapel at

Aldmondbury. A guard always manned the door, at the end of a long path which ended in flagstones. The guard always had to say "Halt — who goes there? Friend or Foe?" When satisfied the oncomer was a friend, the next official statement was "Advance, Friend, and be recognized."

The officer of the unit, Mr Heather, used to go by car to the Newsome post, to check everything was in order, and return to Aldmondbury afterwards. One evening, he marched down the old path towards a new Home Guard man, standing with rifle poised over his shoulder. "Hi" he greeted the officer.

"You shouldn't say things like that," stamped the officer in extreme annoyance — no doubt wondering what the ultimate outcome of the battle would be with such weak guardians of England's outposts on duty. "You should have challenged me," he continued.

"Alright then. Go back and I'll challenge you," countered the guard.

"Don't be impertinent," snapped the officer, disappearing inside Headquarters.

The following week it was Jack's turn to man the door, and Mr Heather went as usual to check at Newsome. The Home Guard who hadn't done his appointed duty was still nattered. "I say, Oldroyd, let me take over," he offered, picking up a rifle. He kept repeating what he should say when the officer reappeared. "Halt — who goes there? Friend or Foe? Advance, Friend and be recognized." He couldn't possibly go wrong this time.

After a while a car drew up, and out stepped the officer. He marched down the path, on to the flags.

"Halt, Mr Heather, who goes there — friend or foe?" asked the repentant Guard in his most stentorian, Put-The-Fear-Of-God-Into-You tones.

Before 1939 Jack was a bell ringer at Aldmondbury church, and a member of the YMCA Soccer Club. No bell ringing went on during the war — few would have had the energy in any case, after working and "leisure time" work. But in 1945 Jack and seven other bell ringers rang no less than 5,000 changes in a joyous, 3 hour 13 minute Victory Peal. It nearly killed him. He was "almost as knackered" as in 1939, when working almost non-stop testing those gears. He has never been in a belfry since.

The group who became friends at the YMCA in 1939 formed themselves into what became known as "The Thirty-Niners", meeting annually to keep the friendship going.

Annie Myers was working at Hopkinson's in 1941. Once, on night shift, she was in an almighty panic when the sirens shrilled. It was ages before she could grab her tin hat which was kept on her machine, because she was in such a dither. Finally she went into the cellar beneath "Hops", where workers congregated until the All Clear sounded. Rumours spread like wildfire. "They're dropping flares like Hell up Rash-cliffe" was one. This was where Annie was living, and her mother was at home looking after Annie's son, Peter. His dad was away at the war. Annie was frightened to death. When morning came, though, everybody was asking, "have you heard what's happened? — a bomb's been dropped in the River Colne at King's Mill Lane." It never exploded.

All the excitement proved too much for Annie, and she left Hopkinson's. Whenever the sirens went off, she and her neighbours congregated together in each other's cellars. They never bothered to lock their house doors, as burglars weren't a problem: there was nothing to steal anyway. Annie couldn't even afford a nightie. One night when the sirens sounded, panic struck worse than ever. Quite forgetting she wore only a vest she grabbed a couple of pillows and ran outside — straight into the arms of air raid warden Stanley Hirst.

But it didn't bother ARP men what they saw. A bit like doctors, if the person was moving then everything was alright. And Annie was certainly moving. "I never thought about a coat," says Annie, "but I did when I got in't cellar!"

Sometimes, if there didn't seem time to go anywhere else, she grabbed Peter and ducked beneath the table. Her husband's grandad, who lived next door, said "thar't a silly bugger", if he happened to be visiting at the time.

When Annie started experiencing sickness, Dr Kennedy diagnosed her condition as being a result of coming off night shift — a tummy upset. Dr Waddy later confirmed that she was three months pregnant. As Christmas Day approached she became very ill, and her sister thought she had better call a doctor. Dr McGibbon took her in his car to the Princess Royal

Hospital, and Annie's husband returned home on compassionate leave.

He sat at her bedside in his khaki uniform. While lying there feeling dreadful, Annie overheard one doctor asking her mother if anyone in the family had died in childbirth ... but everything worked out alright, and a daughter was born on Christmas Day. What a good job the air raid sirens didn't ring out at an awkward moment for the expectant, young and panicky Annie. Gordon, her husband, was so relieved. He gave her an iron crucifix from a dead German. After a while the new baby girl was left at Southgate Nursery during the week, while Annie worked.

August 1941 "Holidays at Home" were in full swing at Greenhead Park. George Herbert Hirst coached boys in cricket at Leeds Road Playing fields, where there was an air raid shelter. One little girl living nearby thought it wonderful to wear her Mickey Mouse gas mask, with its big rubber ears.

Even in summertime, cinema was popular. Flocking to see Peter Lorre at the Rialto, and *Goodbye Mr Chips* at the Theatre Royal.

31 October saw the dreadful disaster of the fire at Booth's clothing firm. Forty-seven people died after girl workers threw themselves from windows. Police war reserves helped recover bodies from the wreckage. They were then kept in a temporary Civil Defence mortuary at Gledholt Bank. Water from Cambridge Road Baths was used to help put out the fire.

However, Greenhead High School speech day was an event to infuse new hope and to lift the heart. Girls traditionally wore white dresses, not uniform, for the event in the Town Hall. That year it was on 20 December.

When we were rehearsing in the Town Hall, the air raid sirens sounded. We all trooped beneath the Hall, where music mistress Edith Spikes continued with the programme, saying "Hitler won't stop Greenhead from singing." Miss Spikes usually wore a dark green crocheted jumper, matching tweed skirt and sensible brown brogues. Alderman Smailes presided the following day, when parents were assembled in the area of the hall and on the balcony, and the VIPs on the platform, which had flowers arranged along it. Someone described the girls in their white dresses as resembling "a bevy of angels", then made a huge *faux pas* by saying he had come to see the "sights of Huddersfield", and one of the first he had seen was Miss Hill.

She, Miss Hill, after regaining her composure, mentioned in her report the many war efforts undertaken by the school since 1939, especially the sale of National Savings certificates during War Weapons Week. She referred to the examination successes, and congratulated "Old Girls" in the forces.

Music, as always, was arranged by Miss Spikes, who was magnificent in her speech day floor length black velvet dress and short white ermine cape. Her iron grey hair was in its usual severe "bun" at the nape of her neck, and her eyes sparkled like diamonds as the beautiful music soared to the rafters of Huddersfield Town Hall. The ceremony opened with the singing of the National Anthem. Vaughan William's "England", Schubert's "To Music", "Motherland", carols of Polish, Czech, French and Dutch origin were also performed, and a Bach chorale was sung by the Senior Choir, with Joan Edwards as the splendid soloist. The accompanist throughout was Mr A. Rooke. Peggy Nowell was another of Greenhead's "star" singers. She sang the descant in "Angels From The Realms Of Glory", and few could ascertain, among the 500 girls, just where the glorious angelic soprano voice was coming from. But she was somewhere up there near the organ.

The piece that brought parents to their feet, clapping and calling for encore after encore was "A Partridge In a Pear Tree", sung with actions. We had been meticulously rehearsed by "Spiky". Five hundred white figures emulated five gold rings (fingers in the air, counting them off), eight maids a milking, eleven lords a leaping — what thuds — and finally every right arm extended in the same direction to a mythical pear tree in the top corner of the hall.

The exuberance was all embracing, and exhilaration filled the air. For once in a long time, thoughts of shortages, inconveniences and terrible accidents were forgotten. Mrs J. T. Broadbent expressed thanks to Mr Mabane, and the programme closed with "Hark, The Herald Angels Sing" and the School Song.

The YMCA had asked people to invite servicemen into their homes over the Christmas period. Having a shop, my parents were in an ideal position to extend hospitality. We always had more than our own rations, as we must never be without sufficient to cater for any

Forces who may come home on leave. Mother telephoned the YMCA asking for as many as they would care to send. The more the merrier was her motto. On Christmas Day a number of soldiers knocked at our back door, the shop being locked and shuttered. Some brought their girlfriends as well. All were welcomed with open arms.

Our "front room" was above the shop, and Dad had fixed fairy lights above the mantlepiece. Balloons wafted gently from the ceiling as the door was opened. The piano stood diagonally across one corner of the room, the radiogram in another corner. As the warmth made balloons wilt they gradually diminished, but high spirits never wilted. There were spam sandwiches galore, corned beef, pickles, pork, apple sauce, mustard sauce, Christmas cake, madeira cake, "pop", ginger ale, tea and coffee.

Games to play included Forfeits, Consequences, Truth or Dare, and, the favourite, Postman's Knock. All the girls, and mother, were dying to have their number called when handsome soldier Bill Bailey was the postman. Cigarettes and Manikin cigars were the prizes for winners of games — and for losers as well. If they weren't good at one thing, Mother would soon suggest something that they could do to merit a little gaily wrapped gift.

Dad attended to putting records on and seeing that everybody was happy, telling silly stories and jokes and singing. He was quite tired, though, as Jimmy the baker had been called up, and Dad had taken over in the bakehouse as well as attending to all the extra Food Office work.

Mother played carols on the piano, with a sea of khaki round her. And on and off throughout the evening we kept Singing "Won't You Come Home, Bill Bailey", as we had a real life Bill Bailey there in the room with us.

Bernard, a somewhat slow, stodgy soldier, created great amusement with his party piece, grunted with extreme concentration so he wouldn't forget the words — "Sylveste, My Brother Sylveste, Got a row of forty medals on his chest, big chest, he takes no rest . . ." with a deadpan expression throughout the many verses. The applause, laughter and clapping encouraged him to give encores.

In the early hours of Boxing Day mother played "Past Three O'Clock, On a Cold and Frosty Morning", but nobody wanted to break the party up, as everybody was enjoying it too much. So after the last carol, "As With Gladness Men of Old, Did their Guiding Star Behold", someone else requested "Angels From the Realms of Glory", then "Once in Royal David's City". And of course we *must* have "While Shepherds Watched" again — and we haven't had "Here we Come a Wassailing" . . .

But sheer tiredness overcomes even the happiest party, and some decided to have a kip on the floor with pillows and blankets as the clock ticked on to 4a.m. Reluctantly, at long last, goodbye kisses were exchanged, as were addresses and promises to write.

Bill was to be posted "Somewhere abroad". It was awful saying goodbye, not knowing if we would ever meet again. But at least there would be airgraphs to look forward to, and the memory would linger on.

We ended 1941 by going to see *Zeigfield Girl* at the Ritz, starring Hedy Lamarr. It was school holidays, so homework could be forgotten for a while, and fantasy could take over. We went to the cinema again on 30 December, to see *Escape* at the Rialto, starring Norma Shearer and Robert Taylor. New Year's Eve was spent at the Empire, to see that marvellous film *Lady Hamilton*, starring Vivien Leigh and Laurence Olivier.

A Christmas parcel had been sent to every Huddersfield "Old Collegian" known to be in the forces, by the College. They must have been heartened to know they were not forgotten.

CHAPTER
FOUR

1942

January 1942 began with a flourish in the town. On the 5th the Princess Royal, in WVS uniform, was entertained to luncheon at the George Hotel by Mr Lawrence Crowther and guests. (No ordinary Huddersfielder ever called the midday meal anything so posh as luncheon — not even lunch. It was dinnertime.) In the afternoon the Princess visited the YMCA canteen, inspected tea cars drawn up in St George's Square, visited Buxton Road Methodist chapel, and Slaithwaite centenary church. A clothing officer at the WVS administrative centre in Station Street expressed her delight at the excellent clothing sent for distribution among air raid victims by the American and Canadian Red Cross. The Princess Royal saw some of the clothing purchased from the £500 allocation sent to Huddersfield by the Lord Mayor of London's National Air Raid Distress Fund. Mention was made of the service given to members of the forces arriving in the town late at night on leave. Directed to the YMCA, they had a place to stay for the night before continuing home the following morning.

Another New Year and another January Sale Time. Joan's, New Street, had "Thousands of Glamorous Frocks for Day and Evening Wear. How about a beautifully embroidered one in contrast on Black Morocain, with an effective bolero? The slim fitting skirt beautifully gored. Usual Price 49s. 11d, Sale Price 23s. 6d." Or what about a swagger fur coat, 10 gns and eighteen coupons.

Mother and I treated ourselves to a pair each of the fashionable new square-toed bootees, covered with shiny black fur, which were exotic, and wonderfully warm in comparison with wellingtons with a pair of thick socks inside. Only when we started walking down Deighton Road together and glanced down at our feet, moving in unison, did the ludicrous nature of both of us wearing identical square-toed, black fur bootees strike us. We must have looked like a couple of abominable snowmen plodding along together.

Huddersfield Music Club suffered a disappointment on Saturday 10 January, owing to the indisposition of Miss Eileen Joyce, who was unable to appear. Fortunately the committee was able to engage the services of Louis Kentner for the piano recital.

Cold and snowy January was the ideal time for Mother to put the gas fire on in the back bedroom and take a basket of mending up, with a bottle of Christmas port near at hand, tucked away in the bottom of the wardrobe, so she could enjoy "a little tot" to help along the tedious darning of socks and repairing of ladders in stockings. That was war work enough for her!

118

Fifteen-year-old Betty Thewlis started her first job at Fireguard Headquarters on Buxton Road, next to the Picturedrome, sending rotas of fire-watching dates to people in the town. Betty had to attend court every Thursday, to prove that she had posted a rota when absconders made out they hadn't been notified. One conscientious objector was summonsed so often that he was sent to prison for six months. Betty worked normal office hours, from 9a.m. to 5p.m.

Betty's husband-to-be Basil Darlington was ordered to be a Bevin Boy after many miners had been called up. He went to Stringer and Jagger's, Emley Moor, before they were nationalized. It was an awful job, but better paid than "ordinary" ones. The lads took a bottle of water with them, or cold tea, to slake their thirst, and sandwiches in their "snap" tins. There were no facilities for washing, and no toilet. Often Basil had to work lying down to get at the seams of coal, and there was a three mile walk to the pit face.

Brighouse Scouts compiled a register for local air raid wardens showing the whereabouts of every householder during air raids, making it one of their service jobs to keep it up to date.

Butchers warned customers not to expect English beef during the week commencing 8 January. Allocation that week was 1s. worth of meat and two pennyworth of corned beef per head.

Nearly 150 children evacuated to Huddersfield from blitzed areas were entertained at the parish church schools by the local Social Welfare Committee. The party was arranged by WVS Evacuees After Care, and the committee chairman was Miss N. Freeman. Alderman and Mrs Arthur Gardiner, mayor and mayoress, attended. Children aged from four to thirteen received presents, and were entertained with a film show, conjurer, then a first class tea, and games.

So as not to crowd out war workers on buses, the public were asked to travel between 10a.m. and 4p.m. In the evenings people still preferred to stumble around in the blackout rather than deny themselves the pleasure of "going to the flicks". Especially as some good films were being shown that January. George Formby was in *Keep Fit* at the Princess, Greer Garson and Laurence Olivier in *Pride and Prejudice*, and Marlene Dietrich in *The Flame of New Orleans*.

Two new Ford emergency food vans were delivered, and received by the Mayor on behalf of the town from a representative of Ford Emergency Food Vans Trust. In total 350 were given to the country to alleviate distress after air raids. Food was carried in special insulated containers, and complete meals could be served in any locality where required. Brockholes Motor Company undertook to garage and maintain them ready for immediate use, day or night, at their own expense. Members of the WVS were to drive them.

Points rationing for certain foods came in, including USA luncheon meats — 3 lb for forty-three points; meat roll or galantine — 3 lb for twenty-one points; and brisket — 4 lb for fifty-seven points.

Besides being a popular venue for dancing and swimming, Cambridge Road Baths held wrestling tournaments. That January, one was held in aid of the

Mayor's Comforts for the Troops Fund. Admission prices were 5s., 5s. 6d., 2s. 6d. or 1s. 6d.

Shops competed with each other: "Spend your Clothing Coupons with Ben Worsley the Tailor. Have your own cloth tailored. Imperial Arcade, open till 7p.m. and 8p.m. on Saturdays."

"Be Coupon Wise, Economise" was the slogan of Joan's of New Street, advertising a well-tailored tweed costume: "Today's Value 4 guineas. Sale Price 46s. 3d."

The "Shrapnels" concert party continued to entertain the troops. At the Fraternity Hall a two hour, non-stop revue of humour, song and dance included Ivan Garside (bass), Harry Walker (baritone), Elsie Jackson (contralto), E. Margaret Brooke (piano), and Kathleen Whitwam and Elaine Stancliffe (dancers).

The second week of the new year was a bad one for fishmongers, many closing as supplies ran out an hour after opening. Poultry was scarce too. The few turkeys left from Christmas were being sold at the controlled price of 3s a pound. Rabbits were in great demand, hares plentiful and popular. A few young partridges helped ring the changes at 2s. 6d. a brace. Some cooking apples made a welcome addition to meagre fruit supplies, sold at the controlled price of 9d. per lb. Pears were 3s. per lb, rhubarb 8d. a stick.

Those Home Guards who owned cars and used them on duty were to be paid 1d. a mile for the first 250 miles in any one calendar month. A motor cyclist with or without sidecar (excluding motor assisted bicycles) was paid 2¼d., while cars up to and including

8 hp and tricars were allowed 4½d. Cars over 10 hp were paid 6d.

Miss Mary Crowdy, of the "Yorkshire Aunties" was staying with Mrs Taylor Dyson at Aldmondbury to see how her scheme was working. "Yorkshire Aunties", promoted by Miss Crowdy, was an organization that aimed to find new homes for children under five from blitzed areas. The scheme was run in conjunction with Children's Country Holidays Fund, Miss Crowdy being the secretary.

At Almondbury on Wednesday 9 January St John's Methodist Bright Hour was held. The Rev. O. W. Smith gave the address, and Mrs H. Lockwood played the piano.

Anything that gave a little brightness in those dark January days was welcome, as bad news was continually received about local men in the forces. For example, the death occurred in the Middle East of Second Lieutenant Peter Mowat Hall, elder son of Mr and Mrs Norman Hall, late of Woodleigh, Edgerton, and grandson of the late Sir John G. Mowat. Such tragedies were all the more galling when it became known that a local man had been fined £5 and ordered to attend for medical examination under the National Service Act. He refused to undergo an examination, and for failing to comply with the Order of the Court was sentenced to twelve months' hard labour.

Black and white films were beginning to be superseded by "Glorious Technicolour" — Greer Garson and Walter Pidgeon were in colour at the Ritz. Films for cameras were difficult to get, and people were longing for a bit of colour in their lives. Some started having studio portraits "tinted", giving the photographer a list of hair, eyes and clothes colouring.

Owing to shortage of staff, the Moldgreen branch of the Halifax Building Society closed from 12 January 1942 until further notice.

Citizens were urged to spur themselves to greater effort in the great national waste paper salvage drive. Returns so far from Huddersfield had been disappointing. Everyone was asked to give old books, ledgers and magazines which "clutter up garrets and storerooms". Schools used second-hand text books.

Daily efforts were made for the war in all kinds of ways. A "Kitchen Shower" was held at the Women's Liberal Rooms, Westgate, selling articles ranging from vegetable soup to scrubbing brushes. A total of £52 was raised by that and a whist drive in the evening.

A military dance at Cambridge Road Baths, with music by the Certo Cito Dance Orchestra (Royal Corps of Signals) was held on 16 January. Proceeds were for local military reception hospitals. There was a licensed bar and buffet, and admission was 2s. (1s. for members of HM forces).

On the fruit stalls, some oranges for children aged under six had appeared. Onions were sold at a controlled price of 5d. per lb.

Brook Motors Ltd War Workers' lunchtime concert was held every Friday, and collections were taken for the Works Comforts Fund. At one, Mr Victor Smythe of the BBC was scouting for talent. He was so impressed with the firm's concert party that he booked it for a broadcast in March.

What would the authorities ask for next? Householders were asked to give, or sell for 25s. a ton, their garden railings, for scrap.

Appeals to patriotism did not go unheard. People were giving, and digging. Approximately 3,500 allotment holders were in Huddersfield by then. The value of vegetables grown during the last season had amounted to at least £35,000.

Make-do-and-mend was second nature by now. A customer was sorting remnants in a shop for patching. After remarks on household economy she said, "at least patches look much nicer than holes, don't you think?" Conceding that, the shop keeper added,

"Yes madam. Especially if they're where they can't be seen."

"Well," replied the buyer, "they won't be seen in wear, but when the shirts are washed and hung out to dry is the time *I'm* thinking about."

I began keeping a small pocket diary in 1942, writing in pencil. A pupil at Greenhead High School, life consisted chiefly of school and homework. But there was just enough space to jot down other things. Listened to Happidrome on the wireless, for example, or going to the Theatre Royal to see Tom Walls, with Mother, Dad, and Mildred (who had taken over from John at our shop when he had to join up.)

Tuesdays were red letter days. When school was over, I ran down to Rushworth's corner, where mother waited for me and we had tea in a café, then went to a show.

On 10 February we had tea in Whiteley's, down Westgate, then went to the Empire to see Charles Boyer in *Hold Back The Dawn*, calling to see Grandma at No. 2 Whitacre Street, on the way home. Grandma, whose eyes were getting bad, had difficulty pulling the blackout curtains on with her walking stick, but insisted on doing it herself. "I have to every other night," she reasoned.

On the 24th there was a choir practice in the hall until 4.45p.m. In the evening I laboriously knitted on four needles, making khaki gloves for a soldier. On 26 February I went to the Rialto, where Judy Garland starred in *Little Nelly Kelly*. Philip, my brother, went on ARP duty at Warrenfield, Sheepridge, until 11p.m. on 4 March.

On 5 March there was deep snow, so I walked to school with Pat Patrick, who was evacuated from Lewes, in Sussex, to live with her grandparents Mr and Mrs Du Lake, who owned the Warrenfield. Pat's southern accent seemed so posh at first. In the evening Mrs Porter came to our house to use the telephone. Bunny, my rabbit, was playing in the kitchen as a change from the hutch.

March

10th.   Greenhead Choir practice at Longdenholme.
15th.   I sowed peas and cauliflowers in the back walled garden.

16th.   After school to see Pat Patrick's rabbits, then she came to see Bunny.

18th.   A soldier came in for supper after Mother had been to the pictures with him.

20th.   Choir practice in school hall till 5.45p.m. evening, played the piano for Bunny, and sang for it.

26th.   Lily Herbert died of TB. Only fourteen. Philip went to the ATC this evening.

29th.   Helping with the stock-taking in our shop. Bought another rabbit from Jim Hawkins, as a companion for Bunny.

30th.   Jim and his brother Sam and sister Pauline built a bigger hutch for Bunny and Beauty.

April

8th.   To the ARP post to have my gas mask mended.

9th.   Cleaned my gloves with petrol.

10th.   My 15th birthday. Played with rabbits and Prince [our collie]. Took Grandma's pension for her. Erected new ledges in the hen huts.

12th.   Gardening.

14th.   Called at Warrenfield ARP Post and talked to Mr Anyon, Chief Warden.

May

7th.   Found kittens in a box in the attic. Hurricane, the proud new mother, looked a bit worn out. Brought them downstairs and made them comfortable by the fire.

27th.   Took some material to Miss Atkinson, dressmaker, at Wasp Nest Road, Fartown.

June

1st.   School. Tea in Whiteley's café with Mother. Then we met Dad and had Horlicks in the Arctic Café until time to go to the Theatre with the free shop pass. It was *David Garrick*. Philip had to go fire-watching at the bank.

7th.   Kathleen Keenan and Jim Hawkins at our house. We watched a chicken being born this evening.

8th.   Cold, windy, drizzly day. Played with kittens, Prince and the chicken.

9th.   School, tea with mother and Prince in Whiteley's Café. We took him to have his photograph taken with us in Geoffrey's afterwards.

13th.   Went with mother who had to register for war work of some kind.

15th.   School. Met mother, tea in Kingsway then another drink in Coletta's Milk Bar.

29th.   Philip worked over at the National Provincial, then fire-watching.

July

1st.   Began swotting for exams.
6th.   John Howarth came up to see about a soap permit for the chapel. Mother caught the old

chap who comes across from the new estate pinching a load of soap from our cellar. He had gone down on the pretext of doing a bit of a job. When he came up, she thought he looked a lot fatter, and was in a hurry to get away. She opened his jacket and waistcoat, and out fell tablets of Fairy soap and Carbolic. Customers banging at the back door frequently this evening, to see if they could wangle anything extra by way of rations.

9th.   Winnie telephoned. Her brother Ernie, my cousin, is reported missing. He is in the Tank Corps.

26th.   To Miss Atkinson to try new pinafore dress on. There were some scraps of pink material over, so I took them home to make matching handkerchiefs.

28th.   Kenneth Halstead called with the Sergeant who has been billeted with them. John Hall went overseas today.

29th.   To the Town Hall this evening, to see the Austerity Flitch.

August

2nd.   Bernard, the soldier who came to our party last Christmas, and his girlfriend Marjorie here again.

19th.   My cousin Ella here for a holiday. We went to Cambridge Road Baths (swimming) and both were flung in. Philip to an ARP meeting.

September

9th.   New "old" books for the new school term have to be backed. So brought them home.

10th.   To Fox's Dancing Academy this evening. We left at 9.45p.m. to catch the last bus.

16th.   In Art we had to draw a cat, a stray that Miss Lloyd had found and put into a cage. Philip fire-watching after Tech.

18th.   Mother went to the Rialto with an RAF man she met at Fox's. We all talked after supper till very late, then he slept in my bed and I slept in an arm chair in the front room. Dad has never been to a dance, and has "flebitus" or something through standing all day on the stone floor in the bakehouse. It never seemed to affect Jimmy, the baker, but he was only young. Dad has varicose veins. But he won't stay in bed, because there is nobody else to do the job.

21st.   School. After finishing my homework rushed back to town on the bus to meet Dad to go to the Theatre. I forgot to take the free shop pass, so we had to pay.

23rd.   Hurricane had three more kittens. Dad drowned them in a deep bucket in the sink. Wish there was some way poor Hurricane needn't have any more.

October

6th.   Philip took his ATC uniform back as he hasn't time to go now, with Tech. for banking exams, fire-watching, and ARP duties. I wrote a long letter to John Hall.

22nd.   School. Evening, to Fox's, dancing. Danced with Jack Fox, then an ATC boy, and a soldier. Walked home with Mildred, we didn't want to have to leave early for the bus when we were enjoying ourselves.

23rd.   Roger Smith is home on leave from the RAF.

24th.   Trying to make a bolero.

28th.   Broke up for half term. Mother and Mildred went to a Police Dance at Cambridge Road. I stayed at home and listened to Victor Sylvester on the wireless.

29th.   Evening, to Fox's with mother, Mildred, Irene Taylor (who's in our form at school). Danced with Jack Fox — he calls his partners "Little Flower" and looks so handsome in his black evening suit, bow tie and starched white shirt and cuffs. And shiny black dancing shoes. It's ever so exciting being close to him, and his hair is so sleekly Brylcreemed back from a centre parting. My heart thumps so hard I can hardly breathe. Then the ATC boy, and Robert Taylor — not the film star, but the greengrocer, and an old man of about forty. Walked back in the moonlight.

November

12th.   At 3.20 till 4.30p.m. at school there was a lecture on the League of Nations. To Fox's this evening. Danced with "Smithy" the soldier who is billeted at the Halsteads', I excused a soldier in the Excuse-Me Quickstep, then another soldier, and danced the slow foxtrot with Jack Fox. Queer him being called Fox as well. Mildred locked out on our return, so she slept at our house.

13th.   School. Tea in the school hall then to the Tudor with a school party to see *The Young Mr Pitt*.

19th.   Didn't go to school, I have a sore throat. Evening, to Fox's dancing. Moonlight, home on the last bus.

21st.   Helping in the shop. Winnie and Bill, the soldier, rode up on bikes to collect the rations.

23rd.   Philip to an ARP meeting at Cambridge Road.

Sometimes there is so much to enter in a diary that there simply isn't enough room, especially if it's only a tiny one. So bare facts had to suffice for the diary, and memories are recalled by them — as what happened on 28 November. *The Desert Song* was to open at the Theatre Royal on the 30th. Little did we imagine that we would be providing hospitality for a French hero more dashing in appearance than any sheik in the musical!

The French were coming to the fore in Huddersfield. Atkin Baker, conductor of the Palace Theatre

Orchestra, paid tribute on the Saturday night to officers and men of the French Fleet. After the close of each performance, after "God Save the King", "Attie" led his orchestra into the stirring strains of the Marseillaise. After recent events in Toulon, the audience appreciated the gesture of gallantry.

We at our shop were to become more intimately connected with the Free French than in our wildest imaginations. Ordinary housewives, searching for "Owt Tempting?" as they leaned disconsolately on the glass topped counter, fingering their dog-eared ration books, or panting in like a Longwood Harrier after hearing that some cigarettes had been delivered, were the usual type of human we encountered. The call had gone out again, with Christmas in the offing, for anyone willing to provide hospitality to servicemen away from home. Mother, naturally, was immediately on the phone to the YMCA, romance and excitement being her *raison d'être*. Could we take a French soldier for a couple of days? Yes, of course we could. It would be a pleasure — no trouble at all. Arrangements were made to meet a certain train at Huddersfield station on Saturday evening. Miss New, our French mistress at Greenhead, would expect stupendous results in my French exams after this!

Jean Tiffany, from the Woolpack Pub, near our shop and the Council School, went to Kaye's College. When she heard about the imminent visit she dashed down to talk about it. We supposedly did our homework in the front room above the shop, practising French verbs with more enthusiasm for once. Mostly we chattered excitedly. What would he be like? Where would he sleep? What if he sleep walked? What if he couldn't understand what we said, or worse, what if we failed to understand him?

Eyes sparkling, Jean accepted Dad's offer to accompany us in a taxi to the station the following evening. Saturday dawned. I "swotted" Geography in bed, the only place where it was reasonably quiet, living at a shop, then helped tidy the house in readiness for our guest. It had been decided that the French soldier would sleep in the little front bedroom, Mother and Dad in the back, as usual, while I would have the Put-U-Up opened out in the upstairs sitting room. Philip would have the camp bed if not fire-watching.

After tea, Jean came down. She had put a bit of lipstick on, but still wore her school tunic, blouse and tie. The taxi arrived in the blackout and off we went, not knowing what to expect. The driver was asked to wait outside the railway station until the reception committee — Dad, Mother, Jean and I — returned with our guest.

We hung around, eyes alert for anyone that could remotely be intended for us. A train puffed its way in, drawing to a shuddering halt. What would he be like? What if we missed him? Oh — surely that wondrous apparition couldn't be the one . . .

"Can you still smell my 'Evening in Paris'?" I nudged Jean as we moved hesitantly towards what, at first sight, looked remarkably like General De Gaulle. Here was certainly no mundane, run-of-the-mill "Frog", as some still jokingly termed the French. Tall peaked hat, officer's uniform, highly polished calf length boots, belt, cane, gloves in hand.

As he leapt lightly from the train a huge navy cape billowed behind the incredible figure. The cape was lined with scarlet; a big hood was flung back. He carried a natty little black attaché case in one hand, the kid gloves in the other. Coal black eyes scanned our small group, then a smile on the tanned classical features showed white, white teeth. He walked jauntily towards us, hand outstretched.

"Monsieur Taylor? Madame — et ma Cherie . . .?"

We all felt completely flustered. Had we strayed in a dream into *The Desert Song*? The platform air was dank and chill, typically November. Jean and I suddenly found ourselves enveloped in the heavy cloak as we hurried down the station steps to the waiting taxi.

Pierre Rabaste, as he was called, sat between Jean and myself in the blacked out taxi, Mother and Dad on seats facing us. Pierre was talking fast in a mixture of broken English and French, mostly French — his hands moved as fast as his words. I heard Jean giggling, then I felt a hand fumbling with my blouse beneath that voluminous cloak, embarrassing beyond all telling, especially with Mother and Dad in the taxi as well. But we had been asked to provide hospitality, and we didn't want him to think us gauche, Northern, unsophisticated non-entities. It was quite a quandary to be in, faced with this glamorous Frenchman with the matinée idol looks.

Neither Jean nor I had ever been out with a boy. Well, I hadn't. At Greenhead High School we were in detention if we so much as walked past the Boys' College in New North Road instead of walking the other way. As for talking with one — Good Heavens, Miss Hill would probably have expelled us on the spot.

I felt I was in an awful dilemma; and didn't know how I ought to behave. I was more at home playing with Prince, the rabbits and our seven cats, or swotting for the imminent School Certificate. On the other hand, how I had day-dreamed about the swarthy good looks of Errol Flynn, and went crackers over the broken French accent of Charles Boyer. Now, here was a combination of the two, but without a moustache, actually with his arm around my waist!

The taxi found its way back to our shop, and we all went round the back and into the big living-kitchen, where one side of the room was taken over with the shop fittings — big open shelves for trays of bread from the bakehouse, and a couple of huge drawers underneath to house drapery. A swishon curtain covered the lot when the shop was closed.

Sometimes a bulge could be seen moving about beneath the curtain, if one of the cats went nosing inside to see if there was anything interesting. A black horsehair sofa lined the side of the room adjoining the shop, and there was a massive sideboard by the window. A large wooden table was in the centre of the room, and two wooden boards propped up at the back of the cellar door could be put down the middle to make it capacious enough for table tennis, or to cater for a funeral tea. There was a recess for the sink, where the washing-up was done, Belling electric oven, and pinky-rose coloured hot water bottles hanging on nails, waiting to be filled to make the cold beds more tolerable.

As we came in from the blackout my face felt to be on fire. And Jean's looked to be. Mother gesticulated, arms sweeping the room with which we were so familiar, and in which we lived comfortably enough.

"Hell Hole", she laughed. Then she mouthed the words more slowly, as the only French words she knew were "Ouvrez la porte" and "Fermez la porte", totally useless in this situation. If a door had been left "ouvre" the air raid warden would have been there in no time.

"Put the damned kettle on, never mind all that," said Dad, grinning broadly. He was lucky; he wasn't in as vulnerable a position as we felt ourselves to be in. He filled the kettle himself and put it on the gas ring. "Now lad, what would you like to eat? What would you like for your supper?" Dad guided Pierre into the adjoining shop. Pierre laughed.

"Ah, oui, mange — everything!" he laughed. We all laughed; the ice was well and truly broken. Yet another soldier had slipped easily into the happy-go-lucky atmosphere of Central Stores.

After supper, sandwiches, lots and lots of tea, madeira and fruit cakes, and non-stop talk and laughter, Pierre indicated that he needed something. Nobody could fathom out what it was. Dad gave him a piece of paper and a pencil. "Draw it," he suggested. What emerged was a safety pin likeness. We had lots. Anything anyone wanted was only next door, in the shop. Ours may not have been a show house, but at least when the shops were closed we had no need to go without anything.

Pierre wanted it for his braces. Then, that problem solved, "dance? You dance?" he asked mother, eyes blazing with anticipation, feet tapping the floor.

"Oh — well, er, I'll try," she replied coyly — as though she wasn't having private lessons in ballroom dancing at Jack Fox's every Tuesday afternoon.

Off we trooped upstairs, except Dad, who stayed downstairs to wash up and to scan the *Examiner*. He was no dancer, preferring a game of billiards. In any case, there was always too much to do now that John Hall, who used to assist in the shop, and Jimmy Walkden, our baker, had been called up.

Pierre took command in the upstairs "front room". Unceremoniously he pushed the three piece suite up against the walls to make a clear space for dancing in the centre. Then he went to the radiogram and selected some records. How I wished we had a camera, so that I could show off Pierre to the girls in my form at school. But where could films be found, even if we had one? And he wouldn't have time to go to Geoffrey's studio on New Street, where you could have "3 for 2s. 6d.". Pierre selected dance music from the Fred Astaire/ Ginger Rogers films *Roberta, The Gay Divorce* and *Top Hat* to begin with, and whirled Mother, Jean and me round the room alternately, giving fleeting little kisses to us all as the music, and our heart-beats, quickened.

Then it was time for bed at last. But not before Pierre initiated a boisterous pillow fight, an international language that we could all understand. By that time we had found out that our guest, in civilian life, was sports editor of *Le Petit Parisien*, which had the largest circulation of any French morning paper. It organized an annual walking race before the war from Paris to Strasbourg, the last one being won by a walker who did 200 miles or so at an average of 5 m.p.h. He completed the walk in forty hours, which included time off for rest, sleep, and eating. No wonder France had a reputation for having such good infantrymen.

Sergeant Pierre Rabaste, aged twenty-nine, belonged to the Camel Corps, an African Regiment of a type similar to the spahis, hence the picturesque cape. He came to England after Dunkirk, where he had been wounded in the head and feet. (No one would have thought it, the nimble way he could quickstep and polka!) After being in hospital in Scotland he had joined the Free French. A Parisian, his sporting interests were cycling, the national sport of France, and after that walking.

Jean, starry-eyed, said "Goodnight", then remembered she knew how to say "Bonsoir", probably feeling that she was in dreamland already. When Dad came back, after seeing her safely home, we all talked again.

Then I suggested I'd get ready for bed first, and said goodnight to Pierre, still feeling a bit of a fool when I thought about being wrapped in his cloak in that blacked out taxi. I wondered if he sleep-walked, having been wounded in the head. Just in case, I put a comb and mirror beneath my pillow, then pretended to be reading my history book when I heard the staircase creak as the unfamiliar light footsteps leapt upstairs. He knew I was there, I knew he was there, and only the door separated us. I hadn't known whether it would look rude to shut it properly, or look like an invitation for him to come in if I left it slightly open. I had decided on the latter, and kept the light on. A minute or so later the door inched open. Pierre had been breathtaking in his uniform, and was even more so in his pyjamas — black satin, with a sinuous purple snake pattern down the front.

He smiled, draping his tall, lithe frame across the Put-U-Up. Gently taking the book from my hand (I hadn't learned a word of it, concentrating as I was on the up-to-the-minute movements in the house) his face came near to mine.

"Baby — je t'adore, cherie . . ." or words to that effect. Every word of French I'd ever learnt completely deserted me. I felt speechless, unable to make up my mind whether I was glad that he'd come into the room again or not. Fear mingled with irresistible excitement. Then — was he trying to choke me? His tongue was in my mouth, and I couldn't speak, in any language. At that moment familiar steps hurried upstairs. Dad came in, smiling affably. He indicated the other room.

"You'll be alright in there, lad", he said.

"Merci," replied Pierre. I felt as though I was the one who ought to be saying *Mercy*. I couldn't wait for the next morning, so I could tell Jean all about Pierre trying to kill me or something.

Sunday dawned, 29 November 1942. After breakfast Pierre took Philip to visit officer friends stationed in

New North Road. Philip, my brother, was good at languages, and this was the first opportunity he'd ever had to talk with a real Frenchman.

That afternoon there was riotous dancing again upstairs. Jean had appeared, and so had Betty Moorhouse, a girl who lived further up the road. All the village had been agog about "that man in a big cloak" they'd seen marching around, who was staying at Taylor's shop.

After tea Pierre had to spend the evening at the Queen Hotel with the other soldiers. Arranging to call for him there later, we went to visit Winnie and Kenneth, and their children Brian and Carol at St John's Road flats. When Pierre left it felt as though the electric light had been suddenly switched off. Philip was fire-watching again at the National Provincial Bank.

We walked to the Queen Hotel for Pierre at the appointed time. As we walked through town he immediately swept me beneath that magic cloak, then we had another taxi ride home in the blackout, and more dancing before bedtime. He must have realized that I'd been in a state of shock the previous night, and Pierre's goodnight kiss was more restrained.

It was a wrench of the greatest magnitude to have to go to school the next morning. But Pierre was still at home when I returned for midday dinner. To my delight he came on the bus to town with Jean and me. When he walked up to the school gates with us, first formers to sixth formers trailed behind him, like rats mesmerized by the Pied Piper. Even the mistresses, even Miss Hill herself, could not raise any objections to a Frenchman. After all, we were being patriotic, offering hospitality to an ally. And just think how our French would improve!

That evening we took Pierre to introduce him to Grandma, then he went to the Queen Hotel again. Grandma was beginning to feel weary, pulling on the blackout curtain laboriously so early those November nights. She wasn't as besotted by our guest as everybody else had been, for she still remarked "I wish the Lord would take me" as she replaced her walking stick by the window.

Next day at Greenhead, to make matters worse, we had a shorthand exam in the morning, geography in the afternoon. At four o'clock out we came. There, at the school gates, exactly as the report in the local newspaper had described him, was Pierre: "A replica of the sheik in *The Desert Song*, currently on at the Theatre Royal."

Resplendent in flat-topped De Gaulle-type hat, billowing cloak — who had ever seen a man in a scarlet lined cloak in Huddersfield before? — and those highly polished boots.

My heart felt to be bursting with pride. That this vision could actually have slept in our house! Under the cloak we went, as many girls as could cram themselves beneath it. Laughing, giggling, joking, nearly all our form went with us on to the railway station platform.

Recklessly, Pierre attempted to pull Edith on to the train with him. I wondered if Edith McLoughlin would ever be seen again as the train prepared to steam out of the station. Kisses were blown from the window — whew — it was like being swept up in a whirlwind. He had his cloak to keep the desert sands out of his eyes. We had nothing at all to keep the stars out of ours.

Home had resumed its usual demeanour by night time, Mother mending socks by the fire and listening to the wireless. Jean came down ostensibly to do her homework with me in the upstairs front room. But mostly we talked, every minute detail about the weekend, Pierre's effect on us, and on everyone else he had come into contact with. How we longed for him to be able to visit us again at Christmas. He had promised he would try.

Jean had news for me. "I've found out about what Pierre did that night, kid," she said. "It's called a French kiss."

CHAPTER
FIVE

1943

After a humdrum life as the local plumber in Deighton, Tom Jessop found himself directed to work in the Tyneside shipyards. His wife, Muriel, worked as a typist at ICI earning "good money" — £4 a week — some of which could be saved for their future, when peace returned.

Muriel was also an air raid warden, as was her neighbour Harry Medley. When the sirens went Muriel was awake at once. Not so Harry. She had to go round and bang on his door, then patrol Deighton Road, to ensure everything and everybody was alright, a bit frightening in the blackout especially when ack-ack guns were noisily spluttering up at Almondbury.

Tom could only go back home infrequently, and Muriel's ears, ever on the alert, listened for the more welcome sound of the train pulling into Deighton Station late at night, bringing her husband home for a brief reunion. Going to chapel helped Muriel, and so many others, withstand the partings that war brought.

Betty Key was happily employed in Boots Library. A musician in her spare time, Betty had been invited to join Ivy Benson's all-girl band. But her father, Lance, thought his high-spirited young daughter would be safer at home than roaming the country — although Betty had already, when twelve, broadcast with the Yorkshire Comedy Players, and at eighteen had been a trombonist with Lindley Boys' Club Band. During the winter pantomime season of 1943, Betty played the trombone at the Theatre Royal.

When she had to think about whether to join the forces, land army, or work in munitions, Betty didn't have to think for long. She didn't fancy having to say "Sir" to anyone, so the services were out. She couldn't have tolerated working on munitions, but she loved all animals. The Labour Exchange agreed that the Land Army would be suitable. So Betty was eventually kitted out with the familiar hat, badge, tie, two cream coloured shirts, two long-sleeved green "V" neck jumpers, two pairs of corded breeches and knee length socks, a couple of pairs of beige dungarees, and a pair of strong, lace up shoes. Black boots, like men's, wellingtons, a hip-length camel hair coat, one oilskin and a sou'wester completed her outfit. Land Army girls provided their own underwear, and a belt to keep the breeches up. Her dad bought the belt.

First "posting" for the new land army girl was at Garbutt's farm near Mirfield. At first Betty felt ridiculous in her new uniform, as though she were in a show of some sort. The only place she dared try it out for the first time was somewhere in the dark, so she walked to the Regent cinema. It didn't take long for the uniform to feel almost like a second skin, though, when it became a bit worn. Indeed, Betty looked the perfect example of an attractive, happy go lucky Land Army girl, and more at home in the uniform then out of it. Pay was £2 10s. a week, with the midday meal included.

Betty soon learned how to muck out, a job that had to be done twice a day, as had milking. After a few weeks Betty transferred to Joe Smith's farm at Lindley. Being in the Land Army meant early rising, for work started at 6.30a.m. There was no need to be frightened in the dark early mornings, because other early morning workers were so friendly — rushing to bus stops with their workmen's return tickets, laughing and chatting their way to various war work. The majority of them had proper air raid shelters or cellars at their places of work should there be an alert. Betty, however — "Oh, I'd get under the nearest cow and hope for the best!" Later on she worked for Mr Fred Kenyon, of Bent-Lea Farm, Meltham.

Haymaking in summer, longer hours, didn't earn any extra money. But nobody went on strike during the war — well, not many. Most pulled together in a common cause. Betty's hot weather wear on the farm was her dungarees, with the sleeves rolled up. Refreshments were a drink of milk from a cow, and sandwiches.

In wintertime, when she delivered milk on her round, customers seemed to pity her outdoor job. "By gum, lass, it's cold," customers exclaimed, holding the door open while Betty measured the milk out into their own jugs. But after all the hard physical work the land girl, though not disputing the observation about it being cold, was sweating. The first time she went on a milk round, in charge of the horse and the milk float, a local wag called out: "Sithee — Kenyon's new jockey!"

Milk was in churns, though there were a few bottles with cardboard tops on, and a little piece in the centre to push out. When the cardboard top was dry, children enjoyed making pom-poms with them, pushing wool round, then cutting the outside while still on the cardboard, and tying a length of wool round the middle to hold it together. Cats loved to play with the pom-poms, tied to a chair arm.

Farmers complained that some of the milk bottles weren't returned. Like most other jobs, there were the occasional "perks", a few eggs and a pint of milk for Betty to take home, for example.

Ivy Kenyon, daughter at the farm, joined up, preferring to see the world rather than staying at home. Betty, a "townie" until the war, loved the life, even the harsh winters — especially coming into the farm from outside to see the farmer's wife boiling up potatoes in a big black pan on the coal fire, and joining in the midday dinner, with lots of talk and laughter.

After a bath in the evening at home, the regulation wartime limit of five inches of water up the side of the bath, Betty had enough energy to go out dancing. One evening I went with her to Cambridge Road Baths. We missed the last bus, so walked to her home on Bradford Road. Betty suggested telephoning our shop, to let them know I was staying the night there. Her parents were in bed, asleep. What about when they woke up in the morning and found a stranger in Betty's bed?

We squeezed into her single bed, Betty hanging on to the edge by, I'm sure, sheer will power alone. It didn't seem long before I heard her getting up again to go to the farm.

"What will your mother say when she sees me in bed?" I whispered.

"Oh, she'll make you some breakfast, then you can go home," was the nonchalant reply as she swung jauntily out of the door, hat at its usual rakish angle.

Mrs Key strolled into the bedroom about 7a.m., and jumped back on seeing a body in her daughter's bed. She insisted that I stayed for breakfast, however. Despite shortages and rations, I enjoyed a tasty repast of fried bread and plenty of HP sauce. Spontaneous hospitality always seems to be the best!

Indeed, there was far less fuss and palaver when there was less to eat, and guests just shared what there was. No airs and graces made wartime meals far more genuine, and when not much was expected no-one was disappointed.

At that time there were many homely talks and hints on the wireless Home Service for those with time to listen — for example, "New Clothes for Old", "The Care of Corsets", and, of course, "Children's Hour".

Huddersfield Corporation was notified by the Ministry of Home Security that to meet demands for indoor shelters of larger capacity than the Morrison table type, a two-tier shelter would be available free to those with no space for an Anderson shelter, and with no strengthened passages in the house, providing earnings (or pension) didn't exceed £350 a year. They could also be bought by the public for £9 15s. and were preferably to be erected on the ground floor, where there was no other form of protection.

While the majority worked full tilt, a few still tried it on. One worker asked for time off work to get his hair cut. When his boss objected, the chap snapped back, "well, it grows in t' firm's time don't it?"

There were inconsistencies leading to petty annoyances at times. An air raid warden, pulled up for wearing ARP gum boots on private affairs, hotly replied, "ah'd have thee know that ah've done plenty of ARP work in me own boo-its."

A Hillhouse woman was summoned under the Fish Act (Maximum Prices Order 1941) for selling kippers at a price exceeding 10d. per 1b, and for failing to display a notice giving the description and price offered for sale. She was represented by Mr Stephen D. Lister, and Mr G. E. Hutchinson prosecuted for the Food Control Authority.

On 24 January George Formby was in a new film, *South American George*, at the Ritz. A Linthwaite insurance manager was knocked down in Buxton Road during the blackout.

Married women with no children and without domestic ties were directed to work in factories. Wives of servicemen were to serve in industry, but were not to be moved away from their homes.

A warden suggested that arms were needed for Civil Defence Workers in case of invasion. At present, all that the warden could do, if enemy troops were in the neighbourhood, would be to "lie low".

Towards the end of January 1942, refugees from Nazi oppression met to hear Mayor Arthur Gardiner open the newly formed Anglo-Refugee Friendship Club in Dundas Street. Flags of the Allied Nations hung from the walls. Deputy Mayor A. E. Sellers appealed to the people of the town to join the club: "One cause of the present atrocities taking place in the world today is that we haven't mixed together sufficiently. We have not had that feeling of comradeship between the nations." Secretary Mr R. Brook appealed for a piano and table tennis set to add to the amenities of the club.

Huddersfield motorists were soon to have the benefit of "cats' eyes" on the roads — helpful in the blackout.

Evacuees in the district were puzzled with many aspects of their strange new lives, not least the dialect, local customs, and food. One child from London was mystified to see a row of queer looking objects hanging on the bread reel. "Oh, what a lot of wash leathers you have," she said to her hostess. The "wash leathers" were newly baked oatcakes hanging up to dry.

A recital for the Red Cross Aid to Russia Fund, in the Town Hall in February, had the attraction of Moiseiwitsch to play compositions of Beethoven, Chopin, Debussy, Rachmaninov and Brahms.

John Crowther and Sons Employees Comforts Fund Dance was held at Cambridge Road Baths on Friday 30 January. The Westbourne Players provided the music. Admission was 2s., and 1s. for HM Forces.

Miss Edith Toms, from the Ministry of Information, gave a talk to Marsh Women's Liberal Club Association entitled "It Might Happen Here".

A group of nine particularly good chums, approaching military age, all in the Junior YMCA, hated the thought of losing contact with each other. So they formed the Contact Club, pledging to keep in touch when the time came for joining up. The membership fee was 6d. a month, and each young man promised to pay wherever he was. The group had their photographs taken, and as the call came they dispersed. Each week, all of them wrote a long letter to the others, care of the central YMCA. The letters were kept in a book there, and when the "Contacters" came on leave they could read the letters and thus keep in touch with each other. The 6d. a month subscription was banked for the club, accumulating for the great day when the faithful nine could celebrate together again.

No matter what the news, Huddersfield's dancing went on and on. Laund Hill Ladies' Hockey Club held a dance in the Fraternity Hall, with the Brooklyn Players providing the music on 30 January, while a "Select Dance" at Cambridge Road Baths, in aid of Group I ARP with the Philip's Personality Players, brought the month to a close.

One of the hazards of attending dances was, for ladies, finding places of safety for their handbags. With all the junk carried around in them — keys, powder compacts, lipstick, handkerchief, money, cloakroom ticket; they were too bulky to carry while dancing. Yet leaving them beneath seats was a bit risky. Leave it with a friend and she couldn't be expected to forego a "May I have this dance?" just to be a handbag attendant. One girl who lost hers advertised, diplomatically, in the local paper, for the "person who took lady's handbag by mistake from the Co-op Hall dance on Wednesday night, to please return to the address inside. Sentimental value."

Thomas Kaye's sale announced that "Thrifty Buyers will readily appreciate the opportunity of securing quality goods at bargain prices, thus enhancing their coupons' value. 21–23 King Street."

Nostalgically, on 1 February at the Princess cinema, Fred Astaire and Eleanor Powell were starring in *Broadway Melody of 1940*. While at the Tudor, Nelson Eddy and Rise Stevens were singing delightfully in *The Chocolate Soldier*. Crowd puller Bette Davis was in *The Great Lie* at the Ritz, with Billy Hobson playing the organ during the interval.

On Tuesday, Wednesday and Thursday evenings a comedy based on Russian communal life, *Squaring the Circle*, was presented by the Co-operative Players in the Fraternity Hall, Alfred Street. While Huddersfield Anglo-Refugees Friendship Club arranged for a celebrated Czechoslovakian pianist to give a recital in the Town Hall on the Wednesday. Another wrestling tournament was scheduled at the Baths for Thursday, a dance in the Town Hall on Saturday.

That day, 7 February 1942, the mayor opened Aid For Russia Week and Flag Day, in the Market Place.

The week closed on the following Sunday with a concert at the Palace Theatre, when Leslie Sarony of the "Two Leslies" fame headed an excellent variety bill. Exhibitions were held in the drapery department of Huddersfield Industrial Society, and in what was formerly W. H. Smith's bookshop, which was headquarters for the week, and where tickets could be obtained for any events. Daily film shows depicting life in the Soviet Union, and a film called *Our Russian Allies* was shown at the Waterloo cinema.

Over 800 boys were registered at the Employment Exchange, and over 40 per cent were already members of either the Home Guard, Civil Defence, Boy Scouts and Boys' clubs.

A famous name, Solomon, gave a piano recital at the Theatre Royal in February. On a more mundane note, the Corporation water works National Economy Campaign announced that taps could be washered free of charge. If a tap leaked, householders should telephone the Waterworks.

News of two Huddersfield prisoners of war was picked up by Geoffrey Cockin, former *Examiner* sports reporter, then in the RAF. He tuned into a Vatican broadcast and heard it announced that Corporal H. H. Hodgson, of Longwood Road, and another soldier named Bradfield, were safe and well.

On the home front, a married man with one child earning not more than £4 a week and with no other income, was not required to pay income tax. A married man with no dependent children in receipt of the same amount was liable to a weekly deduction of 6s. 5d. from his wages. So wrote "Disgusted" in the local paper.

All was not sacrosanct in the realms of the dead. Mr H. Travis Clay, of Rastrick, asked in the parish magazine for anyone objecting to the removal of tomb railings for scrap, to communicate with the vicar. No objections were received, either from the living or the dead.

"Disgusted, Marsh" was still annoyed, however, this time about free milk for children. Instead of using free milk in addition to their usual supply, he knew of some who were making it their sole supply — while widows receiving 10s. a week were having to pay 9d. per quart, and wealthier people were getting free supplies because they had a child.

Early in May a sheep, not directed to the ICI by the Labour Exchange, was found wandering in the ICI grounds. It was taken into the Police Station for the night. In the morning, probably sensitive to the national need for further production, it had produced a lamb. Mother and daughter were reported "both well under Police Protection".

On the food front, rhubarb was still the only type of fruit available. April 1942 had been pronounced the sunniest for forty years.

A Huddersfield farmer objected to having a Land Girl helping him, requesting a shepherd instead, because a shepherdness had once "made a reet mess of it". Asked who she was, the farmer grinned, "Bo-Peep".

On Wednesday 20 May a supply of fresh oranges was available in Huddersfield and district for children, with green ration book. From 15 June ration books had to be marked when tomatoes were bought.

On Tuesday 16 June a British restaurant opened in Northumberland Street, supplying 11d. and 10d. lunches.

A few strawberries arrived on the market at a controlled price of 2s. 3d. per lb. By Friday, the 19th, disappointment — the hoped for tomatoes had failed to turn up. But it was hoped they would be delivered the following week, according to the Central Distributing Agency.

Chief Scout Lord Somers visited Huddersfield on 13 June when thousands of scouts attended a rally to hear him open a National Scout camping ground in Bradley Wood.

Summer. Troise and his Mandoliers appeared at the Palace Theatre, and the Brook Motors Concert Party were entertaining the forces all over the country most Sundays and many evenings. Their producer, Tom Sly, arranged for them to spend their annual holiday in London, entertaining Forces in Southern Command every evening. Una Mellor, one of the "leading lights" of Brook Motors Concert Party, was terribly upset when her dad, an undertaker of Cowlersley, refused to let his sixteen-year-old daughter go with them. She cried all that week. "You know where she'd end up, gadding off to London," Mr Mellor said to his wife, Emma Jane. But no-one ever said where . . .

Una had joined Brook Motors in 1940. Her first morning was in the depths of winter, icy blasts and drifting snow. "You'll have to walk, there are no buses," commanded her father. Marjorie Sykes taught the newcomer rotor winding, and Una earned 12s. 6d. a week at first, and was allowed half a crown spending money.

154

It was hard work pulling wires all day long, but, being wartime, everyone kept their spirits up by singing as they toiled. To save money, Una took sandwiches, usually beetroot. One dinnertime Una was fed up of beetroot, so she didn't eat the last one. She was sitting on one of the bins where bits of wire were thrown in — a suitable receptacle for the damned beetroot sandwich thought Una, so in it went. Bins were usually emptied daily, but for some reason they weren't that day.

Next day she was singing away, having a brief rest, when she heard something rattling about in the bin. She glanced in, then screamed "a rat!" Her screams were echoed by the other workers, who stopped work and stood back. Raymond Gaye came to the rescue, plunging an electric fork, used for testing motors, into the bin. The rat, electrocuted, shot up into the air. When the boss, Mr Bushfield, heard the commotion and found out what had happened, he gave the culprit a "right telling off". Next morning Una called up to her dad — he didn't get up as early as she, having to begin work at 7.30: "what can I put in my sandwiches for a change?"

"Try some arsenic, there's some in't cellar," replied her disciplinarian father, annoyed about the episode. Una had never heard of arsenic before:

"Oh, is it nice?" she wanted to know. Well, when you've had beetroot sandwiches for a week . . .

William Mellor, her dad, went round knocking neighbours up when the air raid sirens went. He wore a tin hat, very different to the tall black silk hat he majestically wore when attending to his funeral business, along with his long black frock coat. Many a time he received no response. "It's like wakening the b — dead, the dozy bugger'll have to stay where he is" was William's reaction after banging to no avail.

By that time, Una, her mother and sister were in their cellar, where three coffin boards were always kept in readiness. Everything always happens in threes, was her father's conviction. Boxes of shrouds were kept in Una's wardrobe.

Every so often the cellar was limed. Coffin boards were outlined more starkly against the pristine whiteness after this was done.

There were lean times when people seemed to go on living forever, and the family rations of everything had to be cut down. Chips and no meat when they were a bit hard up, with nobody dying.

When a "passing" was expected William sat up waiting until about 3a.m. If a call hadn't come by then, the undertaker went to bed, saying to Emma Jane, "they'll keep". A funeral, including the grave diggers, cost about £50.

William's favourite meal was sheeps' brains, or pigs' trotters with butter oozing all over them. When Una looked at those atrocities, all white and twisty, she could have been forgiven for thinking them the originators of the phrase "getting your wires crossed".

Una's dad used to get all steamed up when organizing a funeral. Pacing the floor in his robes of office, muttering "six feet by . . . I wonder if that grave digger made it big enough?", because they'd had a "couple of bad do's" with mistaken calculations. If it went off alright, William sent for a jug of beer to be brought across to his house in Cowlersley Lane.

Often the shout went up, "Emma Jane, you'll never guess who's passed." On hearing the name of the deceased, the unvarying response was "Ee, and I only saw him/her last week!"

Una's mother was a "wonderful knitter but slack", according to her daughter. She used to knit everything, even down to knickers and swimming costumes, with the inevitable disaster of sagging, and that sinking feeling when wet.

William thought he knew best when it came to using clothing coupons. When Una needed a new coat he took her down to the market in Huddersfield and insisted on her having a trench mac. It reached her ankles. "Can't I shorten it?" she pleaded.

"No, watter'll run straight off, leave it as it is," and that was that.

But it was he who instilled a love of singing into his young daughter. His idol was Gracie Fields, his favourite song "Sally". Una, trying to get into his good books, tried to imitate Gracie. William made her a tap dancing board: he was a very good joiner. He also wanted Una to learn to play the piano.

When Tom Sly, organizer of Brook Motors Concert Party, heard Una singing as she worked, he invited her to join the group. Tom was an ex-Manchester singing teacher, a baritone. Others in the party were Mollie Gibson, an assembler, one-time dance band singer, accordionist Arthur Taylor, and the Shakeshaft sisters, Irene and Joan. The latter had been a Tiller girl, giving up the stage for war work. Hilda Armitage, who sang "Ave Maria" beautifully, was also in the concert party, as was Ronnie Daniels, a driller, whose speciality was singing "The Two Gendarmes" with Tom.

Ronnie, of small build, contrasted amusingly with the over 6 ft tall Tom Sly. Sustained applause never failed to reward their "We run 'em in, we run 'em in, we run 'em in, we show them we're the Bold Gendarmes."

Then there was the professional ballet dancer, Julian. He had been directed to work on munitions at Brook Motors. It was quite an eye-opener to watch Julian rehearsing.

It was a dream come true for Una to swap her blue overall and cap (to keep her hair safe from any machinery), to put on a pretty dress and a flower in her hair, then get up on stage and sing. One of the songs Una sang was "The Umbrella Man" and, of course, her imitation of Gracie Fields, which went down well with both workers and troops. Besides singing "Sally", it always caused a laugh when she sang "The Biggest Aspidistra in the World".

For touring to remote places in the blackout, such as Wakefield, Leeds, even as far as Harrogate, wherever the troops were, the Concert Party had a bus — "a right old relic, with a piano in it." The bus windows were painted black, to comply with regulations.

Una sometimes wore a black dress, jazzed up with sequins at the "V" neck. Occasionally someone lent her a dress, to make a change.

The bus driver dropped each member of the party near their home after a show, entertainers having enjoyed sandwiches and coffee or tea in the Officers' Mess before leaving for home. Una's dad was always at his post, peering out of the blackout up Cowlersley Lane, waiting to see his daughter safely back.

The day of the Brook Motors Concert Party Broadcast in March, 1942, William was worked up to the hilt. Did Una know all the words of her songs? He didn't want her to show them all up. But everything went well when Works Wonders No. 63, by War Workers, for War Workers, was on the air. A big piece about it, and Una's photograph, featured in the *Daily Sketch*.

Accordionist Arthur Taylor brought a pal, Bill Pearce, to see one of the concerts. Bill's dad had a farm at Shepherds Thorne, Bradley. Bill was a Petty Officer in the Royal Navy, and was immediately swept off his feet by the delightful young singer, Una Mellor. Bill had had a narrow escape when on a landing craft. "Your shoe lace is undone, Bill", a chum observed. Bill bent to tie it up — and an enemy bullet missed him, passing through the stomach of Bob Fowler, who happened to be standing behind him.

Bill wasn't as lucky in his first encounter with Una's dad. "Which way out do you want to go out — through t'winder or t'door?" he was asked unceremoniously.

Death came to many through battle, but disease could still be a killer. Huddersfield College School magazine sadly had to report the death, from diptheria, of Keith Hellawell in 1942. Included in the Roll of Honour was Sub-Lieutenant John Charles Geoffrey Cranston, RNVR, serving in the *Hermes* at the time of its loss. And condolences were offered to Mr and Mrs E. B. Blakemore, of the Fleece Hotel, Kirkgate, when it was learned that their son Roy was missing.

In peacetime, the summer was a term of great activity at the Boys' College. In wartime, boys experienced a very different way of life to that of pupils in earlier years. The tennis competition was temporarily suspended, and the swimming gala lacked the keenness and atmosphere that were striking features before the war. No longer were there glorious school trips to remote parts of England (such as Filey and Stratford!), and a perpetual anxiety that "Old Boys in the Forces" may have their lives in danger laid a pall over everything.

It was hoped that all boys of fifteen would consider joining the Air Training Corps at the beginning of the autumn term. And that all boys would consider the claims of the Sea Cadets, Home Guard, Civil Defence, and other youth organizations such as the Scouts. Those intending to proceed to universities were encouraged to do so at the earliest possible date.

Mrs C. D. Beatty, Treasurer of the Old Boys' Comforts Fund, was ready to receive donations sent to the College.

The gift of a framed etching of Lord Oxford and Asquith, a pupil of the old Huddersfield College, had been received. Miss E. Willans, sister of Mr J. E. Willans, JP, a distinguished member of Huddersfield Education Committee, became Mrs Asquith, and mother of Lord Oxford and Asquith, who autographed

160

the etching. It was the gift and work of Mr Henry Fieldhouse, distinguished Old Collegian.

On Tuesday 16 June, in the Swimming Sports at Cambridge Road Baths, the house championship was won by Cromwell, with Burleigh the runner-up. Mrs H. G. Barwood distributed prizes.

At Whitsuntide, Scout camps were held at Whitley Beaumont, the weather being even worse than at Easter. Owing to a heavy downpour certain activities had to be cancelled. One two-man hike broke down owing to the collapse of a rucksack. The third hike was washed out by the Whit Monday deluge.

"Holidays at Home", with events in Greenhead Park, weren't a wash-out, even if the weather sometimes was. An active concert party was the Whizz Bangs; the producer of the shows was Mr E. C. R. Chinn. They did their share in Greenhead Park as well as entertaining the Forces. Since the Whizz Bangs were formed they had travelled over 1,000 miles in the blackout, often through the night.

Quality shows continued with the Sadlers Wells Opera Company at the Theatre Royal in September, and Herman Darewski and His Band at the Palace. The orchestra was directed by Mr Atkin Baker. Many patronized the Palace as much for the pleasure of seeing "Attie" in his immaculate evening suit, bow tie, dazzling white shirt, flower in his lapel, and that dimpling, amiable smile as he turned, baton in hand, to acknowledge the applause of his delighted audience. "Attie" encouraged members of his orchestra to get up and take a bow as well.

Thursday 3 September, the third anniversary of the start of war, was a National Day of Prayer. From noon until 1.50p.m., many engineering, factory and office workers, some in their overalls, went straight from work to the nearest church. Employees of Joseph Hoyle, Longwood, and C. & J. Hirst, attended Longwood parish church, then went either home for dinner or back to their canteens.

A special service was held in the works canteen at John Crowther's, Milnsbridge. David Brown employees went across to Crosland Moor parish church, Hopkinson's workpeople to St John's church. There was a special service of intercession in Huddersfield parish church, and High Street Methodist church. Additional masses were said in Roman Catholic churches.

Stories of bravery made the town proud of its lads. Private C. Ingham, Bradley Road, had his gallantry that July recorded in South Eastern Command Army orders. He had stood on the wing of a blazing plane, supporting the pilot's shoulders, while another soldier released the pilot's feet. Then they carried him clear of the burning machine.

Summer was almost over again, and the black, black nights were approaching. It was decreed that the aperture through which light was emitted from a torch should be no more than the size of a halfpenny, and must be covered by one thickness of newspaper or its equivalent. Two pieces of tissue paper were the equivalent of an ordinary piece of newspaper over the torch.

In the interests of fuel economy, the number of illuminated traffic signal lights were to be reduced between 11p.m. and 5.30a.m. from 14 September.

New ideas kept coming forth as to how to raise money. Aldmondbury Branch of the British Legion organized lines of pennies in Westgate, and a collection in Northgate, raising £7 0s. 9d. for Aldmondbury United Effort and Gala. On 9 September a Blitz meal, consisting of stew, steamed pudding and custard, was cooked in the garden of WVS sector leader Mrs Winterbottom, and the meal was enjoyed by thirty people.

For attending all these occasions, ladies could have "perfectly coiffed hair, permed, full head, at Maison Terry, Cross Church Street," for 10s.

No more normal length socks were to be made while the war lasted, they were to be 5 in shorter.

News came through to Huddersfield that Marjorie Heyes, former member of Clifford Garner's Concert Party, now in the ATS, was still entertaining her hut mates with her doll, Jimmy — a ventriloquist's dummy clad in khaki.

Huddersfield-born film star James Mason was starring at the Princess Cinema in *The Night Has Eyes* and Shirley Temple was at the Grand in *Miss Annie Rooney*.

Due to the blackout, four Corporation concerts had been scheduled for Saturday afternoons during the winter season.

Wild produce of the summer had been harvested for use. Foxglove leaves and nettles were being dried at

Ravensknowle Museum under the supervision of Dr John Grainger. Valuable drugs urgently required by hospitals could be obtained from them, and the local collection was to be sent to drug manufacturers. Rose hips had been collected, and also horse chestnuts, which supplied nutritious cattle feed. Girl Guides, Boy Scouts, and anybody else willing to help were invited to organize collection groups.

The public were warned that noises representing firing and bomb explosions might be heard on the night and early morning of Saturday/Sunday 19 and 20 September, as Home Guards were exercising. Should an air raid alert sound during the night, their activities would be immediately suspended.

A local reader was shocked after returning home from the library. She realized that her clothing coupons, which she had been using as a book mark, had been left in her library book. Back she dashed, heart pounding. There was the book. She opened it, and *what* a relief — the coupons were still there.

Dorothy Atha, secretary at Thomas Broadbent's, longed for something different to eat. It always seemed to be spam on the menu. Surely a holiday in Ilkley would break the monotony? It didn't. Spam may have been served up with impeccable elegance, amid refined surroundings — quite unlike the workaday British restaurant on Lord Street — but spam it remained, in various guises.

To make a change from chapel socials, musical chairs, "King William" and ladies trotting out the same old monologues, Dorothy went to CHA dances at the

Co-op Hall. Never really being able to relax there, she was always wondering if there was going to be a siren — half listening for that sound while listening to strains of "White Cliffs of Dover" and "Yours". After the dance was over, there was the walk home to Primrose Hill.

Dorothy's annual holiday was cut to three days as the firm was so busy, but she was paid for the usual fortnight. In the summer girls could go without stockings, thus saving valuable clothing coupons for other items. But Dorothy knew somebody who worked in a draper's shop in town, who let her have a pair of artificial silk stockings every six months. They had to be paid for, but she was excused from giving coupons. Perhaps wartime was the beginning of the phrase "it's not what you know, but who you know." Dorothy liked wearing hats — at least they weren't on coupons.

Her firm, Thomas Broadbent & Sons, of Central Iron Works Huddersfield, made practically all the centrifuges used by the Allies for the manufacture of gun cotton, and also components for thousands of anti-tank guns, spigot mortars, parts for tanks, arrester gear for aircraft landing, watertight bulkhead doors for Corvettes and so on, but the most interesting of all were the four complete X-craft midget submarines that they had to build under conditions of absolute secrecy. Their crews were awarded four VCs and many other awards. Three of the Works staff were awarded the BEM for their work in handling the many difficult production problems involved. Bringing one of the two-man submarines out of the plating shop door at Milford Street at dead of night for transportation, one of the workers had his hand badly crushed when turning the submarine round.

Hats were popular, especially ones that looked like the ones worn by film stars. One shop sold a range with film stars' names on them. Margaret, a postman's daughter, was thrilled with a maroon velour Deanna Durbin hat, which her mother bought for her to wear at Wiggan Lane chapel anniversary. Margaret played the piano at Wiggan Lane. Many of the hats for older ladies had veils, but Margaret was only what was becoming known as a "teenager".

Hymns selected for the anniversary seemed apt for wartime — "Jesus Bids Us Shine, Like a Clear, Pure Light, Like a Little Candle, Burning in the Night . . ."

Walter, commonly known as "Walt", Margaret's dad, was an enthusiastic allotment holder in his spare time. He grew magnificent vegetables in that plot by the bowling green, also chrysanthemums. "Ordinary Elsie", as he affectionately and jokingly called his wife, whose proper name was Audrey Elsie, was presented with flowers every week by her husband. She was so proud of Walt, who had served in the First World War, and who used to entertain friends and neighbours with tall stories about the strange things he had seen, or thought he had seen. Not least of them was the story he recounted with gusto when he and "his lot" were down in Sykes's cellar during an alert, about "a Zulu with two penises". Whether that had been a form of hallucination under strain of battle could never be disproved, but it certainly entertained his Second World War listeners. "Oh, Walt!" "Ordinary Elsie" would say reprovingly, but with an amused little smile playing around her lips nevertheless. Nobody could be frightened of mere bombs when Walt was around, as he made a joke of everything.

Many a time in those wartime winters of deep snows, Walt was almost buried in drifts when delivering post up at Scammonden. But with determination and sheer tenacity of purpose, the mail got through to those remote districts. So grateful to their postman were the inhabitants that they gave him what they could by way of a "thank-you" gift. Many an old hen ended up in his sack, bound for his dinner table. Margaret recalled seeing him plucking one enthusiastically, and she was sure it wasn't dead.

"Ordinary Elsie" used to bake oven bottom cakes for when he came in from the cold, often giving up her own butter ration, so that Walt could enjoy them as he used to do in pre-war days, with lashings of butter. It was a happy marriage that may be summed up in the words of the song, "You'd be so nice to come home to, you'd be so nice by the fire."

When Margaret started having boyfriends Walt took his parental responsibilities as rigorously as he applied himself to his other jobs. With diplomacy, hearing two voices in the blackout outside, he strode down the garden path.

"Is that you, Margaret? Have you a shilling for t'meter, lights have gone out" was his invariable opening when, in reality, the following words were the ones he meant, which were spoken as soon as the khaki-clad figure disappeared into the darkness fast.

"Get in this house, me lass." He wasn't going to have anything go wrong with his one and only daughter, who was earmarked to be a "Hello Girl" telephone operator at the GPO when she was old enough.

"Ordinary Elsie", though she never joined up or anything like that, learned how to manipulate events to her advantage. The kitchen in the row of terrace houses where they lived at Sheepridge was on the gloomy side. When Walt wasn't working, one of his jobs was to watch out for if the searchlights came on at the camp. If Elsie heard the shout go up, "they're coming on", she scuttled off into the kitchen, drew back the blackout curtain, and washed up by searchlight. Such a treat. They lit up the whole kitchen.

Her Walt boasted that he had the finest feet in England. After walking miles delivering the mail, he still enjoyed taking Trixie, the dog, for a long walk.

Walt liked to pretend that he was Romany, and Trixie was Rac (the gypsy raconteur who used to be on Children's Hour on the wireless and his dog). Walt was never idle for a moment. In their cellar was equipment for "cobbling" boots and shoes. Most of the neighbours took their footwear for Walt to mend. Many a time he didn't charge at all, or only a few coppers. Or he'd suggest, "you can buy me a pint."

Every Wednesday his beloved Elsie cooked a meat and potato pie. Margaret dreaded that day. She was detailed to catch the 12.40p.m. bus at Browning Road, carefully carrying her dad's portion of pie, with gravy, in a covered basin. It was a work of art trying to balance it going down Woodhouse Hill, especially if there was any snow and ice on the road.

Walt was waiting to receive the pie outside the GPO then Margaret got back on the bus and went home again. She had completed the Important Mission once more, and was back home in time for school. She never failed to worry about what she would do if the familiar, stocky figure wasn't standing there on Wednesday.

When the day was over, what a comfort to sit in her nightgown, by a coal fire, if it was wintertime, with a big mug full of cocoa, and Trixie, contended, leaning against her leg — dreaming of summer days, when they would ramble in Newhouse Wood again, and Trixie (Rac) could enjoy a drink from the streams that rippled, clear and pure, through the wood. Perhaps the war would be over then, and they wouldn't have to bother about spending nights in a chilly cellar ever again.

In 1942 Renée Hopkinson went to work at Brook Motors. Her boyfriend, Roy Large, worked there. She had previously been at Pat Martin's mill, Lindley, where they turned out a lot of khaki. After the bombs fell on the mill in 1940, Renée was confronted with lengths of cloth hanging out of the windows and all over the place.

Roy's dad encouraged her to learn winding. She worked from 7.30a.m. till 5p.m. and worked over three nights a week till 7.30a.m. There was three-quarters of an hour for dinner; half an hour at tea-time if working over. They also worked Saturday mornings. The canteen, or British restaurant catered for dinners, and for a change Renée went into town for a quick Welsh Rarebit and coffee in Sylvio's café.

Winders sang all the time, and enjoyed "Music While You Work" in the "Duchess Works", making parts for motors in aeroplanes.

Roy worked in the machine shop, and was in the Home Guard, learning how to shoot, at Deer Hill. He went on duty every Sunday morning, walking there and back. The only time Roy didn't work was on a Saturday night: there wasn't much time for courting!

Harold Martin, his boss, also walked to work every day and back home again at night. They thought nothing of it.

On 15 September 1942, fire-watching for women employed at Business Premises came into force, for those between the ages of twenty and forty-five. The Technical College began a canteen cookery course on the 22nd, for those desiring to obtain jobs in works canteens, British restaurants, and other communal feeding centres. The course fee was 10s. and took place on Tuesday afternoons from 2–4p.m., Wednesday from 9.15a.m. to 3.30p.m., for a period of twelve weeks.

At the beginning of December the public was informed what transport would be available at Christmas: weekday services on Christmas Eve, Sunday services on Christmas Day, and weekday services on Boxing Day. The running of extra buses wasn't allowed, and late ones were run exclusively for workers, Mr Muscroft, Transport Manager, stressed. People without permits were not allowed to travel into town from outside termini on those buses. They might start off

170

empty, but picked up passengers throughout the journey into town. If those without permits were allowed to ride on those buses, the position would soon become impossible.

This wasn't the only position that was getting impossible. A hopeful shopper was heard to say outside an empty fish shop, "as ta anny 'ake?" The fed-up fishmonger had a ready reply: "aye, stomach ache."

But as long as there was a new dress to wear at Christmas, the ladies could usually brighten up. Jackson's Stores of No. 5 Queen Street, suggested "Checks for charm, frocks 37s. 6d."

New clothes were the panacea for some; music served the same purpose for others. One local gentleman thought it would be a great privilege to hear the voice of Robert Naylor, famous tenor again "in these dark winter Sunday evenings". He wondered if any musician or singer could get Mr Naylor to visit Huddersfield.

From 7 December at the New Empire, Dorothy Lamour starred in *Beyond The Blue Horizon*. One Huddersfield girl imitated Miss Lamour so much that she could almost have been mistaken for her. From her jet-black long page boy hairstyle, to the eyes thick with mascara, Tattoo tan shade face powder and pouting, vivid red lipsticked mouth. The girl, who worked on munitions, hardly ever allowed herself to smile, maintaining a sultry aloofness that was to her workmates, if not a few mesmerised males, boring in the extreme.

On Sunday 7 December, an appreciative audience of troops was entertained at the YMCA by Miss Gladys

Senior, Evelyn Graham, Mr Arthur McGauvran and Mr Radley Cooper. They enjoyed pianoforte duets, vocal duets, operatic numbers, and folk songs. Mr F. W. Greenwood of Holy Trinity church presided. The usual *Messiah* uplifted the hearts of others in various chapels and churches around the district.

More down-to-earth complaints about food served at Milnsbridge British restaurant were being voiced, particularly about the number of times carrots appeared on the menu. One lorry driver was particularly scathing. "Eat more carrots and see better in the dark, seems to have been strictly adhered to by the Powers-That-Be." He was vicious about the puddings: "sad, heavy, and sticky. Potatoes tasted, and looked, as if they had been mashed in egg preservative, and the carrots — God bless 'em — were there in all their glory, any length up to eight inches."

Meals at Milnsbridge were sent from the kitchen at the Northumberland Street restaurant, and it was finally agreed that there were inadequate facilities to keep warm the food delivered to Milnsbridge British restaurant before 11a.m. The "specials" at 1s. 3d. were about the quality of those that used to be 10d., while those at 10d. "beggared description". Everyone was urged to use as little electricity as possible between 8a.m. and 1p.m., as that was when war factories needed it most. In the battle for fuel, firebricks should be put down each side of all open fires.

By 10 December fishmongers were already more or less on holiday. Supplies were so short that work finished about twenty minutes after the day's supply had arrived. It was not a bright outlook for Christmas.

Wives, children, and other relations of 256 prisoners of war on the books of Huddersfield prisoners of war committee were entertained in the Town Hall on the 9th. Every guest received a gift from a Christmas tree, money gifts delighted the children, and there were games and musical items by the Certo Cito band. Entertainers Clifford Garner, Miss Hilda Broadbent, and Madame Emily Harrop (vocalists) added to the five hour function, as did Mr F. A. Carter, illusionist. At the close, Mrs Thomas Smailes, Chairman of the committee, thanked the Mayor for use of the Town Hall.

Even if there wasn't plenty of fish, there were plenty of jobs. Hay's of Northgate wanted a fourteen-year-old boy to learn clog making, and Brougham National restaurant at Marsden required a porter. Wages offered were £3 5s. a week, plus two meals a day. A "Cinema Boy" was wanted to learn operating at the Rialto, Sheepridge.

Dustmen were doing the rounds as usual in the days leading up to Christmas, knocking on doors hoping for tips. Many householders thought that any money to spare should go to the Red Cross and other war organizations, so they kept doors firmly locked when the dustmen were about, and stayed out of sight.

At Cambridge Road Baths, on Saturday the 12th, Ken Johnson was asked to play the Warsaw Concerto during the interval. Admission to the dance was 3s., and 1s. 6d. for members of HM Forces.

"Eat more potatoes" urged the Ministry of Food, in a burst of Yuletide spirit. If there wasn't much food for the body around, at least there was food in plenty for the soul and spirit with the abundance of wonderful music and musicians then in the town. On Friday 18 December Sir Adrian Boult conducted the Hallé Orchestra in the Town Hall, in a concert that commenced at 6.30p.m.

The public sorely needed such sustenance, as more news of prisoners of war in Italy and the Middle East filtered through.

The good news was that felt was still not on coupons. An old dress could be freshened up for Christmas by making felt necklaces and belts in bright, varied colours. Many girls made artificial flowers out of felt to wear on lapels of coats.

The Red Cross had novelty gifts for sale — ash trays, book ends, vases and so on made out of stone from the blitzed Houses of Parliament, and 25 per cent of the money taken on each article was sent to the Red Cross and St John Fund.

Gramophone records of classical music, and tokens were in big demand, classical being a lot more popular than jazz.

On 10 December Mother met me from school and we went to George Hall's shop to buy my white Speech Day dress. That was the shop, with Kaye's, to buy school uniforms.

In the evening I began to knit khaki gloves, with not much chance of finishing them in time to present Pierre with them if he visited at Christmas. Mother continued with her mending, which seemed endless. She never knitted again after seeing a pattern for a vest in a magazine, using two-ply wool, which took an eternity to knit. Mother began the task, then put it on a chair when a customer came into the shop. Someone sat on the knitting, and all the stitches came off. No one would have had the patience to start that all over again.

Next day there was a choir practice at Greenhead, and great excitement at tea-time: a letter awaited from Pierre. I replied at once, frantically searching for words other than "la plume de ma tante" to convey to him that we would like him to visit us again at Christmas. The khaki gloves were boring. I had some white wool, so started a bolero for myself. Something could always be bought for Pierre; anyway, he wasn't really the type to wear woollen gloves.

The following evening, Jean came down to our house to see if I could translate into French the letter she had written for Pierre.

Next morning we had a Speech Day rehearsal in the Town Hall. On Wednesday 16 December all left school at 11.30a.m., so we would have plenty of time to scrub our necks and get ready for the big event. In the afternoon I sat towards the top of the tiered Town Hall platform, with Joan Farrer at one side of me and Joan Dunworth on the other.

Eagerly we scanned the area and balcony to see if our parents had arrived. Our gas masks lay at our feet. It was a heady experience with "Spiky" conducting, impressive in her Speech Day black velvet dress and white ermine cape. How much time and worry it saves

when you only wear two or three items of clothing —
outerwear, one lot of daytime clothes, and a special
outfit for events. No one bothered that Miss Spikes
never wore any different outfit on Speech Day. Her
music outclassed the most expensive evening dress
anyone could possibly have, as it did again on the
Speech Day of 1942.

On the Sunday we made some ginger wine, then I
went to the Rialto with Betty Moorhouse to see *Swiss
Family Robinson*.

Tension mounted as Christmas approached. There
was never enough time for all we wanted to do. Mother
met me at Rushworth's Corner after school on Monday
the 21st. We had tea in the Kingsway café down King
Street, eating my favourite: baked beans on toast with
little bits of cress on them. In summer we could gaze
down from the table window seats and watch shoppers,
without them realizing they were under surveillance.
Also we could covet the Heatonex coat and bonnet sets
for girls in the windows of Kaye's, hoping they
wouldn't close before we'd finished our tea. It was
infuriating if mother wasted more time having a
cigarette before putting a threepenny bit or sixpence
beneath the plate, then paying the bill at the desk at the
top of the stairs.

I thought that leaving money under a plate was a daft
habit. Who was there to see that the next customer
didn't pocket it? We went down the stairs arguing (well,
I argued) about the time spent in silly smoking, and
then throwing away the tip. Sixpence that could have
gone towards Christmas presents ... But mother

thought that if you were "in" with the waitress you'd receive quicker and better service.

All annoyance evaporated as we went shopping before going to the Palace to see the pantomime *Dick Whittington* at 5.45p.m. The only drawback to the outing was that homework must still be done on the return home.

A Christmas card arrived from Pierre the next day, all in French that none of us could make out, not even Philip. It was scrawled handwriting, almost illegible. So we still didn't know whether to expect him or not. And there was no means of getting in touch with him, somewhere in Surrey.

It was time to put trimmings up in shop, front room, and kitchen. Mother stood on the big wooden table to fix the coloured paper chains we had glued together to the central light fitting. I held the limp weight of the trimmings until she stood on a chair to loop them to the four corners of the room. Dad was out of puff after blowing up umpteen balloons, especially the long sausage-shaped ones. I held my forefinger on the string while he tied the knots. There were pretty Chinese lanterns from years back, and a big Snowman joy bomb: the best kind of bombs to have. Fairy lights were strung across the front room fireplace upstairs, and we all heaved a sigh of relief when they still worked.

Betty, who loved to come across to the shop and help, washed out all the "fittings" in the kitchen with mother. Betty worked at Sheepridge laundry when she left Deighton Council School. Her family was rationed with us.

Miss Tebbs and Miss Watson-Jones, mistresses at the High School, left the following day. So did Mr Atkinson, the caretaker, a familiar figure at Greenhead amid the 500 pupils and mistresses — the only man in sight, unless one came to give a talk.

We heard by letter that Pierre was able to make a fleeting visit after all. Once again we went by taxi to the station, this time mother, Mildred (our shop assistant, who was nicknamed Anna Mae Wong by customers because she resembled the oriental film star) and me.

Dad was too busy in the bakehouse, but we knew who we were looking for this time, so went with more confidence to wait on the platform. The imposing figure, cloak billowing behind him as before, leapt off the train and there were kisses all round, then into the taxi and Mildred beneath the cloak as well.

After a meal at home we took our prize exhibit to the Parochial Hall to a dance. As a safety measure (from the amorous Pierre), Mildred stayed the night with us, sleeping with me in the Put-U-Up.

Early next morning Jean bounded into the shop, having heard that Pierre was back again. She came through into the kitchen, to be warmly embraced by the Sergeant in the Camel Corps. Then we took Pierre to town to look round the shops.

In the afternoon we put the fairly lights on in the front room, drawing the blackout curtains early. It was a truly magical Christmas Eve. Pierre, Jean and I played games, gave each other French and English lessons, and danced to records on the radiogram. Pierre had to spend Christmas Day with his officer friends at

New North Road, but at least we had had the enormous pleasure of his company for a whole night and day.

Jean and I went with Pierre to New North Road, clinging on to every last moment with him. He promised to try and see us again before returning to Surrey, but didn't know on which day.

Gilbert Hardcastle, a local young man and a sailor, was home on leave. He called to see us that evening. Then Mildred, Mother, Irene Taylor, Jean Tiffany, Edith and Joyce McLoughlin, and Margaret Greaves, also a pupil at Greenhead, all went to the Christmas Eve dance at Fox's, Trinity Street, in town. Jean slept at our house. She didn't like her mother to know what time she came home after a dance.

Our house was full on Christmas Day. Six soldiers from the YMCA turned up — alright, but oh so ordinary after the incandescence of Pierre Rabaste.

There'd be no show without Punch, so Jean was among the party. So were Edith McLoughlin and Margaret Greaves, Gilbert, Leslie Moorhouse and Mildred, all preferring the rough and tumble, easy-going atmosphere of our place to their own more orthodox ways of life. Nobody wanted to go home. Fairy lights have a strange effect, especially when there's a blackout outside, and when it's Christmas time. They give an air of unearthly *je ne sais quoi*.

Before the guests arrived, I looked into the oval mirror over the fire, where the lights were strung across. I was wearing my new rich purple, plum coloured velvet dress that Miss Atkinson, the dressmaker, had made for me. The dress was Princess style, in at the waist, with long, tight fitting sleeves, and velvet covered buttons all the way down the front. Touching the soft velvet, anticipating the evening about to begin, was the very essence of being young. For a few moments I looked at my reflection in the mirror, trying, by sheer force of will, to make myself remain fifteen, waiting for the Christmas party to begin, in 1942. Time may stand still, or seem to do, at poignant moments. Then it's off again with a whoosh.

The door burst open and the room was filled with soldiers in khaki battledress. Badinage, laughter, mingled scents of Evening in Paris, Manikin cigars, and all the other heartwarming aromas of the season — which, despite being well into the war, somehow or other our shop had managed to provide.

Mr Schofield, the butcher down the road, could have played his part, as he and Dad did many a deal: pork for us in exchange for a bit of extra tea, butter and sugar for them. Herbert Truelove, who lived at the Toll House, Bradley Bar, often called in with "a bit of something", in the shape of a rabbit or hare. He was a countryman through and through, working for a farmer who, if he asked Herbert to get him a rabbit or hare, usually told him to keep a couple for himself.

I preferred apple sauce and mustard sauce, sage and onion stuffing and the vegetables to the poor dead animals the others tucked into, knowing that once what was on the plates might have felt, as we did, a surge of *joie de vivre* on a bright and frosty morning.

That Christmas I smattered every other sentence with a bit of French. It gave life added piquancy. Gilbert, the sailor, and some of the party gave a bit of trade to the Woolpack as the evening continued its merry way. Mildred came back looking more like Anna Mae Wong than before! Mother played the piano, going through every carol in the book, which had a jolly coloured picture of Santa in bright red outfit (oh, that scarlet lined cloak of Pierre's!) bearing a huge sack, the huge moon bright behind him, and a boisterous quartet of reindeer leaping over the snow. Rooftops in the picture were thick with snow, and Victorian men in top hats and capes played fiddles and sang, holding lanterns to light their way.

"Grand Selection Words, Music, & Tonic Sol-fa" it said at the end of the list of carols. What beautiful words — "Saw you Never in the Twilight", "Nigh Two Thousand Years Ago", "How Beautiful Upon the Mountains", "As With Gladness Men of Old" . . .

They said an armistice was held temporarily for Christmas Day, between both sides at war. This made us feel less guilty about enjoying ourselves while others were fighting.

We had another music book, *Allies' National Anthems*, published around the time of the First World War, by Bovril. On the back were the words "A Requisition from the Front: 'Send me Bovril, urgently wanted'", and "When marching take with you — Bovril Lozenges and Bovril Chocolate." So we all grouped round the piano to roar out the "Marseillaise". Then we had "Rule Britannia", "It's a Long, Long Way to

Tipperary", "Pack up Your Troubles" — but nobody
wanted "Auld Lang Syne". As usual, we wanted
Christmas to go on for ever and ever.

Everybody being in the mood by then, all wanted to
contribute a solo. Mother rummaged in the piano stool
and found "When the Sergeant Major's On Parade".
One of the soldiers volunteered to sing:

> When the sun is shining bright,
> Dispelling all the dews of night,
> With Sam Browne belt and buttons bright
> Behold the Sergeant Major!
> Batman makes my army bed
> And soon my boots a lustre shed
> He turns me out from foot to head,
> A dapper Sergeant Major.
> Then woe to them that meet my eye
> [an ominous rumble on the piano there]
> They never do, they turn and fly.
> [All of us joined in the chorus]
> When I'm here on parade in the Square
> How the folks passing by turn and stare
> For they say "This beats the band",
> The way he handles the men is grand!
> When I shout birds fly out, daisies fade,
> I've a way that must be obeyed
> NCOs say I bite,
> While recruits die of fright
> When the Sergeant Major's on parade.

By this time the tempo had got into us all, and everyone began marching round the room, Prince joining in — barking with delight.

Pick 'em up! Pick 'em up!
What the? Where the? Who?
Pick 'em up! Pick 'em up!
Coal fatigue for you!
Is that the way we won Waterloo?
Come along, come along, Jump to it, my lad!
If you don't, you'll hear me call a spade a spade.
Party, 'shun! The Sergeant Major's on parade!

After the other verses and refrain had been sung, the well handled sheet of music, held together by glued strips from Oxydol packets of soap powder which Mother had thought served the purpose, even though it looked a bit odd reading "Oxydol Makes Richer Suds & Soaks Clothes Whiter" down the centre of the pages.

Eventually, in the early hours of a very happy morning, the soldiers set off to walk back to the YMCA in town. Edith, Margaret and I squashed into the Put-U-Up meant for two, each lying stiffly and still so as not to disturb the other two. Mildred and Jean went to sleep on blankets and pillows scattered about the floor. How true that you can sleep on a tightrope if you are happy, while you will stay awake all night through in the most luxurious bed if you are not.

We didn't see Pierre on Boxing Day. He must, we thought, have returned to his billet. Jean, Betty and I went to Meltham cemetery in the afternoon of the

27th, as one of the other two wanted to put a wreath on a grave. What a disappointment, on returning home, to be told that while we were placing a wreath on some deceased relative's grave, the very much alive Pierre had been and gone. We would never see him again in 1942, maybe never again in all our lives, as war notoriously brings new friends into one's life and takes old ones away. *Au Revoir*, Pierre Rabaste of the Camel Corps.

But, as ever, a trip to the pictures lessened even the bitterest disappointment. We went to the Regent at Fartown Bar, all wishing we were walking beneath that scarlet lined cloak. Next day Gilbert called, and stayed for tea. In the evening Mildred and I went to see the film *Small Town Deb*, starring Jane Withers.

It snowed slightly on New Year's Eve, and we wondered what 1943 would bring, besides snow. Would it be peace? Secretly, did I really want the war to end, if it meant all the soldiers we were getting to know, and Pierre, would go their separate ways, and we would never hear of them again? Even peace had its drawbacks, in a selfish kind of way.

Anyway, there were always letters to be written to keep in touch. Airgraphs cost 3d. Writing as tiny as possible, a great deal of news and what was happening back home could be fitted on one. We had already received some. One, from Driver Hall in transit, was written on 2 November 1942:

Just a few lines to say I am still cracking in steady, hoping you are all doing the same at Central

Stores. I am still in the same place, wondering where I'll be for Xmas. Just fancy, I was home last year, but I'll be having as good a time as possible, and hope you will enjoy yourselves. I'll be missing that little tot of port. Tell Bunter and Pip I hope jolly old Santa does OK for them as usual. Christmas and New Year Greetings, to all, Love, John.

Another arrived from our former shop assistant, written on 21 December 1942:

Dear Hilda and Joe, Here I am again, this time writing to you from yet another part of the world, hoping you are all well at the Stores and longing to hear from you. I have received some mail, from home, but none so far from you. Mother tells me that you and Hazel have written and so maybe I'll be getting those letters before long. This is a desolate place and what a joint to spend Xmas in. How I'll miss my usual tot of port, and what a contrast it will be to last year. I hope you have received my Xmas Greetings I sent you from Durban, as it is a bit late now. However, here's all the best for a Happy and Prosperous New Year, which I hope will see us back home again. Give my regards to all, not forgetting Mrs Haigh, Love, John.

As all airgraphs, it had been "Passed by Censor". "Bunter" was the nickname John used to give me. Both he and Dad loved reading the *Magnet*, which came to the shop every Monday. They enjoyed the exploits of Billy Bunter, and perhaps felt the need of their own resident Bunter. Not that I was fat or ate a great deal, far from it. But it was a term of affection I suppose, as was "Pip" for Philip. We treasured those little airgraphs in a tin box, as one never knew if they would be the last communication in this life.

A New Year party for Channel Island refugees was held at the Town Hall on the 6th. Money had been donated by the *Toronto Evening Chronicle*, dispatching money to London and all over the country.

There was a certain pleasure and sense of achievement in "make do and mend" that even surpassed the transitory joy of buying new clothes, because precious clothing coupons weren't being spent, and it gave gloomy winter months a purpose. In January 1943 I sewed coloured braid on to an old black velvet bolero, and made velvet slippers out of left-over material, while listening to the wireless and talking with Mother, who, when not out dancing, spent much of her time mending the pile of laddered stockings, or darning socks: a pile that never seemed to dwindle, as more were constantly being added to it.

I tried to make one of the new fashionable dirndl skirts from an old dress too. We hadn't a sewing machine, but there were such easy patterns in magazines that advised how to save coupons.

Winter evenings passed quickly when so many letters and airgraphs had to be written, to Pierre, John, Bill

Bailey, and Sergeant Jimmy Walkden, who used to be our baker.

Roger Smith of the RAF came on leave again. With Philip, we spent happy hours playing table tennis on our big kitchen table, with the two wooden leaves added to make it big enough. The cats seemed to enjoy the ping-pong games almost as much as we did. Chairs were drawn up at either side of the table so that Hurricane, Cheeky, Ginger, Waddles and the others could sit there like furry referees, heads swivelling from side to side, the occasional paw thrust out to prod the ball back into play.

On 11 January, Jean came with me to see Leslie Howard in *Pimpernel Smith* at the Rialto, finishing the evening with the usual fish and chips in paper bags from Oddy's, piping hot, to eat on the walk home.

Greenhead High School celebrated its fortieth birthday on the 18th. Although piano lessons had been dropped, mainly because of too much homework, I still enjoyed playing the piano — especially "Selections From Snow White", with its jaunty tunes.

It used to cost half a crown for an hour's piano lesson with Miss Hodgson on Glenfield Avenue. As I left home to walk down Deighton Road in the blackout mother warned me over and over again to be careful, but I thought her warnings superfluous — I could take care of myself.

However, turning the corner of Glenfield Avenue one night, when the moon kept being obliterated by clouds, thinking about the piano lesson where I'd been learning "The Bluebells of Scotland" and clutching my music case as I passed the big stone house hidden by menacing tall trees and shrubs, brilliant car headlights suddenly almost blinded me.

Nobody else was about, and it was total blackout when the moon disappeared. The car pulled up alongside me, coming down the hill from Deighton Road and into Whitacre Street. I saw a hooked nose, piercing blue eyes, and what appeared to be a frizzy ginger wig on the driver's head. At first I thought he-or-she wanted to ask directions. Having been brought up to be polite, I was about to stop when an arm reached out to me.

With speed born of utter terror I took to my heels, heart pounding madly. What if the driver turned the car round and followed? I remembered as I ran for my life that there was a Married Ladies' concert practice in the Sunday school that evening, and Mother should be there. But what if the doors were locked? I hurtled round the corner and burst into the big hall. What a wonderful contrast to the dangerous blackout left behind! On stage was a brilliantly colourful scene. The ladies were dressed as gypsies, one playing the piano as the others grouped round a pretend camp fire, singing:

> Oh play to me gypsy, The moon's up above,
> O play me your serenade,
> The Song I Love
> I'll be your Vagabond, just for tonight . . .

Hand in hand with mother, we walked back home. I never wanted to go to a piano lesson ever again, down that dark road. Dad told us that a policeman had called at our shop earlier, saying that a car had been cruising around, trying to pick up little girls. He thought it would be for the notorious "white slave traffic". That frightened me far more than ever the fear of air raids did! The blackout changed the course of so many lives. But for that I would have continued with piano lessons perhaps, fitting it in with homework enough to be able to entertain as well as mother could.

The sirens went on 22 January. The following day we had a greater shock. Schoolgirl Betty Vaudin had died. I think she was a Channel Island refugee, who had lived round the back of Deighton Council School. Her mother invited friends to take a last look and say farewell to Betty. Jean and I gazed at the young face in her coffin, in the front room of her home, on 26 January 1943. It occurred to me that poor little Betty would never know the outcome of the war.

Every week mother had a private dancing lesson, either with Jack Fox or Mr Brown. Then she had tea either in Whiteley's, Sylvio's, Field's Café or Collinsons. The latter had fat, squashy, heavenly hot muffins, oozing with butter, even during the war — but you were only allowed to have one. Then Mother would either meet Dad and go to the Theatre or Palace, or meet me from school and we'd have tea in a café.

If Mother was enjoying herself at a dance in the evening, she came home in a taxi, sharing with others to make the individual fare cheaper. For some, it was a lovely war!

In February 1943 *Hollywood Cavalcade* was showing at the Regent cinema, and *The Scarlet Pimpernel* at the Rialto, which I saw with evacuee Pat Patrick. Some Saturday mornings I took "points" in to the Food Office to save Dad a journey into town. My cousin Winnie and soldier Bill came for their rations on Saturday afternoons. On the 16th, soldier Bernard and girlfriend Marjorie turned up, staying a long time so that they'd be asked to stay for tea. Another cousin, Billy Haigh, also turned up, saying he was going abroad now that he was in the navy. He promised to write. No wonder there was a paper shortage with all the letters that were written!

There was a Free French meeting in the Town Hall on the evening of the 18th. Naturally Jean and I went. The address was by Lieutenant Colonel J. M. de Lagatinerie.

An airgraph from Driver F. Taylor, 385 Coy RASC, MEF, was written on 22 February 1943:

Dear Joe and Family, Here I am once more sending you an airgraph, to let you know that I am still alive and kicking out here amongst the camels and sands, and not forgetting you, even if I am in a different part of the world whilst we are trying to finish off what someone else started over three years ago.

Well Joe, how are things at your end as regards the shop, I suppose you can hardly get hold of anything to sell. Since I have been out here I have come across one or two lads who work at the

Corporation, but nobody from down our way. Is John Hall still in the old country, or has he been unlucky and got sent overseas, as for myself I wish I was back there. How is Hilda keeping these days, I hope she is keeping well, and of course Philip and Hazel. Anyway, if all goes well I hope to see you all again very soon.

So Cheerio, and I would like to hear from you.

Yours Sincerely, Frank.

Frank, before being called up, worked on the buses, and loved nothing better than coming into our shop when off duty for a "packet of fags and a 'cal" (slang for bit of conversation), smoking the first Woodbine or Capstan as he leaned across the counter in his navy blue bus conductor uniform, cracking a few "gags" and "telling the tale".

Laughter was never far away. Frank was thin as a lath; his straight black hair was Brylcreemed and his head was thrown back every now and again to blow happy, lazy smoke rings into the air. It was quite an art form, that, blowing those rings in disciplined formation.

Alas, we had been so busy that we hadn't had time to write to Frank for some time. Then, one morning, the postman hadn't long gone past the shop, when Mrs Taylor, his mother, came weeping into the shop, wiping her eyes on her pinafore every now and then. Her mob cap covered the Dinky curling pins in her greying hair.

"What's up, lass?" Dad asked, pushing the Bentwood chair beneath her, as she seemed in a state of near collapse.

"It's our Frank," she blurted out, "our lad — he's missing." Another gulp; her handkerchief was already sodden and the pinafore took over.

Frank Taylor, the young lad who'd bobbed in and out of the shop every day until he went to be a soldier, while he, like most other youths of the village, had done odd jobs around the house, shop and bakehouse. Even on Sundays he could never resist coming round to the back door on the excuse that he'd "run out of fags". There was always a glass of Tizer, or Dandelion and Burdock for whoever called; and all the latest news and gossip, our shop being the hub of what went on in the village.

Mother immediately went into the kitchen to put the kettle on, her own eyes overflowing with tears. She couldn't even bear the thought of anything happening to Philip, her own son, when he was on ARP duty or fire-watching. And here was another Mrs Taylor, mother of Frank, to whom it had actually happened. So far away, too, and with no chance of comforting her dying son, or saying goodbye. How do people bear the unbearable? Maybe, it is hoped, with the support of friends and neighbours, who, after the tears, do all in their power to bring laughter to their eyes again. That is what Frank and all those others would have wanted: consolation for those left behind, to know we had contributed in some small way to their happiness while living.

As Mrs Taylor calmed down and sipped her tea, we could almost feel Frank there, leaning over the counter, saying "Na then Joe lad, tell her I'm OK now". Indeed, as his mother took a long, shuddering sigh before managing to eat a tempting looking jam tart and having another drink of tea, flanked with her friends either side of her, she saw, with obvious amazement, tears flowing down Mother's face.

"Well, we look a right couple o'bonny uns if any of them smart commercial travellers come in, don't we?" Mrs Taylor said, with a trembly little smile. And the two of them smiled warmly at each other. Everything would be alright in time, they knew, deep in their hearts — no matter what the terrible war may bring.

West Riding Police held a pigeon show at the Tramways Social Club, John William Street, to help the Red Cross. For an admission fee of 6d., the cream of Britain's racing pigeons, 350 entries, could be viewed.

Later that year, two pigeons bred and trained by Flight Sergeant Douglas Kendal of No. 153 Longwood Road, distinguished themselves in the Middle East. A Baltimore, returning from reconnaissance, flashed an SOS that its engines were petering out over the sea. Rescue planes searched for four and a half hours, but nothing could be seen of the airmen. It was feared they had gone down with their plane.

A few hours later, one of Kendal's pigeons flew into the loft of the Royal Corps of Signals, with a message stating that the crew of four were safe in a dinghy at a spot four miles away from that given in the SOS. A rescue launch found the crew, and brought them safely ashore. This was the first time in the Middle East that a pigeon had saved the crew of a crashed plane. And that pigeon was Huddersfield born and bred!

Another of Flight Sergeant Kendal's pigeons, six and a half months old, carried an important message 500 miles through dust storms and over waterless country — a performance never equalled. Flight Sergeant Kendal, in the Pigeon Service of the Royal Corps of Signals, had served since volunteering early in the war. A keen and successful pigeon fancier, he was a member of the Huddersfield and Longwood Homing Societies before the war, and President of the Longwood Homing Society at the time of his enlistment.

Every little helps, as the saying goes. By taking their old newspapers and magazines to the *Examiner* office, householders could earn a few coppers, a penny for every 3 lb.

A warning went out to cigarette smokers not to use coloured pool petrol for lighters, as it contained lead. And the ruling came in that all railway engines had to be painted black for the duration of the war.

Money was raised for David Brown's Comforts Fund by a collection during the midnight break in the canteen, from those on night shift. £2 17s. was raised. Music was by the Works dance band, Earl Farrar and his Peers.

The nursery in the grounds of the Princess Royal Maternity Home was open from 7a.m. until 6.30p.m. Each morning youngsters were examined by nurses for any illness, and then bathed. For the rest of the day they wore Corporation clothes, attractive ones, then changed for home before they were collected by their working mothers.

It was resolved by the Finance Committee of Huddersfield Corporation that all rate books up to and including 1919–20 should be destroyed, to help the waste paper salvage drive.

At the Motor Exchange, Leeds Road, a new Wartime 5-ton Bedford dropside lorry was for sale in February 1943, for £448 (in primer); chassis and cab for £405.

In February 1943 the National Fire Service concert at the Ritz was proud to have Wilfred Pickles as its guest. That month Miss Dawn, one of the English mistresses at Greenhead High School for Girls, left to become Senior mistress at Ilkley Grammar School. Huddersfield Art Gallery, to the annoyance of many, was only to be opened during the summer months due to the difficulty of blacking it out.

Mollie Moorhouse began working on munitions at Roberts' Castings. Employees had to wear gloves, as there was so much black sand and grease at the core makers. Hours were 7.30a.m. until 4.30p.m., with half an hour's break midday. Mollie earned £2 5s. a week. Many of the workers wore clogs and trousers; Mollie had some brown brogues with clog irons fitted to them. There was no holiday pay, and holidays were staggered in order to maintain continuous production.

Mollie never went away on holiday during the war, and went barelegged to work winter and summer alike. She bought a smart black leather gas mask case, one with enough room to push lipstick and things inside. Elizabeth, her mother, was becoming even more innovative with her sewing — bleaching flour bags, then making handkerchiefs out of them. Hettie McLoughlin of Lockwood, spent her working days at Rippon Bros acetylene-welding aluminium aeroplane fuel tanks, which arrived, damaged, with bullet holes in them. She wore welding glasses besides the usual protective clothing. Hettie took sandwiches for her dinner. Working hours were from 7.30a.m. to 5p.m. Before starting work she had to take her small daughter, Anne, to Greenhead Nursery, and then collected her at the end of the day. The nursery cost 1s. a day. Matron was Mrs Edith Bentley, State Registered Nurse and certified midwife. Miss Eileen R. Brooke taught the children singing and dancing, and arranged concerts for them to "star" in.

Joyce, Hettie's younger sister, began her working life as a junior in Longwood Co-op, in the Drapery department. Though work was not as arduous as on munitions, hours were equally long. Work began for Joyce at 8.15a.m., ending at 6p.m. from Monday to Thursday, at 7p.m. on Fridays, and 4p.m. on Saturdays. Three nights a week she had to attend Technical College for Retail Distribution, English and Arithmetic classes.

By the time war was declared in 1939 Joyce had become the manageress. The day after, a Monday, she was on her own at the Co-op, and had to dash round finding black sateen and getting it ready to pin up with drawing pins until a permanent blackout could be made.

There wasn't time to go home for tea on Tech. nights, or Tuesdays either, when she enjoyed going to the Co-op Hall dances with her friends, so she usually made do with a bar of chocolate or another sandwich before getting ready. Joyce followed the fashion of plucking her eyebrows, then pencilling a fine, surprised looking arch where they had been — to resemble Marlene Dietrich and Greta Garbo.

Joyce only earned 10s. 6d. at first, per week, so expenditure on make-up was minimal. Pond's Vanishing Cream, an occasional 6d. bottle of Evening in Paris, or Californian Poppy from Woolworth's, sometimes Jockey Club or Devon Violets for a change, was all she could afford. What a boon Woolworth's was, the "Nothing Over Sixpence" store.

Industrial workers received extra clothing coupons. Joyce wore an overall at work. Her mother made all her daughters' dresses.

Aylwin Secker and his pals from Primrose Hill also favoured the Co-op Hall on Tuesdays, dancing to the catchy tunes of Glenn Miller, Joe Loss and others. "In The Mood" and "American Patrol" gave dancers plenty of time to get to know a new and pretty partner: just as you were thinking of relinquishing the hold, off the music started again — and again, and again.

Aylwin first met the dark haired, attractive Joyce at one of the Tuesday evening dances. He had volunteered for the RAF, and was eventually sent to Padgate; then Joyce was directed to work in the Land Army — she didn't fancy that at all. One way of escaping such a fate was to marry, which she and Aylwin had already decided they would like to do.

6 March 1943 was the date set for the wedding. Ronnie Dyson, an air-gunner in the RAF, also from Primrose Hill, agreed to be a groomsman.

Mrs Secker and Mrs McLoughlin went with Joyce one Wednesday afternoon, half-day closing at the Co-op, to select a dress in Leeds. The veil was bought from Huddersfield Co-op, and a friend offered to lend a bridesmaid dress to Edith, Joyce's youngest sister. Edith was then a fifth former at Greenhead High School.

Mrs McLoughlin baked the wedding cake, while Joyce managed to get icing sugar from the bakery department at Longwood Co-op, and had help acquiring the other ingredients.

If anything "vital" had cropped up, such as an invasion, the bridegroom and his groomsman would have had to leave the bride waiting at the church. No-one ever knew for certain. Right up to the Friday night before the Saturday wedding, Joyce wasn't absolutely sure that they would get leave. But the Boys in Blue arrived home in Huddersfield that Friday evening.

A reception was held at Huddersfield Co-op Hall Restaurant: a splendid repast for war time — chicken salad, cream buns, sherry; not forgetting the impressive wedding cake.

Edith had made a fashionable "pill box" hat for her sister to wear for going away on her honeymoon — a wonderful creation, with little ermine tails sewed all round it.

Aylwin had worked at Weaver to Wearer, Gents' Outfitters, before exchanging one of their suits for a dashing RAF uniform. His mother, Doris, was a part-time post lady. To save her ordinary shoes wearing out too soon she wore wooden-soled ones for walking around in. They made a bit of a clomp, clomp, clomping sound as she walked up garden paths, but who cared, if wooden-soled shoes saved coupons?

Mr Secker was employed with Jarrett, Pyrah and Armitage, timber merchants. Norman Hall, best man, worked in the Westgate office of Bentley and Shaw.

Joyce and Aylwin moved from Huddersfield to begin their married life. Sadly their groomsman, Ronnie, was shot down and killed after he returned to duty.

Edith and a lot of her form friends were at Lockwood church that Saturday morning to watch the handsome RAF man marry her sister — wishing that they were old enough to be standing there, in a long white dress, with a brand new husband in uniform standing beside them, instead of mouldy old School Certificate examinations to swot for.

In a general knowledge paper at a local school one of the questions was "Who is the Patron Saint of England?" The teacher ought not to have been unduly surprised when one of the answers was "Winston Churchill".

Figures for those killed in the previous year as a result of the blackout were twenty killed and 260 injured, and double that killed in 1941.

Bus passengers were supposed to place the tickets in a box provided on the bus, to save paper. However, only 40 per cent issued were recovered.

Annie Mallinson was too young for the forces or munitions, so when she left school at fourteen she became a trainee shop assistant at Thomas Kaye's, King Street, working in the ladies' underwear and baby linen department under Miss Hellawell.

Every morning Annie, being the youngest, had to go into one of the two fitting rooms, where customers tried on corsets and other garments, and mix a glass of Sanatogen powder with cold water. When it was mixed — it was always consumed mid-morning — Annie had to say to her superior, "Miss Hellawell, your Sanatogen is ready."

As she was under sixteen, Annie had a milk allowance which was delivered to Kaye's. She went to the staff room, at the top of the building, to drink it. Often when she arrived, much of the milk had already been used, older assistants putting some in their coffee. But younger assistants didn't dare say anything to older ones — it was a bit like the infantry being cowed and subdued by a fearsome sergeant major.

None of the girls were called by their first name; it was always "Miss" even if you were only fourteen and fresh from school. Wednesday was half day closing, at 1p.m. Miss Mallinson and Miss Hall, from Haberdashery, had a snack, then went to the pictures — always referring to each other as "Miss" even when not at work. It was the done thing when you were employed by Kaye's.

All the female staff at Kaye's wore black or navy dresses with white collars and cuffs. They had to be clean on each morning, so were lightly tacked on to the dress the night before. Annie's didn't retain their pristine whiteness on Monday mornings, when she had to dust all the cardboard boxes in the stock room until dinnertime.

An hour was allowed for dinner, and Annie spent her time eating her sandwiches and reading in the staff room.

In one upstairs room sat an employee, sewing blackout curtain orders throughout the war.

Miss Holgate was the lady employed to work the big old-fashioned lift, with a handle, calling out the name of each department when it stopped at different floors. When Miss Holgate went for her dinner, Miss Mallinson stepped in for her, calling out, somewhat self-consciously at first, "Ladies Underwear", "Bedding", and so on, standing to one side as Kaye's esteemed customers stepped in or out.

One day, when Annie was in charge of the lift, it stuck between floors — something that terrified her far more than ever hearing the air raid signal did!

After six months of training, Miss Hellawell went up to Annie, and, as though handing Annie the Crown Jewels, half smiled in a coy manner and announced: "Miss Mallinson, you may now go and serve on the counter. Baby bootees."

After a few days selling those, then Morning Sets, Annie progressed to what she thought the best department of all — the children's, where bonnets, trimmed with ribbons and artificial flowers, were bought by fond mamas for Easter and Whitsuntide. There were panama hats for older girls, and "halo" hats.

On one of the Most Important Days of the Year, old Mr Kaye's birthday, all the juniors, from both that shop and Alfred Kaye's, had to line up outside his office. The door had been firmly closed after his morning arrival. At 9a.m. precisely, the Juniors sang in perfect unison, "Happy Birthday to Mr Kaye". When they had finished, the door was graciously opened, and the old gentleman said "Thank you".

Once a year he treated the staff from both shops to a show at the Theatre Royal. One year it was *Yeoman of the Guard*.

Being a well brought-up young lady, and with the reputation of Thomas Kaye's to uphold even in private life, Golcar "Lib" was absolutely taboo for dancing to such as Miss Mallinson. Soldiers swarmed there on Saturday nights from Slaithwaite Barracks, and even coloured GIs from Penistone turned up there. But Mr Mallinson would have tied his daughter to a chair rather than allow her to frequent such a Den of Iniquity.

Bobby Twentyman, the local police officer, carried a huge torch, and used to sweep the rays of it all over Golcar "rec", where couples were laid out on a Saturday night canoodling in the grass outside the Liberal Club.

It was a very different set up at Golcar Conservative Club's Friday evening dances. Annie was allowed to go there, and her dad was always outside the door to take her home prompt at 10p.m. The "Sunrise Swingtet" sometimes played with Golcar Youth Band.

Mrs Mallinson worked at Thornton and Ross, pharmaceutical manufacturers. One evening Annie and her mother, having returned home from work and had their tea, were "throng washing" as they termed it, when the wireless stopped — a sure sign that enemy aeroplanes were over the coast. It would be about 7.30p.m., and they soon heard and felt the vibrations of the naval gun, "Big Bertha", at Aldmondbury. Over at Bolster Moor the searchlights were picking planes out, then guns were shooting at them over the Huddersfield area.

Annie and her mother dashed into their cellar, then, when it quietened down for a few moments, up they came to put another garment through the mangle. This went on for some time, but they hadn't time to rest on the camp bed in the cellar. They were far too busy washing that night.

Annie was a member of Golcar Youth Club. There was a wonderful outing on Easter Monday 1943, spent in Mollicar Woods with all her friends from the club. They went to Huddersfield by bus first, then walked to the woods. There was plenty of amusement — paddling in the streams, climbing trees, playing cricket, with sandwiches for both dinner and tea, and books to read — but no "silly work".

There was plenty of silly stuff at the local cinemas. The merry month of May 1943 included Arthur Askey, Richard "Stinker" Murdoch, Jack Hylton and his Boys in *Band Waggon* at the Waterloo. At the Plaza, Thornton Lodge, Charlie Chaplin appeared in *The Gold Rush*. For those preferring sentiment to slapstick, Greer Garson starred in *Random Harvest* at the Ritz. Those listening to the wireless may have heard a man singing to his tobacco: "Love, Could I Only Tell Thee, How Dear Thou Art To Me."

The reduction in the blackout period until 14 August was a morale booster, and Wings for Victory Week, 7–15 May, was hoped to raise money through Savings Bonds, National War Bonds, Defence Bonds, National Savings Certificates, and also National Savings Stamps at 6d., 2s. 6d., and 5s.

An Outlane man was fined £40 at the magistrates' court for making toys in his garage and selling them at a profit of at least 50 per cent. Operations on old established toy manufacturers had been drastically restricted. Specimens of his toys included a tank, and an aeroplane. They were handed to Stipendiary Magistrate Waldo R. Briggs, who remarked that they appeared to be made of solid metal.

When Private Bertram Walker returned home to No. 56 Commercial Street after being a prisoner of war in Italy for two years, he told how parcels he had received from the Red Cross had been pilfered. Walker had had an altercation with an Italian guard, and had struck him, for which he was sentenced to five years in prison — but Mussolini pardoned him. The soldier, who had been wounded, was attending the infirmary to undergo his fourteenth operation after being repatriated at the end of April.

The sufferings of those in the Forces made those who misbehaved while in comparative comfort at home all the more distasteful. A thief stole a knife and two spoons from the canteen at Bank Bottom Mills, Marsden, and was fined 40s. How petty thieving was in comparison with the gallantry shown by others. Corporal Edward Hennigan of the Reconnaissance Corps, whose home was at Kirkburton, had been awarded the Military Medal for gallant and distinguished service in North Africa.

Kirkburton had a Wings For Victory Week at the same time as Huddersfield, beginning Sunday 9 May, with a Drumhead Service.

Little drops of water, little grains of sand,
Make the Mighty Ocean and the Pleasant Land

were the sentiments put forward to encourage every contribution, however seemingly insignificant. Even children's pennies would help. Banners proclaimed: "If Huddersfield will set about the task of raising that million pounds with its characteristic energy and determination, there can be little doubt that the target will be reached."

Meltham Wings for Victory Week had a target of £50,000, their slogan being "Now is the Time for the 'Many' to Help the 'Few'".

Some products were being kept before the public eye with current wireless catchphrases, one being — "In the Interests of the Nation — TIZER THE APPETIZER has Gone for the Duration". "Funf" and Mrs Mopp came out with phrases that caught the listening public's fancy in ITMA, with Tommy Handley.

The New Co-op Hall arranged a Summer series of Wednesday night dances. On the opening night, 12 May, there was a chance to hear the "Immaculate music of Eric Pearson and His Ballroom Orchestra, playing in correct tempo the tunes you prefer. And Jack Parker, BBC vocalist, singing all the latest songs of stage, screen and radio. 7.30–11p.m. Admission 2s., Forces 1s."

Checking one's diary to see if it would be moonlight to walk home by hadn't the importance for summertime dances. A film at the Tudor was about that Godsend of the blackout, entitled *Dangerous Moonlight*, and starring Anton Walbrook and Sally Gray. Another good idea to help the forces in the area was a "Share Your Newspaper" scheme. When people had finished reading the paper they could drop it into one of four boxes — two at the station, one at the George Hotel, another outside the YMCA. The YMCA then collected and distributed the newspapers to the forces.

No matter what happened in the world, everything seemed to be alright once inside the cocoon of a cinema, surrounded with lilting melodies and happiness on screen. Besides, you might find yourself sitting next to an attractive soldier . . .

Judy Garland was in a film packed with tuneful melodies, *For Me and My Girl* at the Picture House. The Lyceum, Moldgreen, showed Barbara Stanwyck and George Brent in *The Gay Sisters*, and also "War News From All Fronts". Should you prefer something more bloodcurdling, Boris Karloff played the monster in *The Bride of Frankenstein* at the Grand. For the more intellectually inclined, there was Huddersfield Chess Club. Mr Alfred M. Lee had been recently elected its president.

Early that May was a Wings for Victory auction sale at the Town Hall during the dance interval. A basket of strawberries was bid for, and sold for £8 15s., each strawberry therefore costing 16s. 6d.! They had been bought three times, then put up for auction again at once. Photographs of film stars sold well. Anna Neagle and one of Leslie Howard went for £4 10s. each; topped by Anthony Eden at £5. Sir William Beveridge's photo sold for £3, Mrs Churchill's for £4. These were also put into the auction again, reselling for another two guineas. A huge cucumber — real, not photographed — brought in a guinea, and a model of a Spitfire £3 15s. The whist drive, dance, and auction was organized by ladies of Huddersfield Savings Sub-Committee. Dancing was to the music of the Detonators (Royal Engineers) Dance Orchestra by permission of Lieutenant Colonel D. B. Watson. The orchestra's leader, Corporal Harry Kahn, was formerly music arranger for Joe Loss. Mr E. C. R. Chinn was Master of Ceremonies. Refreshments were served in the mayor's reception room.

Wings For Victory Week dancing in the Co-op Hall on Friday 14 May, had Mr A. Wilkinson's No. 1 Spitfire Dance Band, with vocalists Mollie Gibson and Chris Doughty.

More news came in of Huddersfield's boys in battle. Private J. Swan, of the Boy and Barrel Inn, Beast Market, was a POW in Japanese hands. So was Dr T. A. Divine, formerly of Fartown, while Private William Sykes, of No. 16 Maypole Road, Sheepridge, was wounded in North Africa.

A woman conscientious objector, of Kirkheaton, refused to pay £3 that had been imposed for failing to comply with conditions of her registration — that she undertake full-time chiropody work in a hospital, or work in the laundry or on the domestic staff of a hospital or institution. She declined to undertake any work to which she was directed, saying she must have "perfect freedom and liberty at all times to do the will and work of God". She was a "Four Square Gospeller".

When committed to prison for a month she was asked if she had anything to say.

"God says no," said the defendant.

"How do you know God says no?" asked the magistrate. "It is very convenient to blame God for what we don't want to do, isn't it?" How, one wonders, would she have retained that freedom under Hitler?

Southgate Nursery, where young children stayed while mothers worked on munitions or other war work, was hardly in the best situation, with ugly buildings and hardly anywhere to play outside. Some suggested it should be converted into a small park, where a really adequate nursery school could be built. At St Patrick's Parochial Hall the Women's Junior Air Corps appeared in "W.J.A.C. Off Parade", which included a one act play, *The Apple Tree*, which contained fine characterization by Sergeant Josephine Rickett. The production gained second place in a Youth Club competition.

On 11 May the Wings for Victory Target was reached — £1,000,000: "The Borough Gets Its Wings".

While most did all they could to help, others did the opposite — stealing instead of giving. During the last year 282 forks, 102 spoons, 71 salt pourers, and 20 vinegar bottles were stolen from Lindon Smith's Dining Rooms on Shambles Lane.

A Cockney evacuee, watching his foster parent planting seed potatoes, was completely mystified by the seemingly senseless carry-on.

"Cor, we can't get potatoes in London, and 'ere you bury 'em," he said.

Utility furniture became obtainable at Harrops of No. 30 King Street. "Bring us your permits and call for free advice on how to obtain same."

Local people were outraged by a bus strike that May, asking: "Could the lads of the Tunisian Campaign strike on account of their pay, which is very little more than drivers are seeking as a rise." Miners and munition workers were faced with having to walk to work or turn back home. Enraged mothers of lads abroad fighting thought that bus crews should receive their call-up papers if they failed to return to work within twenty-four hours. Wives and mothers of drivers put forward the argument that those working on buses had an onerous job, walking home in the blackout after driving others home and taking the buses back to their depots.

Girls of Greenhead High School gave a gymnastic display in the Town Hall, all kneeling down before the interval to form the words "Wings For Victory". The demonstration had been arranged by gym and games mistress Miss C. M. Thackray, who was presented with a bouquet. Miss Lloyd, art mistress, had made the costumes worn in the folk dancing.

On 18 May Albert Nutter and His Crazy Gang held a Grand Carnival and Crazy Night at the Co-op Hall, admission costing 1s. 7½d., and 1s. 0½d. to members of HM Forces. There was a jitterbug competition, but no jitterbug dancing was allowed during quick-step numbers.

Before Frank Lindley was called up he taught Interior Design at Huddersfield Technical College, and was a signwriter at Huddersfield Co-op. His wife Doris worked a Burroughs Adding Machine at Hillhouse Co-op, and they lived at Springdale Street, Thornton Lodge. Frank had hopes of being a pilot, but when he signed on down by the Palace Theatre he was told that he was too old to train as a pilot. He could, however, be a rear gunner.

Frank's call-up had been deferred three times, and he was thirty-two when at last it came. He soon became responsible for the automatic pilot nicknamed "George". Something went wrong with "George" once, so Frank had to go up in the aeroplane, standing between the pilot and navigator, who were both sitting down. Suddenly they went downwards, and Frank went up — it was worse than being on Blackpool's Big Dipper, and certainly gave him a feeling of doing the jitterbug!

Meanwhile, home in Huddersfield, Doris escaped being roped in to work at David Brown's when she discovered she was pregnant. They wouldn't have pregnant women working there. But she kept busy and occupied, making all sorts of things on her new electric sewing machine that Frank had bought for her before he left. She sewed every evening, buying material from George Hall's King Street or Berry's in the Top Market, swapping and "doing deals" with a friend who also had a sewing machine. When clothes rationing came in and she had a baby son, Doris cut up Frank's old plus fours to make a little outfit for David. A pair of slacks for herself was fashioned from her husband's wide white tennis flannels. Her sewing friend remarked, "your husband will have nowt to wear when he comes back!"

Before she had the baby, Doris, Nora Armitage and another friend, Kathleen, used to link arms in the blackout every Saturday night and go to the Premier cinema, Paddock Head. Other evenings were spent making all sorts of things for Christmas and birthday presents — lots of soft toys, a Scottie dog, elephants, rabbits dressed in big baggy trousers and dolls, with bits of wool glued on for hair. Celluloid faces could be bought from a dolls' hospital in town.

Frank never went short of home-knitted socks, pullovers, and balaclavas, all in air force blue. His mother used to knit socks with double heels on, so Doris did too. It was an enjoyable way of spending evenings by herself, as there were such interesting programmes on the wireless to listen to while she sewed or knitted.

Doris managed alright for food, especially as she knew the manager of the Co-op. Before Frank went into the RAF the manager used to say to him, "tell your Doris we've some tins of salmon in", or whatever other little luxury had arrived.

The Anderson shelter was at the bottom of the garden, and the night Sheffield was bombed neighbours were banging at Dora's door, she being the only one whose husband had joined up from the immediate few houses.

"Come on, Doris," they yelled, "get up, and we'll join you in your air raid shelter."

The young wife could see flames in the sky, and a red glow. She ran downstairs, then dashed back into the bedroom to get the case which had Frank's best suit in, and other special bits and pieces. The case wasn't locked and it burst open, spilling the contents all down the staircase.

In winter, Doris kept the coal fire in all through the night, there being no other form of heating in the house.

Sometimes Doris shut the house up in Thornton Lodge and went to join her husband for a few weeks. One place, out in the wilds, had an outside lavatory, and worse, a 60 ft deep well in the garden — especially frightening as there was a blackout in force and she had a young toddler. But out in the country they were never short of food, with cold pork for breakfast occasionally.

A roll of bacon hung from the ceiling, and they even had partridge.

In another digs where Frank was stationed, the bed they shared when he wasn't on duty had awful creaky springs. Every time they turned over, the baby wakened. The only night he slept through was when a line of tanks was going past. There was a Yorkshire range with side oven, and a paraffin stove which took ages to get going.

In Huddersfield, Barker's shop sent young Mrs Lindley a card whenever Dinky cars came in. Little boys were mad about them, and, like everything else, they were hard to find in wartime.

No matter what hardships people went through, there were funny happenings to laugh about. When Frank was in the Home Guard before joining the RAF, he heard a noise one night when he was on duty in the Brewery Yard, Lockwood.

"Who goes there?" Frank asked. A horse, whinnying, was the reply.

When eventually Frank was issued with a demob suit Doris thought it looked terrible. "The material was so rough it must have rubbed his backside sore," she laughed. Still, as she had transformed every other garment he owned while he was away, he had to wear it.

Spelling Bees were all the rage, and so were Current Affairs Bees. We had one at Greenhead in the hall on the 25th. We always kept up to date with what was on at the pictures. Jean, Pat and I went to see Greer Garson in *Mrs Miniver*, sniffing and wiping tears from our eyes as we emerged into the blackout, agreeing how lovely it had been, and wishing we could watch it all over again.

On 3 March there was a Warden's Meeting at the Warrenfield, which Philip attended. A couple of days later Jean and I first went to the Empire, then for fish and chips in Lindon Smith's, ending the evening with milkshakes at the Arctic. Mock Matriculation examinations were due to commence on the 15th, so "swotting" would be the order of the day — and night — for some time to come.

Around that time another lad from the village, Bert Senior, went to Berwick on Tweed for his first posting as a soldier.

What temptations there were in the town and district. Towards the end of March I noted in my diary: "Saw Vision, the officer from Longdenholme." Officers had taken over the house which used to belong to Greenhead, further up the road. Far from being promiscuous, though, my best friend Edith and I worshipped from afar, blushing furiously simply at the sight of him swinging majestically down Greenhead Road as we returned to school in the afternoons. We never spoke to him and never even knew his name, apart from the nickname we had given him — Vision. But daydreams are better than reality; well, at nearly sixteen they are.

On the 26th, Greenhead High School girls went to hear the Hallé Orchestra at the Town Hall in the morning. Next day I made some beads from glitter wax, and stayed up till midnight ministering to poor little Ginger, who was poorly. I gave her castor oil, but she passed away the next day.

End of March was stock-taking time in the shop. Lots of customers came in to lend a hand, but dad could add up in his head, with no need to jot prices down on paper behind the counter. It was like a holiday. All sat round the kitchen table for meals, laughing and talking in between getting down to it again.

April, and another of Philip's pals, John Sykes, joined the Army and was posted to Rhyl. I made French mistress Miss New and also Miss Laverick, into April Fools by saying a drawing pin was on their chair, making them leap up just as they were about to sit down. No one dared try on anything like that with Miss Hill.

On 3 April, Pussy Bakehouse, the stray who had been allowed to stay on condition she lived in the bakehouse to keep down any mice or blackclocks, had kittens. From that day on she was allowed to relinquish her duties in the bakehouse, and remain comfortably in the house with the other seven cats. Clocks were altered to double summertime.

With Easter not far away I embroidered flowers on to a bolero and the pockets of a skirt. *Sweater Girl* was on at the Rialto, and on Good Friday, *The Man Born to be King* was on the wireless. Greer Garson, an increasingly popular film star, starred in *Random Harvest* at the Ritz.

At the beginning of May, with "mock matric" behind us, Edith and I went to Brown's, near the Empire, dancing. A group of soldiers offered us cigarettes. When I refused, saying I didn't want one, they called me a "sissy" — but I wouldn't be made to do anything that I didn't want to do.

We walked up to Fox's at the interval, to see who was there. Oh, for the ability to be in two or three places at once!

Unlike an Elland girl at that time, we were not ready to think of marriage. The girl, aged seventeen, had fallen in love with a Canadian Air Force man. Her family went to the Pentecostal church to ask the pastor whether their daughter ought to marry and go to live in Canada. He suggested that they should all pray about it, which they did, and when the time came, the girl embarked, with her fiancé, on a new life in Canada. It turned out to be a very happy and faithful marriage.

Young Molly Hever, of Rawthorpe, preferred to stay in England, even though many a mealtime consisted of "Chips and Point" — point being where the meat used to be. Her mother, Agnes, bought a sheep's head occasionally, the butcher telling her to "leave the eyes in, so it'll see you through the week." Agnes took pity on the old man who lived next door, and saved the sheep's brains for him, popping them in a bag and taking them round so he could have them on toast for his breakfast.

John, of Town Avenue, Leeds Road, and his family eked out meals when rations had been eaten by reverting to the kitchens at the back of the George Hotel. His mother took a basin and was given dripping, "from chips or owt". Sometimes they had bread and dripping for breakfast, dinner and tea. What with that *and* the National loaf, that tasted of sawdust . . .

They were rationed at the Town Avenue Café, and fruit came from Harry Hewitt's, next door. Meat rations were from Argentine, King Street. John's mother stored tinned stuff in a top cupboard, including corned beef. She bought egg powder: you couldn't have a *boiled* egg from it but it made passable fried ones.

Though John survived the war, in some ways he was one of the unlucky ones. He joined up in the Drill Hall, Page Street, and after an accident in which his leg was smashed up, he was in Manchester Royal Infirmary, leg encased in plaster, when the sirens went. The lights went out, a land mine had scored a direct hit, that blew his bed to the other side of the ward, where the ceiling came crashing down on to his already injured legs. That night ninety-nine were killed, including doctors and nurses.

When John returned home to Town Avenue, there were two evacuees installed, sisters aged six and ten. His mother had collected the terrified children, who had been blitzed in London. They only had their gas masks, labels with names on coat lapels, black stockings, flat shoes, and a small attaché case. Both were in such a frightened state that they used to wake up screaming regularly, and frequently wet the bed. But they were never more frightened than when they went for a walk by Canker Lane. They dashed back screaming their heads off.

"We saw these 'ere monsters," they gasped. On investigation, these turned out to be cows — something they had never seen before.

John recalls the cow that was killed by flying shrapnel at the top of Kilner Bank, and the bomb that fell near Robert Airey's, unexploded in the River Colne. After it had been made safe (the bomb was 7 or 8 ft high), it was put on show in Huddersfield.

John volunteered to go back into the Army again nine times. But the reply was always the same: "You've done your bit. Don't bother coming back as the war will be over in a couple of months."

The evacuees were billeted with his family from 1943 until the end of the war. When their parents came up from London to take their daughters home there was an emotional scene on the station platform, scene of so many grieving partings and joyous reunions. The sisters cried their eyes out when they saw their mother and father. Then they all went back to Town Avenue for a final meal. They were thanked for what they had done, and were never seen again.

A well-known face, and voice, of wartime Huddersfield was Lena McManus. Married on the eleventh hour of the eleventh month, in 1939, Lena thought how odd it was to be saying "I Do" at 11a.m. that November morning when, in other years, mill hooters boomed out, and Big Ben struck the hour, to be followed at once by complete silence. For two minutes, when busy life came to a standstill, heads were bowed in the streets and men removed bowlers and flat caps, to remember the dead of the First World War.

For her wedding, at St Patrick's, Lena wore a borrowed fox fur, maroon-coloured coat and matching hat. She and her bridegroom Paddy couldn't afford flowers, so they wore Remembrance poppies in their lapels. All their worldly finances amounted to 35s. between them, which they blew after the ceremony at the Social Club on Green Street.

Up to July 1940, Lena had been a "doffer" at Jessie Lumb's mill. But she didn't like the work: it was too noisy, and a 6.30a.m. start. Lindon Smith's fruit and vegetable stall on Shambles Lane was more to her liking, even though as an assistant, she had to stand on the pavement in wintry weather without a coat. Assistants wore white overalls all the time, but were allowed to wear a scarf and fingerless mittens — boots as well if snow and rain turned pavements into sloshy rivers.

Lena and Paddy continued to live with her mother at No. 29 Victoria Road, Lockwood, then the young husband was called up.

At Lindon Smith's work commenced between 8 and 8.30a.m. The young men still not in the forces heaved the boxes of fruit and vegetables into the display areas. For a bit of warmth, wooden crates were burned on a little fire at the back, assistants nipping in for a quick warm when custom was slack. Sometimes, if another of Lindon Smith's businesses was short staffed, Lena helped out at the fish and chip shop and café.

At midday Lena and her chums went to Jessie's Tea Rooms on Victoria Lane to buy a sandwich and a pot of tea. If you chose to have a pint pot, the tea cost 4d. The café belonged to two Miss Boothroyds, but was managed by Jessie. Assistants took their own pot to Jessie's mid-afternoon for another bit of refreshment. In the forties Shambles Lane was a hive of activity, with Porter's fish shop, the Dolls' Hospital, joke shop, and a shop which sold overalls. Hardwick's, nearby on Victoria Street, was a busy boot and shoe shop with wellingtons, clogs and other wares hanging outside.

When deliveries were made at Lindon Smith's, customers seemed to appear from nowhere. Once a swarm of would-be customers began jostling and pushing each other in an attempt to obtain some onions that had appeared on the stall. The shoving got so out of hand that someone went to fetch the mayor, to try and calm them down.

People almost *went* bananas if they caught sight of any of those! A busy "black market" went on in the area. Fruit was sold in exchange for something from the local grocers, perhaps a tin of salmon.

Management made sure that their staff got a share first, then the fish shop assistants. Lena used to put her hand out twice. "Well, I work at both shops at times," she reasoned.

One of the qualities needed if you were to work at Lindon Smith's out there on the pavement alongside the fruit and vegetables, was the ability to shout and bawl. Lena became extremely proficent at this, so much so that some of the other shopkeepers shouted out "Oh, shurrup you, we can't hear ourselves speak."

After working all day, Lena had to take her turn fire-watching in the Top Market, with Jessie. "Have I to bring some beer in?" Lena used to ask, after leaving Lindon Smith's at 6p.m.

"No, make a cup of tea," was the usual reply as they chatted in the upstairs café. Lena enjoyed fire-watching evenings, as it meant that she didn't have to trail home to Lockwood to make tea.

There was plenty to gossip about. Once, a young married woman was walking in town with her coloured boyfriend. Her husband, home on leave, shot and killed the coloured soldier.

When selling fruit and veg. it was too much of a bother to fiddle about with halfpennies, so Lena charged to the nearest penny instead.

In 1943 Lena left work to have her son David. When he was six months old she took him to Greenhead Nursery every day, either pushing the pram up Chapel Hill, or carrying him: almost a day's work before she even started the job! Lena was usually first at the nursery and last out. After returning home to put the baby to bed, she had to rush back to serve fish and chips at Lindon Smith's, or to be a waitress in the upstairs café.

Mrs Leonard was the cashier and "gaffer", who cooked as well if someone didn't turn up. Lena sometimes found a threepenny bit under a plate for a tip, even a tanner (6d.) occasionally.

In winter, when snow lay deep, contrasting sharply with the bright yellow mimosa heralding spring along Shambles Lane, Lena was troubled with chilblains. On Saturday evenings poorer people went into town late, to buy fruit and vegetables at a reduced price before

Lindon Smith's closed for the weekend. Lena put the goods into bags and called out her wares, at the top of her voice. Prisoners of war with patches on their sleeves sauntered by on Saturdays mingling with the crowds. Wednesday was half-day closing, and how odd and lifeless Shambles Lane looked and sounded when the shutters came down at one o'clock.

When you have a commodity to barter for something you want, it may not be fair, but it made wartime shortages easier for many. At Central Stores, our grocer's and baker's shop, one of the flour travellers occasionally managed to allow us a sack of real, pure white flour when the National loaf was all we were supposed to have. So anxious about being in possession of such an illegal treasure was Dad that it was hidden beneath the double bed until a secret baking session was due. Only tried and trusted friends and relations were invited to taste white bread again on the rare occasions some was baked.

In return, the traveller, a Jew who came from Leeds, cajoled mother every time he turned up: "Fry me some bacon and eggs SA." Even in peacetime Maurice was not supposed to eat pig. "SA", I found out from Philip, was an abbreviation for Sex Appeal. The traveller demanded a kiss as well, and one from me if he was there when I came in from school. All thought it a good bargain.

Dad enjoyed cooking meals and baking. Suppertime was often pea soup, in a huge black pan that simmered "mushy" peas and ham shank for ages. Anticipation and aroma conveyed a sense of security and well-being that no "quick fix" can ever do.

Roger Smith, who worked in the Midland Bank before joining the RAF, strolled in yet again after we thought he had gone abroad. He had had German measles, then been in a plane crash, so made for our shop and another game of ping pong as soon as he returned.

Villagers were worked up to the hilt when they thought cigarettes were due to be delivered to our shop. When Mrs Brook had hers safely she pounded out the "Sabre Dance" on her piano, in sheer exuberance and delight. We could hear her a couple of houses away down Deighton Road.

We had to become proficient liars, maintaining there were no cigarettes in the shop at all, which was often true — Mother having hidden them all away in a top cupboard in the kitchen, for herself and her "favourites".

School Certificate French oral examination coincided with our four day holiday in Blackpool. Headmistress Miss Hill had a long and earnest conversation with Dad on the telephone. There was no alternative but for me to return to Huddersfield on the day of the examination, then go back to Blackpool on the train immediately after the five minute exam.

My parents and Philip saw me off at Blackpool. It was the first time I'd been alone on a train, and in wartime too. One would have thought I was off on an expedition to the North Pole, the anxiety to be felt on that station platform!

Soon the brief holiday was over, and I was glad to make a tour of inspection of my Dig For Victory allotment in the walled garden at the side of the shop. There was always a willing customer to look after our hens, being invited to take any eggs for their own use; and they always received "A Present From Blackpool" on our return.

We were shocked on 3 June 1943 to hear that film star Leslie Howard had been shot down and killed in an aeroplane. My mind was so teeming with events — that sad death, examination, my allotment, the airgraphs to write, that I absent-mindedly fell off the bus that afternoon. I only grazed my knees, but how foolish to be on one's knees before passing soldiers, trying to look as though nothing had happened.

Art, English and History were my best subjects, but most in the fifth form were leaving and not going on to University. I didn't want to be odd man out, and besides, we all thought what a lot we would be missing if we spent the next couple of years studying, when so much was happening in our own town. Wartime Huddersfield was a terrific place to live in. Marvellous musicians visited; strangers abounded in uniform at dances — our youth would be gone if we went away to university.

Stuart Hirst Commercial Art studio in Leeds, offered me a position as artist after seeing a portfolio of my work. Dad came with me. It was exactly what I would have enjoyed, but timidity overcame me. I'd have been terrified having to travel all the way to Leeds and back every day on the train, with all the soldiers shoving and pushing, and the blackout, and fear of air raids in a strange place.

Security was what people went for in a job. And Dad thought an office position at the British Dyes would be well paid, as well as being within walking distance, getting on for two miles. Some of my friends were to be interviewed, so I decided I might as well try it.

What a mistake that decision was! But, in the meantime, there would be the summer holidays to look forward to when School Certificate exams were over. 14 June was Whit Monday: Pat Patrick and I had the rabbits out to play, cleaned the hutches out and, after going for a walk, went to see *Gone With The Wind* with Clark Gable and Vivien Leigh, at the Majestic. We looked at *Illustrated* and *Picture Goer* magazines later at home.

Chapel anniversaries amid the news of battle lent an air of serenity to life. On 27 June we attended the Children's Demonstration service in the morning, walked home for dinner, back to chapel in the afternoon, home for tea, and back again for evensong. Mary Barker sang a solo: "Sanctuary of the Heart" was divine — she had a voice equally as beautiful as Deanna Durbin's I thought. The parson prayed for peace, and all gained inner strength and resolution after such a lovely day. School Certificate examinations commenced on 2 July at Greenhead High School for Girls. Concentration faltered for me when my cousin telephoned to say that Ernie, her brother in the Tank Corps, was blown up on the day he was reported missing in 1942, and was buried in the desert. Strange that while we grew old, Ernie and others would remain forever, in the mind's eye, debonair and young, in the peak of condition before war blew them apart.

A silent prayer to say we would not forget, then work in hand had to be attended to. Miss Spikes enlisted the help of Edith, Vesta, Molly, Eileen and myself to help her glue pages of old music books together, as they could not be replaced while the war was on.

Last day at Greenhead was 21 July 1943. I shook hands with Miss Hill and other mistresses, and asked them to autograph my book, then walked through the school gates in my navy blue striped blazer, satchel over my shoulder, for the last time.

Goodbyes are always devastating, especially when the future is so uncertain, but creative activities help. Our rabbit hutches were enlivened with a coat of bright green paint the next day. One of the rabbits showed its displeasure, and was posted missing. Consternation was rife.

Clouds lifted when the postman brought a letter from singing film star Nelson Eddy, whom I'd written to asking for his autograph. And Miss Hill telephoned with the news that I had passed School Certificate, with credits in Art, English Language, English Literature, History, and passes in French and Geography. Predictably I failed in commercial subjects.

And there was I, going to work in the office at British Dyes. I had my interview and a medical, then went immediately to enrol for Commercial Art at Technical College for a couple of evenings a week. To dull the awful prospect of the working future I ate my ration of toffees all at one go.

John Hall sent a pretty blue handkerchief from Libya. A hectic round of dances, fund raising and all manner of events went on in town and district that September, including Moldgreen and Dalton Carnival in aid of the Red Cross Fund and prisoners of war. Miss Patricia Crosland was crowned Rose Queen. Entry fee for the dog show was 1s. "It is not necessary for a dog to be registered," read the programme, "so enter your pal." Secretary of the dog section was Mr H. Senior, of No. 24 Lyncroft Avenue, Dalton. Then there was the inevitable rabbit show, and Tradesmen's Turnouts. Nora Bray's pupils gave a dancing display, and there were side shows, pony racing and sports. Admission to the field was 6d. for adults, 3d. for children. Teas were served in St Paul's Methodist School and Grove Place Schoolrooms.

On the anniversary of the outbreak of war, 3 September, Golcar "Lib" held a dance, with Aubrey Hirst and his band, with "Big" Bill Turner as M C. More must have been going off than usual, as there was also a Jitterbug contest. Girls were swung and swooped round, skirts swirling out to show their underwear to cheers from the onlookers; sometimes they disappeared beneath the legs of their khaki clad partners, to reappear the other side, grinning and ready for more.

Posters and adverts everywhere urged people to give up their old diaries, ledgers, files and papers in Huddersfield Book Drive. The target was 250,000 books, and secrecy was guaranteed in destruction.

Sport lovers were saddened to hear about the death of Yorkshire and England test cricketer Hedley Verity, who died of wounds on 31 July.

However, music hath charms to soothe, and who better to perform that task than the New Hallé Orchestra, with Barbirolli, visiting the Town Hall on 15 September.

There was good news for knitters. Greenwoods, of No. 13 Victoria Street, let it be known that the New Board of Trade Regulations were to release for sale some 10,000 lb of various quality, coupon-free knitting yarns — a splendid opportunity to obtain stocks of wools for winter knitting.

News of another cricketer came through to Huddersfield. West Indies cricketer Leary Constantine had been asked to move his family from a London hotel, following a colour bar incident on the Saturday before August Bank Holiday.

The war had not waned enthusiasm for football or rugby. Huddersfield versus Oldham at Fartown Saturday 4 September. Admission for men was 1s. 6d.; for women and members of HM Forces it was 7d. Kick-off was at 3.30p.m.

Good natured noises and cheering at a football match was one thing, but listening to church bells clanging if you were a night worker trying to sleep was another. One such complained about the clanging of bells on Sundays, after the ban on their ringing had been lifted: "one used to be able to get a bit of peace on Sundays."

There was praise, however, for Huddersfield Transport Services from a visitor to the town from Luton, who remarked on the efficiency and courtesy of operators, and also the cleanliness of buses.

In connection with the National Day of Prayer that September, there was a United Methodist Service of Thanksgiving at Queen Street Mission. Conducted by the Minister, the Rev. E. J. Nuttall, who read the lesson from Psalm 46, "God is Our Refuge and Strength". The sermon was delivered by the Rev. Ernest H. Johnson, Minister of Brunswick Street Methodist church. Miss H. Pullon played the organ, and five hymns were sung, including "All People That On Earth Do Dwell", and "Lord, Thou Hast Been Our Dwelling Place".

One of the largest convoys of reinforcement troops for the Canadian Army overseas to leave Canada since the start of the war arrived safely at a British Port — news to please Huddersfield girls who were enjoying the chewing gum and gifts of nylons from those already here.

The Grand cinema showed a new recruit in *Old Mother Riley Joins Up*. It was announced that the Moldgreen and Dalton Carnival had been a great success, not least in the contribution made by ten-year-old spaniel Frin, "in charge of Mrs J. W. Jackson, of Dalton". Frin, wearing a pannier consisting of two collecting boxes over a Red Cross blanket, and with a miniature nurse's cap on his head, collected over 50s. It was the second occasion the little working dog had assisted in the cause of the Red Cross. Two weeks earlier he had made his stage début at the Waterloo cinema in aid of the same fund.

With clothes on coupons, dry cleaning was a popular option instead of buying new ones. Klenerite, Paddock, advertised "Dry Cleaning in 7 Days for Winter. Ladies' Coats and Plain Wool Dresses, 1s. 9d. Suits and costumes, 1s. 11d. and 2s. 6d."

People had to begin planning toys for Christmas in good time, when they were scarce and of poor quality in the shops. Adverts began to appear in autumn, both with toys for sale, and wanted. One request was for a doll, black or white, suitable for a child aged six or seven, and also a baby's buffer car. Many who before the war would never have dreamed of buying secondhand clothes, now scanned "For Sale" columns avidly to make a change to their wardrobes not entailing the use of precious clothing coupons. A bargain was a "Gent's blue swagger overcoat, £2".

A teetotaller wanted to know why, when everything else seemed to be rationed, beer wasn't. He thought it disgraceful that sugar was employed for alcoholic purposes.

Nellie Wallace, famous comedienne, came to the Palace Theatre on the 7th. There was more to take minds off the war on Sunday 12 September, during an afternoon vocal and instrumental recital at St Paul's church by Winifred M. Smith, organ; Madame Hylda O. West, soprano; Mr George E. Crowther, cello. The programme included works by Handel, Haydn, Bach and Elgar.

One of the worst things that could happen to anyone was to lose their ration book. A reward was put out for the return of one (with clothing coupons also lost) by the owner, who lived at No. 101 Moorbottom Road, Thornton Lodge. There would, doubtless, be nightmares of walking the streets naked and hungry unless they were returned.

Stealing could be resorted to by those so inclined. Not much hope could be held out by the shoe shop assistant, who appealed to "Person who took two pairs of shoes, value 14s. 1d. and 16s. 4d. from the shop in town," to please call to see him.

Short rations sharpened the wits of some. In court, the magistrate pronounced "Thirty Days". "Hath September", flashed back the accused. Shortages even brought out the poet in others, as in this reply to "Disgusted" concerning the sugar in beer:

O Noble Teetotaller, I wish you no ill
I like you to live in what manner you will
But noble teetotaller, you look down on me
As you bury your snout in your coffee and tea
Well kindly recall that your coffee and tea
Though noble, no doubt, must come over the sea
While the liquids I like, though they may cross
   the bar,
Do not at the moment, endanger the tar
So be glad of the madness of human affairs,
And drink what you like, but don't give yourself
   airs.

Hopes were raised, then dashed so many times. The Royal Artillery Records Office notified Mrs Margaret Crosland, of No. 51 Bromley Road, Birkby, that her husband, Gunner Harold L. Crosland must again be regarded as missing. He had been reported missing the previous September; then his wife had heard only once, in February, when she received a letter-card dated 26 October. Gunner Crosland was being transferred from North Africa to Italy as a prisoner of war when the ship he was on sank, with no information of survivors.

Huddersfield Authors' Circle members should never have been short of material to write about in those unpredictable times. They met at the Pack Horse Hotel monthly. One speaker that autumn was Mr Oliver Smith, his subject George Bernard Shaw. Thanks were expressed for the talk by Mr E. J. Adkins, seconded by Mrs Blatch, of Primrose Hill.

A minor catastrophe was averted when the new manager of the Regal cinema, who should have arrived at the Borough Police Court by 11a.m., but didn't, was fortunate that members of the licensing bench stayed behind to grant the transfer licence to him. John Woodhead, new manager, ironically was showing the film *Look Up and Laugh* — it might have been a case of *Sit down and Cry* had Moldgreen not been able to have its cinema that night.

Good news on the food front included potted shrimps, no points, 1s. 3d. a carton, at Trawler Shops. Rabbits cost from 2s. to 10s.; also eighteen boxes containing fifty mice £2 to clear. It was not clear, however, whether the mice were pet ones, or were like horse-flesh, to eke out the meat ration . . .

Hats remained unrationed, so "why be perverse and go without one?" Rushworth's of Westgate wanted to know. "Think what a difference it makes to know you are wearing a hat that really suits you. It helps you to put up more cheerfully with restrictions and other things."

Praise was forthcoming for the women of Huddersfield who, as early as 7a.m., swung through garden gates with a smiling face and cheery "Good Morning", then rolled out householders' dustbins and collected the salvage. One of them was a mother of nine children, and a grandmother as well.

Such hard workers could be forgiven for occasional lapses of current affairs knowledge. "Nazis claim capture of Mussolini" — one offered the latest news to another.

"Where's that?" asked her friend.

Over 1,400 women born in 1896 registered in Huddersfield and District under the Registration for Employment Order 1941. About 40 per cent were already in full time employment. Mr F. E. B. Gabbutt, of the Ministry of Labour and National Service, pointed out that so many were in employment, rebutting the contention that grandmothers were being called up.

Lascelles Hall Working Men's Club held a Red Cabbage Show, with money prizes for the best, to weigh 1 lb or over. Everybody was so busy and involved that some couldn't even bear to stop when at a concert.

One woman caused havoc by knitting during a Hallé concert, the clicking of her needles almost driving those nearby to murder. Her excuse was that she was knitting for the Forces.

Popular Blackpool organist Reginald Dixon came to the Ritz on Sunday 26 September, along with other entertainers. The concert began at 6.30p.m. in order to end in time for the audience to catch buses to all parts.

A tricky situation came up with Huddersfield girls and coloured American soldiers stationed around the town. They were to be found in shop doorways, quiet side streets, and in lorries. But officials stressed that "the men are our guests, and strangers in our land". Before long the first half-castes were being born. Mr W. Ellis, acting secretary of the YMCA, said that some of the coloured troops visited the town on weekend leave; others on all night leave. White fellows were really chummy with the coloured men in the YMCA hostel.

Away from the seedy side of the war, Deanna Durbin starred at the Princess in *The Amazing Mrs Holliday*, and at the Picture House the audience could see stars heard so often on the wireless in *Happidrome*, with Harry Korris, Robbie Vincent, Cecil Frederick, Bunty Meadows — and a host of guest artists. It was fascinating to actually see pictures of what was going on in the war on the news at the cinema.

Dances were in full swing again as autumn continued, and the nights drew in. The Messenger Corps Dance at the Town Hall was organized by the Civil Defence Messenger Corps, and proceeds, approximately £15, were devoted to the Corps Welfare

Fund. Dancing was to the Certo Cito Orchestra. Mr C. E. Dryden was MC, spot dance was won by Mr J. Buckley and Miss M. Oliver, while Mr T. Dale and Miss M. Brook won the Elimination Dance.

Blamires' Comforts Fund Dance was at the Co-op Hall, with Rawlins Rhythmics. Benjamin Shaw & Sons Employees Comforts Fund, with a Military Whist Drive, was held in Woodhouse Church Schools.

The doyen of all the dancing venues, Cambridge Road Baths, had its Grand Opening of the season on Saturday 9 October, with Britain's pioneers of jazz — Lew Stone and his full broadcasting band; also Alec Wilkinson and his Spitfire dance band. Tickets were 5s. from Kenneth Levell's.

Presentation of the Broadbent Cup took place at the Drill Hall when Lieutenant Colonel R. Rippon presided, explaining that the cup was to be competed for annually by the Huddersfield Home Guard Battalions. In its first year it had been won by "A" Company of his own battalion.

To save time and conserve energy people were asked to prefix a local number on the telephone by first asking the operator for Huddersfield. At present, if a caller omitted Huddersfield the operator always said the word.

Meanwhile, my wartime working life began, and I hated it, especially the 8.30a.m. start at British Dyes, the awful smell as one approached it on Leeds Road almost made me put my gas mask on, and midday dinner in the canteen, with the stench of workers' overalls. One morning I had to count hundreds of filthy canteen tickets with Joyce Gannon.

Although days from 8.30a.m. till 5.30p.m. felt like an eternity, I felt rich taking home my first wage packet, containing 30s. On the first morning, 13 September 1943, Maurice Marshall instructed me in the office work. I wasn't the slightest bit interested. On 14 October I obtained a release form from Mr Milnes.

Philip, my brother, had high hopes of joining the RAF as his friend Roger had done. But when he went for his medical, he passed Grade four, owing to an accident he had had when fourteen. He had bought a second-hand bike and the lad who sold it had patched the brakes up with a rusty nail. When Philip swerved to stop the mad ride downhill, the handle bars punctured his spleen. Some who wanted to join up couldn't; others who didn't want to were compelled to.

Though deliriously relieved to be working my notice, the Labour Exchange had nothing in my line. With the paper shortage, there was not much use considering anything in the art line. Then they suggested that the Halifax Building Society wanted another Junior. This was office work again, but it would be in the town centre, and there wouldn't be that terrible stench of the Dyes. I had an interview with manager Mr Nash, and my second office position since leaving Greenhead began on 1 November. Some of the others were part-timers, who were working there as their contribution to the war effort while their husbands were in the Forces.

We wore dark green overalls, the men in smart suits, white shirts and ties. When not out delivering post, I sat at a Dickensian, wooden sloping desk with a ledger on it. Miss Mellor, a grey haired lady, was next to me on another high stool.

Margaret Bennett, one of the other juniors, had her hair in the new short, razored Liberty Cut style. It was enjoyable going round solicitors' offices and banks with documents for them, then collecting orders from the staff at Halifax Building Society for their mid-morning break. Many brought flasks for their tea or coffee, but they wanted either jam tarts or custards from the confectioners in the arcade opposite. How I hoped their quota wouldn't expire before my turn in the queue arrived!

It was strange having Wednesday half-day holiday instead of Saturday. On the first one I went to Telfer's, wholesaler, in Dundas Street, Huddersfield, with mother, to buy pixie hoods and vests to sell in our shop. Then we had tea in the Ritz café.

Mother's friend, Betty Davidson, was a clever seamstress. She made a coat for mother, out of a grey blanket. It was then dyed red.

With Christmas not far away again, I began making presents out of felt, which wasn't on clothing coupons — including a red handbag for mother, secretly stitching it by hand when she was at a chapel concert rehearsal, dance, or at the "pictures".

8 December was the first night of Deighton Married Ladies' concert. It was better than any pantomime. One of the "numbers" was so hilarious that the

husband of one tubby lady had to be assisted out of the schoolroom to calm down. Mrs Muffet, slightly bow legged, was dressed, like the others, in white cricket trousers. She wore her husband's cast-offs.

Each chorus, the ladies circled the stage, and the audience waited for the corpulent tummy to appear again, with top button undone. It was too much for Mr Muffet. He laughed till he shook, and tears ran down his face. Nobody, watching that show, would have known there was a war on. Never have so many laughed so uproariously, for so long, at so few. It was a "wizard" evening, especially when a hungry mouse found its way on to the stage during a sketch, and Edith Wood, wife of the fish and chip shop man in the village, leapt on to a small table and stayed there, shrieking.

Next day an air of sadness hovered over the office. Mr Hirst said goodbye; he was joining the Navy.

But there were always the art classes at Tech — evenings to look forward to. Jeanne Wood, who worked as a tracer at Hopkinson's, sat by me at Tech. That evening, when we were in lettering class, head of the School of Art, Noel Spencer, called us into his office, to tell us off for talking too much. But there was never enough time for all we had to say. Then when we waited for the bus home, the No. 10 for Sheepridge, or the No. 20 for Woodhouse, on New Street, there was always a young man in the Marsden queue opposite, who whistled Clair de Lune when he saw us. It was all very exciting, bumping into soldiers with our drawing boards, pretending it was the fault of the blackout.

238

Mother had made friends with a soldier billeted at Bradley Lane camp, Sergeant Syme. He had a little black moustache, like Hitler's. Like the others, he came and went as he liked. It was "Open House".

I had a go making Mintos one evening: two tablespoons of sugar, two of syrup, a few drops of peppermint essence, and five tablespoons of dried milk. Boil in pan for a minute before adding the dried milk. When thoroughly mixed, cool, then roll into shapes.

Manager Mr Nash gave me a £1 "Christmas Box" when he went round the office wishing us all a "Merry Christmas". Dad took time off from dealing with rationing and baking to play billiards at the club with Sergeant Syme. As usual we had fish and chips for supper then talked till midnight. I'm sure talking kept people sane in those days.

A couple of days before Christmas Dad worked all through the night in the bakehouse with local butcher Mr Schofield, baking pork pies.

I admired a lovely black velvet "V"-necked dress, with puff sleeves, in Paige's on New Street. It cost £5. Mother came to the side door of the Halifax one afternoon and I went with her to try it on. She bought it for my Christmas present. I couldn't wait to wear it next time I went to a dance at the Baths, with a red felt flower I'd made, or the pink feathery cluster I'd bought.

For Dad, I decided on a record of Richard Tauber singing "Smiling Thro" and, on the other side, "A Little Love, a Little Kiss"; and a shaving brush.

1943 had been an interesting year in Huddersfield. October had seen a concert at the Ritz in aid of John

Lockwood Comforts Fund, with famous ITMA personalities, Dorothy Summers, Dino Galvani, Kenneth Bygott, and other well-known artistes. Corporation Lunch Hour Recitals in the Town Hall included one by the Zorian String Quartet.

News had been received of many soldiers from Huddersfield and district, a number having met friends and relatives by chance in the Middle East.

A concert in aid of St Dunstan's was given in Fields Congregational Church School, Kirkheaton. Vocal items were contributed by Miss Joan Donnolly, Marjorie Haywood, Dorothy Rix and Jean Kent, all pupils of Madame Hylda O. West, who arranged the concert.

In a Forces Family Letter-Box over German radio, Sergeant Lawrence Ramsden of No. 48 Kaye Lane, Aldmondbury, was brought to the microphone. He had baled out during a raid on Berlin, and wanted his fiancée, Miss Margaret Brooke, of No. 84 Eldon Road, Marsh, to know he was fit, and had no complaints.

There were complaints in some Huddersfield schools when the cold weather came. They had no central heating, and also children were deprived of biscuits with their school milk, now biscuits were on "points". Yet the Ministry of Food still permitted biscuits to be sold in pubs.

The public was exhorted to save coal, and order coke instead. And Mr Oliver Rodgers, Secretary of the Wartime Dairymen's Association, warned householders that they may have a new milkman. To conserve manpower, petrol, rubber and wear and tear of vehicles, milkmen were being re-directed.

Members of the WVS Housewives Service bought three bicycles, to be kept at the YMCA for the use of servicemen arriving in town late at night. The only stipulation to their use was that they had to be returned.

November, and Cambridge Road Baths began having Personality Parades. One of the personalities was Miss Elsa Wells, Star Amateur champion, British Tango champion, and a blonde with a charming personality. And what a dancer!

Huddersfield Glee and Madrigal Society obtained the services of a brilliant young composer-pianist, Benjamin Britten, to conduct the Society in his *Hymn to St Cecilia*.

Due to austerity, November Remembrance poppies, once made of wire, were fashioned from cardboard, the metal centres replaced with paper. One purchaser of a new poppy was sure he'd been cheated.

Crowds surged to the Baths to dance and listen to the Squadronaires, number one dance orchestra of the RAF, on Monday 6 December 1943. Dancers thronged round the dais, applauding each number and solo with great enthusiasm. They paid 5s. admission, and the dance lasted from 7p.m. to 11p.m.

Rawicz and Landauer "On Two Pianos" were at the Theatre Royal on 6 November, with the National Philharmonic Orchestra.

That week Huddersfield-born film star James Mason starred in one of his finest roles at the Princess, *The Man in Grey*.

As Christmas approached, glum faces were to be seen at shops when it became known that customers would be lucky if there was one turkey between every ten who wanted one. None would be on offer in the shops, as those there were had been "spoken for" a long time before. Game and poultry dealers were in an unenviable position.

What few toys there were in shops were "only fit to be burned", in the words of one disappointed customer. In desperation, many bought gift vouchers. Cosmetics, the old standby, were scarce and expensive. Lipsticks in ordinary metal cases cost 12s. 6d. each. Face creams were often of poor or unknown quality and make. Brand names had to be kept before the public, though scarce: "Nivea Creme — Work of National Importance Must Come First. Nivea is always packed in our branded containers, so you can be sure it is genuine Nivea Creme. Please make Nivea last as long as you can."

Another advert, so different to peace-time wording, read: "He's on leave. You can have off duty beauty. In wartime, above all, it's Snowfire Beauty Preparations you need. Even a little does a lot of beautifying. Worth waiting for. Prices 4d. to 2s. 1d. (Including Tax.)"

People could still get "Lavvo For Spotless Lavatories, 10½d." which was annoying when creams to camouflage spots on faces were scarce as the fairy on top of the Christmas tree ... That good old standby, Miner's

Liquid Make Up Foundation, 10½d. and 2s. 7½d., gave a healthy tan to pallid wartime winter faces and legs.

Even headaches had to be rationed! "Anadin tablets — owing to priority calls, your nearest chemist may occasionally be out of stock." But two 3d. blocks of Monkey Brand, for one coupon, could clean your cooker fifty times.

Better not to have tummy upsets over Christmas, 1943. Capensis toilet paper, 300 sheets in each pack, was 8½d. per roll, but retailers were sometimes temporarily out of stock, so they asked customers' "indulgence in these difficult times". At one pre-Christmas party a local chap insisted on showing his hostess his own sheets, just in case, he said, she had counted her own. All were acutely aware of the Squander Bug, so were urged to buy Savings Certificates for gifts. At 15s., one would be worth 20s. 6d. in ten years, its increase free of income tax.

Young girls would not be thinking about ten years hence, though, when youth would have flown, especially when an advert by Eve Toilet soap (3d. including Purchase Tax, one coupon), asked, "How old will you look when rationing is a memory? Young and lovely if your skin has been cared for by Eve Toilet Soap."

Huddersfield people, as others all over the country, wanting to decorate their homes for Christmas, turned to stippling rooms if they couldn't get wallpaper. Goods may be scarce; ideas weren't.

Fishnet — no coupons — could be made into snoods and turbans, old ballroom dresses into underwear or children's dresses. But oh, how galling to read about a way of life out of reach to wartime girls: "As warm as a tropical night, as Romantic as Red Roses, As mysterious as a Hindu Goddess, As ecstatic as a love affair, As Hedy as Lamarr — Californian Poppy Perfume."

At least they were never bored. They were too busy trying to concoct clothes and accessories out of something and nothing. In town shops, "off ration" collars and belts, collar and cuff sets, and suede belts decorated with gold studs proved popular gifts, as did headscarves, even though one had to forego a precious clothing coupon as well as money. Indeed, you felt extra virtuous handing over a present that had cost coupons besides cash. Fully-fashioned stockings were practically unavailable. But girls were getting used to the new seamless stockings at only one and a half coupons a pair.

Pupils of Longley Hall Central School had made toys for children of Southgate Nursery, also sending several parcels to two ships "adopted" by the school. Headmistress Miss D. A. Finch proudly told how her girls had also sent Christmas parcels to the Red Cross, POW Fund, Merchant Navy Comforts Fund, and the Society for Shipwrecked Mariners.

At Greenhead Speech Day, Miss Hill gave the usual glowing report of pupils' achievements, past and present, including Old Girls now in the forces, School Certificate and Higher School Certificate results. Among the many charities contributed to were the New Hospital at Stalingrad (6 gns), "Our Ship", (£10) the

Red Cross Fund (£100). Sacks of woollies had been sent to the ship, and also toys to the Cinderella Society.

While all this benevolence was extended to others, it appeared as though a meagre Christmas was the outlook for most at home. No pork had been issued for three weeks, to conserve supplies for the festive period. However, on Christmas Day itself, there were parties at St Luke's Hospital, Crosland Moor, and all institutions — with beef, roast pork, potatoes, turnip, cabbage, plum pudding and sauce; beer, mineral waters, tobacco, cigarettes, and chicken for the sick. A shilling each was given from the Mayor's Fund to residents and sick patients, and toys were given to children at Mill Hill, some from the Cinderella Society. At the Royal Infirmary there were carols on Christmas Eve, and a large decorated tree in the children's ward. At Buxton Road chapel YMCA, members of the forces were served with tea and biscuits on Christmas morning.

Some members of the Home Guard had to report for duty, but nothing could dim the excitement of the Christmas Eve dance at Cambridge Road Baths. Girls who could find a bit of mistletoe pinned it provocatively in their hair, and danced the night away to Alex Wilkinson and his band. Some had passouts stamped on their hands so they could take a breather outside with a dancing partner, or nip on to the Sportsman for a drink.

Most girls took silver or gold dancing shoes, wrapped in brown paper or a carrier bag, to change into. It was a nuisance paying 2d. for a cloakroom ticket, then at the end queuing for ages to retrieve outdoor clothes. Sometimes, if you waited too long to join the cloakroom queue, the last bus would have gone and it meant walking home in the blackout — or moonlight if you were lucky. It was infuriating when the attendant was slow moving, or couldn't find your coat, and went on to look for the next girl's in the queue.

Handbags were another nuisance, until long straps became fashionable and you could dance with it slung over your shoulder. Until then, it was such a panic if, after a hectic "In the Mood" or smoochy waltz, noses needed repowdering and fresh lipstick applied (if it had been kissed off) — and a handbag left under a seat had disappeared.

Possibly the best position at the Baths was leaning over the balcony, with a bird's eye view of who was dancing, and earmarking which good-looking dancer to excuse in the next "Excuse me Quickstep", or to stand next to in a "Paul Jones".

Most girls wouldn't have been seen dead wearing wellingtons or flat shoes when going to a dance. It was court shoes or high heels even if it was snowing. Some took walking shoes in case they missed the last bus, but only to be changed into if a boyfriend wasn't to accompany them, and then only when out of sight of the dance hall. The disappointment of not having a handsome escort to walk one home was made up for by being able to walk comfortably, not staggering along awkwardly in smart but unsuitable high heels.

There again, who wanted to walk quickly if with a handsome Polish airman or gum-chewing Canadian or

GI. On Christmas Eve especially, a girl wanted to look just like a film star. The more extrovert, good looking ones were given spontaneous gifts by new admirers from across the sea. Nylons especially were greatly coveted.

No wonder the "boys" felt romantic and generous, gliding round the polished dance floor to "Moonlight Serenade" or high spirits intoxicated even further, jiving around to "Chattanooga Choo Choo" and "Don't Go Walking Down Lovers' Lane, with anyone else but me, anyone else but me, till I come marching home." Some hope!

Many dancing partners made no secret of continuing to chew gum after the opening gambit, "do you come here often?"

Indeed, it was part of the devil-may-care charm of the Yanks, making a wartime Christmas different from any before. Some of the more daring, adventurous Huddersfield girls used to visit boyfriends at Burtonwood in Lancashire, where American forces were stationed. One girl even went as far as Bangor in Wales most weekends to meet her "Yank".

That Christmas Eve many converged on Golcar "Lib" where Ronnie Kenyon and his band played. Others went to the Greenhead Masonic, St Pat's or the Co-op Hall, and the Town Hall.

CHAPTER SIX

1944

On New Year's Day 1944, we were given a half day holiday after the morning's work at Halifax Building Society. People were bringing in passbooks for the audit. The free afternoon gave me the opportunity of writing letters and packing parcels for our friends in the forces: Bill Bailey, Jimmy, John and the others.

The audit meant overtime working after that. Hundreds of passbooks were set out in long trays in front of the counter after they had been dealt with. Being the latest junior, I was always the last to leave. If the staff didn't balance the books straightaway, even if only a halfpenny was "out", it had to be put right no matter how long it took. Then I took the postbag to the GPO.

Two ladies, lost in fog on 15 January, called at a house to ask their way. The householder lent them a cycle flashlamp, which they promised to return to the address he gave them. Neither ladies nor lamp were seen again.

The Jigwood Ltd Social Club held a dance at the Town Hall on Friday the 28th, with Bert Nutter's Rhythm Aces and a cabaret by Nora Bray's "Young Ladies", all for 2s., forces 1s.

John Perris, No. 52 New Street, had a remnant day, with many items at reduced coupon rate on the Saturday. The latest fad to save material was for suits with no pockets, infuriating men — who hadn't reached the point of carrying a handbag; but where to put anything?

All annoyances were soothed away next day for those who went to hear a choir of twenty-four American soldiers sing a programme of negro spirituals. When listening to "Steal Away for Jesus" at Queen Street Mission it was neither here nor there whether you had pockets in your suit or not, as long as you had a hankie or two up your sleeve. The choir was never completely silent, keeping up a melodious humming in between songs. Then, at a movement from the conductor's hand, the singers took up the new refrain.

Back in the real world, towards the end of that first month of 1944, there was a shortage of fish, the worst since 1939, and there weren't even any rabbits. Another supply of oranges was in town, however. And there was another weepie at the Ritz — Bette Davis, Paul Heinried and Claude Rains were starring in *Now, Voyager*, with Billy Hobson at the organ during the interval. Everybody could be heard singing the theme song of the film in factories, mills and shops afterwards: "Wrong, would it be wrong to stay, here in your arms this way . . ." and lighting cigarettes from each other's cigarette as the stars had done in the picture.

Margaret Hellawell's real life romance was with Ronnie Atkins. Her family had a baker's and confectioner's shop at Bradley, closing one day a year only, Christmas Day, until shortages decreed otherwise. Ronnie was an apprentice mechanic, earning 3s. 3d. a day when war began, at George Sykes, Crosland Moor. He was in the Territorials then, aged nineteen. No uniforms were ready when hostilities commenced, so some had to make do with First World War uniforms, that smelt of moth balls. Some of the territorials stayed in the Drill Hall, having meals in the Co-op café that first week. They signed on for twelve years, but wartime service counted double.

While Ronnie was away, Margaret had her photograph taken at Dumont's studio on New Street every year, to send to her fiancé. Margaret used to curl her hair with pipe cleaners, and treated herself to a coat from Goodson's, King Street, to wear on one of the photographs to her sweetheart, adding a regimental "fob" to her coat lapel.

Hanging about waiting their turn to learn to drive at Bradley were Belgian soldiers. Margaret, feeling sorry for them out there in the cold, often invited them into the shop and gave them tea or coffee.

The main Sunday trade during summer at Hellawell's shop was for ice-cream. They heard the news towards the end of the war that allocation of fats for catering was to be cut yet again, so it would have been a waste of time opening with not much to sell.

When the shop closed on both Saturday afternoons and Sundays, it was wonderful for Margaret to have all that free time; then a ruling came in that shops must close at 6.30p.m. to save electricity.

Margaret's time passed happily in the bakehouse, switching on the wireless as soon as she began work, and not turning it off until work was over. She enjoyed "Workers Playtime" especially.

Meanwhile, no "Blues Dress Uniform" was issued, and soldiers weren't supposed to wear civilian clothes. But Ronnie wanted to be smart on a photograph taken to send to Margaret, so he bought a uniform from another chap when in Walton Hospital, Liverpool. He was there as a result of burning his face — not in battle, but while cooking a meal!

Girls dolled themselves up more than usual when going to Cambridge Road Baths to a dance on Thursday 3 February. A £3 prize was at stake — to be awarded to the Most Beautiful Girl, to be known as "Miss Huddersfield". Another attraction was Clarie Wears and his All Coloured South American Dance Band.

Big names continued to come to Huddersfield. A song recital at the Music Club featured famous singer Isobel Baillie, at St Patrick's Hall on the 5th at 2.30 in the afternoon. Dame Myra Hess was billed for another programme.

Europe's greatest swing clarinettist, Carl Barriteau and his Dance Orchestra packed them in again at the Baths, with the slogan "Jive to American Swing Music, played in the American Style."

Frank Randle was in another "Gay Somewhere" comedy, *Somewhere in Civvies*, with Suzette Tarri, showing at the Tudor. Anton Walbrook and Deborah Kerr were in *The Life and Death of Colonel Blimp* at the Princess; Annabella and John Sutton were in *Tonight We Raid Calais* at the Picture House.

Another Huddersfield "Star" was Lesley Brook, who appeared in *I'll Walk Beside You* at the Palace, Milnsbridge, with the London Symphony Orchestra and John McHugh, brilliant young tenor.

Away from all the showbiz razzmatazz, blackout material, coupon free, was on sale at John Perris, 2s. 6½d. a yard. And during January and February repairs to respirators were free of charge. A warden in each area visited homes to inspect them.

With many houses having rooms empty, as members of families were away in the forces, some people offered accommodation. For example, a soldier's wife was willing to share her home for company, and an officer was looking for accommodation with a private family.

Rushworth's Repair Service offered skilled repairs to knickers, vests, pants, nightdresses and pyjamas. Laddered stockings could be invisibly mended. The repair service was on the ground floor, near the Westgate entrance.

Huddersfield postman John Roebuck had earned the Imperial Service Medal, as had Harold Pearson, of Holmfirth sub-post office. Killed in action in Italy, Captain Frank Ellis, Royal Field Artillery, had been a member of the Borough Police Force when war began.

The Citizens' Advice Bureau opened a letter-writing service, to deal with applicants' correspondence, both official and private, for those who found difficulty in expressing themselves on paper.

In February staff of the Halifax Building Society were still working overtime, even on one Wednesday afternoon. How dead the town looked when all the shops were closed! I was not the only one complaining about having too much work.

I made another pair of felt slippers. On Maundy Thursday Mother and I had polyfotos taken in Leeds, forty-eight different expressions on one sheet: super for cutting out and giving to anyone asking for a "snap", and to send in letters. I was delighted with the fawn, fluffy "Teddy Bear" jigger coat with big padded shoulders that Mother bought for me.

One didn't need to be on active service to receive wounds from ammunition. Aldmondbury Grammar schoolboy Reginald Munt injured his hand when a piece of live ammunition exploded near him.

That spring news arrived of Leslie Clark, of South Crosland. He had received his wings, and commission as a pilot officer. Mr Clark had been employed by Hopkinson's before the war, and had been a server at Holy Trinity church, South Crosland.

The Princess Royal paid another visit to the town in 1944. This time she was shown a lady's costume made from a man's morning suit, that made its first and last appearance thirty years before. She also saw rugs made from silk stocking bits, fur backed gloves with the backs from home-cured rabbit skins, and slippers with soles of knitted string. Mrs J. Lodge, of Glenthorpe, Holmfirth, had made the costume, retaining the black silk lapels of the original frock coat in the costume coat. Mrs F. Boocock, Thongsbridge, had created dolls' furniture from matchboxes covered with odd bits of velvet.

Some are better at doing nothing — even *that* could win a prize. At St Thomas's Club Popular Dance, cash prizes were awarded in the Statue Dance competition, to the couple standing still long enough to resemble statues, when J. Vivian Rawlins and his New Rhythmics stopped playing.

One evening Dad was dealing with points and rations till 9.30p.m., the big kitchen table covered with bits of paper. Philip was busy fire-watching after work at the National Provincial, and with ARP duties.

Mrs Davidson made a dress for me out of an old brocade curtain. Dyed strawberry pink, with a drawstring neckline and puff sleeves, it made a change from the black velvet dress. I made another felt handbag with shoulder strap, and another from French knitting, using odd scraps of wool.

A break from handing out passbooks in the building society, up Cloth Hall Street, came one day in March when Mr Drake sent Winifred and me on the bus to the Comptometer School in Leeds, to take back a broken comptometer.

Audrey Armitage had her hair Liberty Cut, very short. I wondered how everyone suddenly wearing short hair was going to win the war. On 2 April, Double Summer Time began again. Next day Bert Senior, home on leave, called to see us. We all went to the Theatre, to see *Wuthering Heights*, finishing as usual with a fish and chip supper in Lindon Smiths. On Wednesday, my half-day, we went to the Ritz to see Robert Donat and Greer Garson in *Goodbye Mr Chips*, and then had tea in Collinson's café with Mildred.

A Grand Charity Concert at the Ritz included "Hutch" (Leslie Hutchinson) in "Songs at the Piano", as well as Don Wilson and his Broadcasting Band. This was in aid of the AA Brigade RA Welfare Fund. It was very hot on Whit Monday, 29 May. After sitting in the garden writing letters all morning, we decided to take a picnic to Holmbridge. As the afternoon wore on ominous looking black clouds gathered; then there was a violent, protracted thunderstorm. We left the area as quickly as possible, and in the evening went to the Theatre to see *Madame Butterfly*. Joan Hammond was the principal singer.

We were astounded to learn later about the devastation caused by the storm. As we heard and watched the tragedy on stage, we little knew of the real tragedy we had been so fortunate to escape. News that may have been of interest to the enemy was kept to a minimum before release to the public.

The devastation that hit Holmfirth and surrounding districts that Whit Monday had nothing to do with any enemy except nature. In the cloudburst, which was at its height in the late afternoon and early evening, the river rose to a height of more than 18 ft in places. Mills were badly damaged, offices and shops brought down, hundreds of houses and buildings flooded. Floating in the swollen river were hen huts, furniture, shop equipment, and water dammed up against wooden buildings of Riverside Mills, which collapsed in a few minutes. A powerful stream swept through the yard, taking 200 bales of wool away. An air raid shelter near the bus garage was submerged. The electric clock at Albion Mills stopped at 6.45p.m., and the river seeped through garden walls of houses below the Sunday School, nearly up to the embankment of the mill dam on the opposite side. It was 1 ft deep in the mill yard.

Roaring and crashing emanated from the mills; buildings seemed to be struck by multiple streaks of lightning, followed by huge thunderclaps. The Perseverance mill dam was covered, and around 6p.m. bales were floating down. Penny Bank went down some time later. The bridge to Hollowgate was under water all the time.

The grandfather clock in the mill office at Bottoms Mill stopped, water lapping up to the pendulum 3 ft from the floor, rising another 2 ft before falling. Bales struck two bays of the weaving shed belonging to H. & S. Butterworth, bringing part of the building down. The whole mill was flooded. At Brockholes, Rock Mills, clocks stopped at 7.25p.m., the river rose to 9 ft, finishing up against sheds which were smashed. Water rose 9 ft at Smithy Place Mills, 4 ft at Crossley Mills, Honley, and surged to 10 ft at Queen's Square Mill between 7.30 and 7.45p.m.

Donald Riley, foreman of the electricity department of Holmfirth Council, and his son Geoffrey, endeavoured to save an eighty-year-old lady from drowning. In doing so, Mr Riley was drowned, his body being recovered about 9p.m. near Lower Mytholmbridge Mill, where the flood rose to 12 ft, within 1 ft of the bridge parapet. It was almost 9 ft deep at the bottom of the mill yard.

The hardly recognizable body of Miss Maud Wimpenny, of Victoria, Holmfirth, was recovered from near a mill on the banks of the River Holme.

Mr G. H. Smith, who lived near the Shoulder of Mutton Inn, said that shortly before the flood, rats left the river bank. He saw droves of them running across the top of a 5 ft high wall at the back of the inn. How, one wonders, did they sense the imminent calamity?

Royal Engineers erected a bridge suitable for heavy traffic from the main road to H. & S. Butterworth Lower Mills, to replace the one destroyed by the flood. It was ready in three hours.

It was estimated that nearly 150 tons of sludge was removed from Thongsbridge cricket ground. The district may not have been blitzed by bombs to the extent of other places, but the water blitz proved equally devastating. Mr Brian Broadbent, Central Ironworks, Huddersfield was chairman of the local reconstruction panel for war damage, and made necessary arrangements to get the mills working again after the flood.

"D" Company Platoon of the Home Guard was formed by Broadbents. Brian Broadbent was also on the Sea Cadet Committee, besides being Chairman of the raid spotting association.

Fate seemed to have it in for the locality, as though to make up for the relatively easy time Huddersfield had had during the war. On 31 May a large fire in a six-storey mill on Northgate destroyed fifty Rolls Royce cars, and hundreds of new tyres belonging to Rippon Brothers.

On 6 June, "Invasion Day" as it was called by some, Greenhead High School held a short prayer service in the hall. The next terror from the skies was Doodle Bugs — the dreaded flying bombs, with no pilot. As long as the awful sound carried on, it was alright. But if it stopped . . . They began their reign of terror on 13 June 1944. One exploded over Grange Moor at Christmas, and Mary Oxley recalls her stepfather, a joiner, taking sandwiches and spending the day repairing the damage. It wasn't as though the family were having a splendid festive meal, though. He used to keep poultry, but there had been no corn to feed them with, so they had rabbit instead.

Some ATS were billeted at Highburton, and Royal Corps of Signals. One day people in the vicinity of Lepton thought there was an air raid going on, but it was an explosion at Lion Fireworks.

On 13 June, thirty-three soldiers who had been wounded on the Normandy bridgehead arrived in Huddersfield. Some were sent to St Luke's, others to the Royal Infirmary. Mr Edward Hirst, Beaumont Park, returned after special service with the Royal Navy, bringing a splinter from a German bomb he had found on the Normandy beach.

With Campaign Medals beginning to be issued to the forces, some munition workers asked why they could not have them too.

Everyone had been asked earlier to get rid of their books for salvage, but now they were asked to contribute them for the forces' libraries.

Greed showed its ugly face when a small quantity of nuts were issued to health food stores for vegetarians. When they went for them, meat eaters had often been there before them.

Some struck lucky in other ways. One lady found three yolks in one of her egg ration — better than finding gold!

A touring "Brains Trust", which included Professor Julian Huxley, visited Huddersfield Town Hall on 29 June. War workers were allocated priority seats. Very different to the popular Beetle Drives was the Bug Drive in the town, a war against unpleasant insects infesting old buildings.

The top floor of John Crowther and Sons, Union Mills, Milnsbridge, collapsed on 6 July. Tons of masonry and four scribbling machines killed one man and trapped thirty others. They thought they had been struck by a flying bomb at first. Two more workers died the next day.

Another 400 evacuee children arrived from southern England, from areas affected by the diabolical bombs.

At least there was a good supply of fish at the time. Trawler shops notified the public, but asked them to bring their own wrapping paper.

Chancellor of the Exchequer Sir John Anderson sent thanks for the £385 7s. 6d. raised by the people of Huddersfield in Salute The Soldier Week.

Captain Noel Wimpenny was awarded the Military Cross for gallantry in the fighting on the Anzio beachhead. Leading telegraphist Gilbert Haigh was given the Distinguished Service Medal for outstanding courage, endurance, and devotion to duty in His Hellenic Majesty's ship *Adrias*. The King approved the award of the DFM to another "Old Boy" of Huddersfield College, Flight Sergeant D. A. Watkins, for gallantry and devotion to duty during operations. Unfortunately, he failed to return from his sixty-fourth operational flight in November 1943.

Major Jack Brunyate, another Old Collegian, had been appointed Controller of Textiles to the Iraqi Government.

During Youth Week celebrations, July 1944, the ATC Squadron was reviewed by Lord Harewood, KG, in Greenhead Park.

Deaths at sea of two ex soccer-playing members, W. S. Leitch and J. C. Cranston, and death on active service of J. Beasley were recorded in Huddersfield College magazine.

Everyone had different talents and qualities which added to Huddersfield at War. Bernard Tracey wrote the words of a hymn, "God Bless Our Army and Our Navy" which the organist of St Andrew's church composed a tune for. It was sung every Sunday afterwards:

TWILIGHT VESPER

Bless our army and our navy
And our merchantmen at sea
Give them strength that knows no dangers
Let their fight be just for Thee.
Bless our airmen who face perils
As o'er land and sea they fly
May they feel Thy strong protection
Ever know that Thou art nigh.
Guard our homes and all our loved ones
From war's perils set us free
But if danger would beset us
We will face it, Lord, with Thee.
So when out of all war's chaos,
Peace emerges from the strife,
Let us try to live a better
And a truer, Christian life.

Bernard's mother was terrified if the sirens went, and he used to leave Anne, his wife, to go and look after his mother — who was quite a handful to deal with. When a warden tried to fit a gas mask on her, she repeatedly yanked it off again.

When the war first started, Anne worked at Glendinnings mill, making grey blankets. Then she was sent to Brook Motors, where she was paid 38s. a week. She also used to fire-watch at the gas works. Before she married, Anne lodged with an old lady on Leeds Road, who produced delicious mutton stews and porridge, the secret being leaving them in the Yorkshire range oven for a long time, cooking slowly. Anne gave her £1 a week for board.

Queuing for biscuits in Woolworth's one dinnertime with a friend from work, a chair had to be brought for the other girl, as she almost passed out with waiting so long. Another pal was horrified when she found she had scabies, caused by proximity to her soldier boyfriend's uniform.

There was a good response when people were asked to return their Morrison shelters for areas where there was a greater need.

That August, Maurice Berlin, flour traveller from Leeds, who used to take Mother and Dad riding in his car sometimes on half-day closing, for a treat, announced that he had managed to get some "damned good cloth" for Dad and Philip to have new suits made up. How strange, I thought, for him to have the surname of the enemy capital.

Despite summer weather, *Phantom of the Opera* at the Princess cinema, starring Nelson Eddy, Claude Rains and Susanna Foster, was retained for a further six days.

Often there were phantom food supplies. Early in August the Food Office had to adjust whatever food was available with the arrival of great numbers of evacuees. There was also a slight beer shortage, due to the warm weather and holidays at home. So it couldn't have been intoxication that prompted one lady to remark how she had had to leave London, "as them jitterbugs were going over night and day".

A happier note was struck at the Ritz when Reginald Dixon played non-stop for forty-five minutes at the Wurlitzer in connection with Holidays at Home.

A former pupil of Greenhead High School, a Miss Darby, was the first girl in the country to be awarded the Amy Johnson Aeronautical Scholarship. She was working in a northern aircraft factory to gain practical experience. Girls with fewer special talents could earn 25s. weekly at Woolworth's, at the age of fourteen.

In September 1944, former Huddersfield man Mr J. Harold Wilson, aged twenty-eight, was adopted as prospective Labour candidate for the Ormskirk Division of Lancashire.

On the 3rd of the month, High Street Methodist and Brunswick Street churches amalgamated, with a Home Guard band to accompany the hymns. On the 17th there was good news: from then on, no fireguard duties needed to be performed, and there was easing of blackout regulations. Street lights could be switched on. That Sunday there was a Civil Defence Parade to the parish church.

It wasn't too early to be thinking about Christmas. The Nora Bray School of Dancing required girls of twelve or over for the pantomime, also a couple of "refined girls" for the chorus.

But oh, the *pièce de résistance* in the Huddersfield music world that year was surely the concert in the Town Hall on Wednesday 27 September, with the Colne Valley Male Voice Choir, and guest conductor Mr H. Bardgett and soloist Heddle Nash. He enthralled his audience with "Silent Worship" and

Schubert's "The Night is Cloudless and Serene", before inviting the listeners to decide whether the famous serenade "Don Pasquale" should be sung in Italian or English. Unanimously, it was decided the former.

Heddle also sang "Waft Her Angels", then "Sound an Alarm" with a jubilant encore, "Il Mio Tesora" from Mozart's *Don Giovanni*. Ernest Cooper accompanied on the organ. Taking part also was Moura Lympany.

Another time the Town Hall hosted the Corporation Passenger Transport Comforts Fund, with a Massed Band concert, including Brighouse and Rastrick, Carlton Main Frickley Colliery, with guest conductor Harry Mortimer. The Fletcher Singers also took part.

There was a United Aid to China Week in September 1944, a sixth form party went to a meeting in the Town Hall with Greenhead's Miss Cocker, on behalf of the China Fund.

Christmas came round again with more than usual optimism and hope for the New Year.

On 17 December, the Cripples Special Service and Dinner was held, toys, cigarettes, footwear, clothes or money being collected beforehand. At the annual Mayoress's (Mrs Sidney Kaye's) "At Home" the lady was a charming hostess, in gown of powder blue crêpe, with black fur cape and matching black hat, trimmed with veiling. She held a bouquet of pink carnations and foliage.

The usual Christmas and New Year Fair began at Great Northern Street on 22 December, and many adverts were put in local papers either wanting, or selling, outgrown toys. Many dolls' houses and dolls' prams brightened Christmas morning for Huddersfield children who otherwise, if depending on the shops, would have been disappointed.

Oaklands, Dalton, a large detached house that the Corporation had allowed Ilford Day Nursery to occupy when it was evacuated to Huddersfield because of the "Buzz Bomb Blitz", had to be vacated at the end of the year. They were unable to get staff to look after the children.

On 15 December Glenn Miller disappeared on a flight to Paris. Everyone was stunned to hear this, and would feel saddened when "Woodpecker Ball", "American Patrol", and other hits of Glenn's were played in future.

There was a keen frost all Christmas, with 17 degrees on Christmas Eve.

It was an extra special Christmas for the parents of Moldgreen airman LAC Walter Holland, RAF West Africa, who broadcast to them on the General Forces programme.

Those having parties at home could buy containers of ice-cream for 12s. 6d. each, from Coletta's, Bradford Road — to be collected about two hours before it was required for consumption. Refrigerators for "ordinary" families were an almost unheard-of luxury.

Evacuee children in Bradley and Deighton enjoyed a party at Bradley Rest Centre: householders they were billeted with were invited with them. Over seventy children played games, sang carols, received a gift, paper cap, whistle, and a new sixpence each. Guests included Mr H. A. Willis, Director of Social Welfare, and his wife, Hon. Sec. of the WVS Evacuee After Care Committee. Mr E. Lamb entertained the evacuees.

As the war began to draw to its close, troops returning home received "Demob Suits". Young Dorothy Carter had the task of sewing fly buttons on them at Paviour's, tailors, on Cross Church Street. She began work at 8a.m., going into a "dark hole" to brew tea for everyone at 10a.m. There was just about time to walk to Woolworth's for a break at midday before returning to the long room with windows at one side, and treadle sewing machines. Dorothy can't recall any fire escapes. The suits were either brown with white pin stripes, or navy with pin stripes. Dorothy earned 19s. a week, finishing work at 5p.m. each day.

CHAPTER
SEVEN

1945

With the old year gone, 1945 began at the Ritz with Bette Davis in *Old Acquaintance*. Beatrice Stephenson's had their winter sale, but if you had no clothing coupons left and not much money, a Make Do and Mend class may have been a better idea. In one class, older ladies were to receive instruction in glove making.

"Aren't we rather old for that sort of thing?" was the anxious query of one.

"Too old for glove making?" asked the teacher.

"Oh — I thought you said love-making", sighed the worried pupil with obvious relief.

Staff Sergeant James Haigh of No. 22 Garlick Street, Rastrick, also heard news with relief. He was one of the lucky 627 in the second "leave draw" for men from the Middle East, and hoped to be home soon.

ICI employees' children were treated to a matinée at the Palace. On presentation of their tickets they received 1s. and a greeting card. Stark tragedy engulfed the few who had lost their tickets, but at pantomime time magic and goodness prevails, and the tearful youngsters received their gifts.

Miss Norah Jennings was awarded the British Empire Medal for saving a farmer from being gored by a bull. She joined the Land Army in 1941. Miss Jennings also received a proficiency badge for milking, presented by Lady Astor.

There was a plea for Willow Lane to be sanded in frosty weather. The area was used extensively by horse traffic, which could frequently be seen slipping and sliding in treacherous weather.

Months of silence were giving way to news of men, once prisoners of war, returning home to Huddersfield, or thereabouts. Private Hubert Dyson, RAOC of Long Lane, Dalton, formerly employed at the Corporation Gas Office, was a POW in Japanese hands.

By January 12,000 people had visited the *Examiner* war exhibition in the art gallery. The public was urged to cut down use of electricity between 8 and 10a.m. in cold weather.

But best of all, for young people, the winter dancing season was in full swing to keep them warm. Joan Bertram, a pretty eighteen-year-old evacuee from St Peter Port, Channel Islands, came to live near our shop. She became a "regular" at the Baths and other dance halls in town. We often walked home together, as we did after the Squadronaires had appeared again at Cambridge Road on 15 January. It was packed. We went to a supper dance at the Princess another Saturday evening, sharing a taxi home as we wore long evening dresses.

For most, however, the Baths had an irresistible pull, as more members of the forces went there. I met a smashing RAF Target Instructor there on the 27th. Deep snow on the 29th, with drifts in places, didn't deter us from going to the Theatre Royal, or on another evening to see Deanna Durbin in *Christmas Holiday* at the Princess. Getting warm walking home, stopping at Oddy's for fish and chips on Sheepridge Road, with fingers beginning to freeze as gloves were removed to eat them was all part of the fun of an evening out.

John Barbirolli conducted the Hallé Orchestra at the Town Hall that month.

The upbeat tempo of 1945, when the end of hostilities truly appeared to be a reality, was reflected by some of the shows, Tommy Trinder and Stanley Holloway in *Champagne Charlie* at the Empire, for instance. There was an air of hopeful expectation in the air.

Yet there were still irritations — such as troops on leave from overseas having to walk the fifteen or so miles from Leeds of Huddersfield late at night. One gentleman offered a lift on certain nights or early mornings, saying he would go anywhere to pick them up. But he received a letter in reply, saying that under regulations his offer could not be made use of. It was later suggested that petrol should be allowed to any car owner who would offer this service, but driver and car had to be registered so that authorities could check up.

The process of winding up the war had begun. A Huddersfield firm donated a supply of discarded blankets that had been used for fire-watching to the

Citizens' Advice Bureau. They were given to poor people. The bureau also requested balaclava helmets, far better for keeping ears warm that flat caps. Former air raid wardens were asked if they could spare any.

A letter from a crippled man, confined to his home, asked if a soldier or other disabled person could sit with him occasionally. Even the wireless palls after too long alone.

At the annual dinner of the Fire Guard area captains, held at the Pack Horse Hotel there was a presentation to Chief Constable and Fire Guard Officer Mr James Chadwick. Among the guests were Captain J. A. Irons, Head Warden.

That cold January a gentleman lost a fur-back gauntlet glove, between Kirkburton and Dogley Bar. Its partner missed it so much that a reward was offered if it was returned to the Waterloo Inn.

Granville Wheeler, from Linthwaite, joined the Signals in Catterick, and was posted to Germany in 1945. He was on the Danish border during the summer, and took his Brownie camera with him.

Many Huddersfield people won gallantry awards, including Acting Flight Lieutenant Robert Geoffrey Blamires of No. 103 Tunnacliffe Road, Newsome. He was awarded the DFC.

LACW Jessie Daniel, No. 592 Quarry Bank, Mount, was mentioned in dispatches. Before joining the WAAFs Mrs Daniel was on the staff of James Sykes, Stafford Mills, Milnsbridge.

A Grand Concert at the Ritz on Sunday 28 January, in aid of the League of Firemen and Civil Defenders had entertainers Issy Bonn and Donald Peers. Commencing at 6.30p.m., seats for the concert cost 5s., 4s., 3s. 6d., or 2s. 6d.

The fact that wounded soldiers had to pay on buses irked many. They could ill afford it on a meagre pay of 10s. a week.

Paddock was the first district of Huddersfield to have a clock which showed the time in the dark since the ban on illuminating public clock faces was lifted. People were thrilled to see it lit up — some could tell the time from as far away as Manchester Road.

"Russians only 40 miles away from Berlin", I wrote triumphantly in my diary on 5 February. We could hardly wait to hear at length, not just on a tiny airgraph, what it had *really* been like.

People would be returning to normal life before the year was over, perhaps. Lives had been turned topsy turvey when Hitler dominated the world stage. Even hairdresser Vera Moore, who had many famous clients, including Dinah Sheridan, had driven an ambulance in the war years.

Land Army girl Betty Key was a fan of Donald Peers, so I took her to hear him at the Palace with our free pass on the 9th.

I bought a camel hair coat at Leader's, New Street, hoping that before long we would be able to buy whatever clothes we fancied if we could afford them, without having to wonder, "have I enough clothing coupons?" That would be Heaven on Earth! When I went to June Harries's for tea I wore my new coat. A couple of Belgian soldiers, Pierre and Constant, were also invited. We played records afterwards. They liked the "Ink Spots" singing "Don't Get Around Much Anymore", and "Trees".

Many Belgian soldiers were around Huddersfield in 1945. Emile and Marcel called in at our shop once to buy cigarettes, and thereafter treated it as a second home.

Jeanne Wood and I teamed up with a couple, Louis and Geoff, we met when walking with our dogs in Greenhead Park. In the Princess cinema on our first "date" with them I was more interested in the mini drama going on in the dark of the back seats. Jeanne wore a blouse of parachute silk, with a huge floppy bow at the neckline. Geoff kept trying to undo it, but Jeanne, flustered and agitated, immediately tied it up again.

Variety was indeed the spice of life in wartime Huddersfield. June Harries and I danced with Canadian Air Force men at the Baths on 23 February, then they walked us home, having to walk back nearly three miles into town after kissing us goodnight.

Enjoying ourselves did not lessen our dismay for those experiencing the horrors of war. For example, the splinter effect of a mortar gun necessitated the removal of Rifleman Thomas Albert Smith's right eye, and inflicted wounds to his arm and leg. He was formerly employed by Lindon Smith's.

Mayor Sidney Kaye made an appeal for King George's Fund for Sailors, and a collection for them was taken up by Sea Cadets of the local unit at the Ritz on 6 March. Under the command of Sub Lieutenant

L. V. Haigh, RNVR they marched through the audience, then formed a Guard of Honour on the stage, carrying out drill movements in brisk fashion.

Spring brides scanned the For Sale columns trying to help out clothing coupons. A model white lace wedding gown, couponless, for £5, must have been a boon for one lucky girl. A dusky pink two piece, also £5, and a wedding veil and head-dress were going for £1. A new brown costume was 10 gns. For sale, also, was an all wool tailored coat, no coupons; and a girl's blue Heatonex coat and hat. Another bargain was a fur coat, musquash flank, for £30.

A mother of two little girls "with thick hair" resorted to the Citizens' Advice Bureau, having failed to purchase a comb in Huddersfield. They were in short supply.

The Town Hall held a Dig for Victory exhibition, opened on 8 March by Mayor Sidney Kaye. The Chairman of Huddersfield Agricultural Committee Alderman W. A. Meadows presided. Allotment holders put on a magnificent show of vegetables; and there was a display by the Corporation Parks Department of vegetables produced in parks and at hospitals and sanitorium. There were demonstrations of fruit bottling, cookery and skin curing, talks by experts, and film shows. A Brain's Trust relating to gardening, pig keeping, and suchlike activities was also held, Mr Victor Smythe from the BBC being the question master.

The Fireguard Plan in Huddersfield was abolished. All fires, whether by enemy action or otherwise, were in future to be reported to the National Fire Service. All instructions, leaflets and notices under the Fireguard Plan were to be cancelled and destroyed.

King George approved the award of the Military Cross for Gallant and Distinguished services in Italy to Lieutenant Basil Edward Scrivener King, of the North Irish Horse Royal Armoured Corps.

At Castle Hill, Aldmondbury, was a camp for Italian POWs, much more interesting to girls than the archaeological digs that used to be conducted round there! "Going for a walk" had added interest when swarthy skins and gleaming white teeth and foreign accents could be seen and heard from the "Ities", who wolf whistled as they sauntered by. Fraternizing at a distance could be fun.

For a few brief happy months, after getting bored with office work at Halifax Building Society — though liking the staff — I'd been a full time art student at the Technical College. But Philip thought it wasn't right for him to be working and me to be a student.

So, reluctantly, I left and began working at Leach's, Brighouse that March, ostensibly to learn photo-tinting. But, like everything else, air brushes were in short supply. There was only one available in the section I worked in. So from 8a.m. until 6p.m. most days I was "spotting" photographs. I sat between a couple of pinafored, disciplinarian "Little Hitlers" who forbade any talking whatsoever, which made me almost yearn to be in a prison camp — at least talking would be allowed, surely.

Customers wrote hair and skin colour, eyes, and colours of clothes, which the artists then interpreted as well as they could. Many were wartime wedding photographs that came in to be tinted.

It was too far to go home for midday dinner, so I went to the British restaurant, where I queued for stodgy food. Then it was back to the enforced silence of the grave, or so it seemed.

Often something good comes out of a bad. I bought a set of special photograph oil paints, and started to get my own orders from our shop at home. Before colour films came in, it was an engrossing and enjoyable occupation. Quite a number of wedding photographs of Huddersfield people were coloured by me. I was modest in charges, 1s. or 1s. 6d., depending on whether it was a single or group photograph.

Appropriately-named films turned up on screens towards the end of the war in Europe. For example, Myrna Loy and William Powell in *The Thin Man Goes Home* at the Ritz in April; and George Formby in *He Snoops to Conquer* at the Tudor.

The Town Council decided there would be no street lighting during Double Summer Time. All gas lamps had to be turned off individually by a lamplighter man, who walked round with a long pole — a job begun over the weekend owing to shortage of staff. There were only seventeen men to attend to them, compared with forty-five in peacetime, and 2,700 lamps had to be turned off. All electric street lighting under automatic control was suspended. The Council also debated whether to extend licensing hours when Victory Celebrations began, the feeling among some being that many would prefer to go to their nearest church to offer prayers and thank God that the ordeal was over.

A reminder of sirens — a test of all electric and steam sirens — was scheduled for the following Monday at 10a.m.

Fascinating stories were being recounted by people about their experiences during the war; also from the forces returning home — stories they would be able to tell to their grandchildren, fifty years on. Harry Dyson told of the time when, living in a cottage at Newsome, he and his uncle heard guns at Aldmondbury, and saw a searchlight catch the tail of a German aeroplane in its beam. The pilot, to make a quicker getaway, dropped all his bombs and incendiaries. Harry heard them coming down, and dived into the brick coal place with his uncle to take cover. They were "just like Kentucky Minstrels" when the All Clear went. Harry was never as frightened in all his life. Two big holes were in a field, which was full of cows, who "went crackers — they didn't half perform!" Shrapnel was found at Berry Brow and "Mucky Lane", Newsome — marvellous finds for schoolboys, who treasured them.

Private Walter Roberts of No. 4 Briggs Terrace, Moldgreen, member of the Duke of Wellington's Regiment and former sand blaster at Britannia Works, Birkby, was on the dangerously ill list in February 1945. Aged thirty, he had his left leg amputated.

Sergeant Ronald Hallas of No. 122 Cowcliffe Hill Road, received the Military Medal. On 28 July 1944 his troops were held up by a minefield covering the diversion of a blown up bridge. Hallas took out a patrol of three men, and after a half hour search located the observation post covering the area, capturing four of its six members. This spirited action on his part allowed the mines to be cleared, and advance to continue by daylight.

In the same general area, owing to an enemy bazooka post covering the road, it was not possible for vehicles to continue their advance. The leading car of Sergeant Hallas's patrol located the post and he again organized a foot patrol from his two cars, and led it forward to destroy the post and their weapons, then continued the advance.

On 6 August 1944, in the area of Castellonchio, a vehicle of his patrol, put out of action by enemy mortar, had to be abandoned. Thirty minutes after the car was hit, Sergeant Hallas proceeded to it and ensured that no maps or code lists were in the vehicle — his own initiative as patrol commander, showing tenacity and initiative beyond the call of duty.

George Earnshaw was decorated by King George VI at an investiture in Buckingham Palace, among returning forces, for his act of bravery under fire in the invasion off the coast of Normandy. The Golcar Marine, formerly employed by Messrs J. Lockwood, Milnsbridge, was a member of Golcar Providence church, Golcar Central Liberal Club, and a playing member of the cricket and bowling club.

Private Jack Blakey, bandsman of the Duke of Wellington's Regiment, who had been missing since June 1940, was reported in March as being in allied hands. Blakey was formerly employed as a painter by

Lunn and Cardno. He played with Honley and Aldmondbury Bands, as well as with a number of local dance bands.

7a.m. — cup of "ersatz" (imitation) coffee; 10.30 — small piece of bread and cheese; 4.30p.m. — rice and water. For fifteen months this had been the daily fare of Signalman Lister Peace, Royal Corps of Signals, former member of the *Examiner* machine room staff. Signalman Peace, whose parents lived at No. 19 High Croft Crescent, Aldmondbury, was captured by Germans at Tobruk in June 1942, and was then transferred to a camp in Italy, which was overcrowded and lacking in sanitary arrangements. Red Cross parcels kept them going.

When the Italians gave in, prisoners, including Peace, forced the gates and escaped. In September 1943 he was living behind the lines with Italian patriots, getting food and shelter when and where he could, dodging Fascist groups in search of the men. He was caught on one occasion, but managed to get away again.

By December 1944 Peace was through to the British lines, and had six weeks leave after arriving back in England in early February 1945. Signalman Peace saw his little daughter, four years old, for the first time. She was born in November 1940, five months after he was sent overseas. His wife had been informed by the War Office of her husband's escape, and that he was living in the mountains. Almost a year went by with no word of him. It would have been too risky for him to write.

Home from a German Prison Camp was Trooper Robert Proctor, Royal Tank Regiment, formerly of No.

101 Moorbottom Road, Thornton Lodge. He arrived in the Hospital Ship *Letitia*. Proctor had fought with the Eighth Army. In the retreat to El Alamein he was wounded, and taken prisoner at El Agheila. Then he was transferred to hospital in Italy, remaining there till September 1943. On the Italian Armistice the hospitals were evacuated, and Trooper Proctor was taken to a prison camp in Germany. The menu there was, early morning, ersatz coffee; mid-morning, soup and potatoes; late afternoon, bread and margarine. Meat appeared once every six months, and there were occasional Red Cross parcels. How wonderful the six weeks leave at home would be!

LAC G. Hewer, RAF, of No. 72 Northgate, Aldmondbury, sent a photograph home of himself in Camp Bangalore, India, with George and Beryl Formby.

Private Frank Beaumont of No. 8 Fartown Green Road, arrived home after liberation from Stalag XIB, which had a starvation diet, the worst of the four camps he had been in. Frank, a bass singer, was a medallist in 1939 Mrs Sunderland's Musical Competition. He was formerly employed by the Corporation gas works, and had been a member of Birkby Baptist church choir.

Lance Corporal Lockwood, of No. 498 Wakefield Road, outwitted the Gestapo. He had a crystal set which fitted into a pill box, as he was determined to listen to the BBC. When the Gestapo inspected he sat on the box, and the radio was never found.

What adventures, and scenes they would never have believed they would see! I had a young cousin in

Australia, Ernie Haigh, who came over during the war. We would never have met under normal circumstances. Blackpool, or at the furthest, Torquay, was where most Huddersfield people ventured until 1939.

One returning POW told how one of the crew on board ship developed smallpox. All the passengers had to be vaccinated before they could leave for home. He was now waiting for pay accumulated during the time he had been a prisoner.

When there was a bombing attack by Russian planes on a town in East Prussia, Private Wilfred Kaye, of Hade Edge, Holmfirth, took the opportunity to slip away from his guards to freedom.

By 6 April there was a steady demand for streamers and flags in town shops, and, at the Empire *Our Hearts Were Young and Gay*, starring Gail Russell.

A concert broadcast from Huddersfield Town Hall on the 17th featured the star contralto, Kathleen Ferrier, with guest conductor Leslie Woodgate.

New North Road Baptist Mens' Fellowship and Contact Club was addressed by Lewis Marsden, mechanical and chemical engineer with ICI, who spoke about nylon. So far, little work had been done on peacetime development of nylon yarns.

"Hooray! You can get Reckitt's Blue anywhere now!" joyously proclaimed adverts. Jeanette MacDonald and Nelson Eddy were singing that lovely, haunting duet "Sweetheart — will you love me, Ever . . ." in *Maytime* at a cinema in town. And, three cheers, on that same May Day, 1945, we heard it rumoured on the wireless that Hitler was dead. As someone said, "what does it matter how he dies, as long as he doesn't die of one complaint — old age?"

Among the homecoming ex-prisoners of war was our old pal Bert Senior, who had been in a camp in Germany. Though peace was imminent, scars of war would remain with many for the rest of their lives. Sydney Gregory, of Cowlersley, on duty with the Home Guard, fell into a steep quarry at Crosland Hill in the blackout. He lay there till dawn. From that night on, he always walked with one shoulder slightly higher than the other.

On 7 May at 3p.m., the Germans surrendered unconditionally. Word spread like wildfire. As a minute gesture of triumph, we at Leach's were allowed to finish at 5.30 instead of 6p.m. Like other firms, we were given two days' Victory Holiday. Some decorated their machines with flags and bunting, and wrote slogans, such as "There'll Always Be An England" across them.

Paid holidays commenced one hour after the actual time of declaration. I had time to go to the Theatre Royal that evening to see *As You Like It*, finishing off the eventful day with an everyday fish and chip supper in Lindon Smith's with Betty Key.

Mrs Mary Brown, widow of Percy, Talbot Avenue, as a token of gratitude for the successful termination of war in Europe, gave £5 to every baby born on VE Day and VE Day plus one. Money was to go into the Post Office Savings Bank. To qualify, babies had to survive one month.

On 8 May 1945 I listened to Prime Minister Winston Churchill's speech on the wireless, as did most of the population. Betty Key, local boy Sydney Pike, and I met at 6.30p.m. to attend the Victory Dance in Huddersfield Town Hall. Queues stretched for what seemed to be miles — it was 8.30p.m. when we finally went inside.

It was a lovely warm evening. We had a smashing time. At the end of the dance we sauntered through town, lots of people were singing, shouting, jigging about. A sense of almost tangible euphoria was in the air. Many were gathered outside the Ritz cinema, playing "King William". We joined in, everybody joining hands. No one could be a stranger in that happy crowd.

"Choose in the East, choose in the West" they chanted, slowly walking round. A dashing Free Frenchman chose me — "Down on this carpet you will kneel, while the grass grows round your feet . . ."

The road, unlike a carpet, was hard. But we were all delirious with relief and joy. It was a magical night, as though life was bound to be wonderful forever, now that we had beaten the Germans.

Somewhere among the crowds Annie Myers was dancing VE Night away too, probably down on *her* knees, thanking God that soon Woodbines would be freely on sale in the shops, and rotten old Pasha cigarettes would be a thing of the past.

There were fairy lights in Greenhead Park, and the War Memorial was floodlit. Families took their children into the town to see the lights being switched on, many never having seen the town lit up before. An illuminated trolley bus wound its way proudly through town and suburbs on VE Day, and the Town Hall was illuminated with a huge "V" sign in front of the building.

On 8 May there was a spirit of quiet satisfaction, not rowdiness. People were beribboned, with obvious joy in their hearts; glad smiles taking the place of war weariness from their faces. But there was no undue boisterousness.

Despite heavy rain, crowds jostled in the streets, housewives eager to get in what provisions they could to make a suitable "spread" for the first days of peace. From the early hours queues formed, good-naturedly, outside food shops.

At midday the bells of Huddersfield parish church rang out a magnificent Victory Peal, and a service of Thanksgiving took place. At 6p.m. the Rev. J. W. Park spoke to the crowds from the Union Jack-bedecked balcony; then a minute's silence was observed in memory of the fallen. Tears of sorrow mingled with those of joy in the silence.

Later on, Ramsden Street, New Street and Market Place were particularly lively spots. Crowds surged round, arm-in-arm with strangers as well as friends, kissing all and sundry, singing First World War songs as well as the current ones: "Tipperary", "Pack up Your Troubles", "Land of Hope and Glory", "Roses of Picardy". Then someone struck up "There'll Always Be an England", and it was taken up by one and all. Sombre songs and silly songs followed rapidly after each other: "Run, Rabbit, Run"; "We're Gonna Hang out the Washing on the Siegfried Line, if the Siegfried line's still there . . ."

What a party! "Now is the Hour, for me to say Goodbye" could have indicated the breakup of the joyful crowd, but it didn't — far from it. They started all over again. High spirits didn't need any artificial stimulus. Some fireworks were set off in the streets, even the occasional "Little Demon" that made a shattering noise, but they only added to the sense of enjoyment. That night the police were celebrating Victory too, so they were tolerant and turned a deaf ear to them.

Both nights there was dancing outside the Ritz cinema to radio music relayed through loudspeakers. The front was floodlit, and a huge spotlight on the roof swept over the jubilant, dancing throng.

Rubber paving in front of the Ritz almost reached sizzling point as merry-making continued into the early hours, and somebody turned up with a big drum to add to the celebrations.

It was a hollow victory for those whose relations didn't make it, though. While most were putting their victory flags and trimmings up, ATS girl Clara Carter was accidentally killed in a street accident in Brussels. The twenty-six-year-old had attended Bradley Church School, and before joining up had been employed by Messrs Boothroyd Rugs Ltd, Thongsbridge Mills. In fog, the Bradley route public transport was usually the first to stop running buses. Many a time Clara had walked to work at Thongsbridge and back, thinking nothing of it. A hardy breed, those of the Second World War. Clara had lost her life in trying to help another. Celebrating the courage of those who gave the ultimate sacrifice, besides the Victory in Europe, was what those heart-warming scenes on the streets of Huddersfield were about.

Al Shaw and his band took their instruments on to the street outside the Palace Theatre, including a grand piano, electric guitar, and xylophone. Up to 3,000 people sang and danced, then Mrs Shaw went round the crowd with a bucket, collecting for the Red Cross.

Bonfires ringed the town on both nights, with dancing round the blazing piles, on Castle Hill and other places. Many included effigies of Hitler. The Manager of the "Lounge" contributed a few ancient cinema seats and a length of film, to get the blaze off to a brilliant start.

Children enjoyed Victory Tea Parties in the open air — looking forward, probably, to more than fish paste sandwiches in the near future.

The mayor congratulated the people of Huddersfield when celebrations were over for the way they had conducted themselves. He congratulated them on their self control.

On the evening of VE Day, as the ceremony was about to begin at the Town Hall, with Mayor Sidney Kaye speaking to the townspeople, there was a sudden burst of sunshine, which lasted through most of the proceedings.

Huddersfield Examiner's War Correspondent, Alfred M. Lee, went to the officers' prison camp, Offlag 79, one of the POW camps liberated with the capture of Brunswick. Their press jeep drew up to the wire gates, and a few minutes later he was celebrating with champagne the freeing of four Huddersfield officers.

Mr. Lee and the others were cheered as they rode up the road to the camp among the trees. He wished everyone could have seen the men's faces and felt the handshakes. He wished all could have heard their words of gratitude and immense pleasure at "seeing someone from home". At the gates one of the prisoners said, as though it was too good to be true, hardly daring to believe it, "You're from Huddersfield . . ." The other three from the home town were rounded up, and in a hut they drank to "Freedom — and Huddersfield", out of tin cans. But "never, before or after, did champagne taste so grand," said Mr Lee.

News of their liberation first came with the arrival of three American Jeeps. In the last few days German civilians had pushed a little food through the wire enclosure. But there were examples of Germans keeping up spite to the bitter end. At a camp for other ranks, Alfred Lee talked with Englishmen who had only a stone floor on which to sleep in a brewery, after being marched seven or eight hundred miles to Brunswick. The brewery manager provided straw and wood slats, enabling them to keep clear of the water on the floor. He had complained about them being there, saying it was unfit for animals. But the Nazis over-ruled him.

In Huddersfield, life began to resume near normality. At St Patrick's Hall on 14 May was a Crooning Competition: someone could win a month's engagement with Aub Hirst and his Band.

The world was waiting for VJ Day. In the meantime, the Co-op Hall suggested "Work Hard, Play Hard — and Dance at the New Co-op Hall every Monday to Stan Robinson's Dance Orchestra. With Doreen, Nightingale of the North."

It had been the worst of times for many, the best of times for some. But, as down all the ages, one of the hymns sung in churches and chapels at that time said it all:

> The day Thou gavest, Lord, is ended,
> The darkness falls at Thy behest;
> To Thee our morning hymns ascended,
> Thy praise shall sanctify our rest.

As long as there'll always be an England, we will survive.

Also available in ISIS Large Print:

Hackney Memories

Alan Wilson

"*The days of my Hackney childhood were lived under a perpetual hazy canopy the colour of lentil soup.*"

This is Hackney seen through the eyes of a young working class boy, Alan Wilson, who grew up in the area in the 1930s. It was an age when trams trundled down the streets, accompanied by the clatter of horses' hooves as they pulled brewers' drays and coal carts; an age of art deco cinemas and lidos. Life was simple: school in the week and visiting nearby relatives at the weekends.

Then fascists appeared on the streets of Hackney and barrage balloons, searchlights and guns were to be seen in Victoria Park. War was on the horizon. At the time of the Munich Crisis, the author fulfilled his ambition to win a scholarship to a local grammar only for the Second World War to come along and change everything . . .

ISBN 978-0-7531-9386-0 (hb)
ISBN 978-0-7531-9387-7 (pb)

Diary of a Lollipop Lady

Hazel Wheeler

"No wonder people weren't rushing to be crossing wardens, I thought ruefully next morning, a foggy first of February."

In February 1966, beset with money troubles and with a young family, Hazel Wheeler began work as a Lollipop Lady at the princely wage of £3 14s 6d a week. During her year spent shepherding schoolchildren over the crossing, she met many new people, young and old, and heard all about the ups and downs of their daily lives.

Hazel recorded her own experiences, together with the varying fortunes of her own family, in her diary, which forms the basis for this delightful and faithful memoir of her time on the "Lollipop Beat".

ISBN 978-0-7531-9392-1 (hb)
ISBN 978-0-7531-9393-8 (pb)

Before the Last All Clear

Ray Evans

"*Except for Mam and Dad, none of us had ever been out of Liverpool before, never mind on a train.*"

This is the story of one young boy from Liverpool, whose family was sent to the Welsh town of Llanelli for the duration of the war. Separated from his mother, and brothers and sisters, six-year-old Raymond Evans was shunted from pillar to post. At first he had a miserable time, unwanted and largely unloved, and it appeared that his war would be spent without any family — real or surrogate. Ray's world is one of ration books, black-out curtains, air-raid sirens and sudden death; a world in which humanity triumphs despite its own shortcomings.

ISBN 978-0-7531-9380-8 (hb)
ISBN 978-0-7531-9381-5 (pb)

Living on Tick

Hazel Wheeler

"Part of our war effort at Central Stores must surely have been in helping to keep people's spirits up. Even in wartime there has to be humour or we'd all be dead. Not from bullets but from sheer monotony."

The corner shop in the 1920s and '30s was much more than just a place to buy the groceries. It was a meeting place where familiar faces, on both sides of the counter, swapped stories and helped each other out. People bought groceries daily, so visits to the shop were a frequent occurrence and when times were hard it was common for a customer to ask for, and usually get, goods "on tick". Hazel Wheeler grew up in her father's shop in Deighton near Huddersfield and recalls her memories of those times. She remembers the people, the goods they sold in the shop and a way of life that has now vanished.

ISBN 978-0-7531-9362-4 (hb)
ISBN 978-0-7531-9363-1 (pb)

The Way We Were

Toni Savage

"*Everything had two alternatives for us. The season was either summer or winter. The days were either good or bad. There was out or in. Out was most of the time.*"

An only child, Toni Savage was evacuated from London in September 1939. She was to spend over four years in the Surrey countryside, living in a country mansion with seven other children, under the watchful eyes of Mrs Parrot, Miss Bailey and the governess Mrs Samuel.

Although her life as an evacuee was often one of fun and laughter, full of new friends and the wonders of childhood, it was also lived in the shadow of the war, with both bombs and soldiers a common sight.

ISBN 978-0-7531-9344-0 (hb)
ISBN 978-0-7531-9345-7 (pb)

ISIS publish a wide range of books in large print, from fiction to biography. Any suggestions for books you would like to see in large print or audio are always welcome. Please send to the Editorial Department at:

ISIS Publishing Limited
7 Centremead
Osney Mead
Oxford OX2 0ES

A full list of titles is available free of charge from:

Ulverscroft Large Print Books Limited

(UK)
The Green
Bradgate Road, Anstey
Leicester LE7 7FU
Tel: (0116) 236 4325

(Australia)
P.O. Box 314
St Leonards
NSW 1590
Tel: (02) 9436 2622

(USA)
P.O. Box 1230
West Seneca
N.Y. 14224-1230
Tel: (716) 674 4270

(Canada)
P.O. Box 80038
Burlington
Ontario L7L 6B1
Tel: (905) 637 8734

(New Zealand)
P.O. Box 456
Feilding
Tel: (06) 323 6828

Details of **ISIS** complete and unabridged audio books are also available from these offices. Alternatively, contact your local library for details of their collection of **ISIS** large print and unabridged audio books.